MW00327242

DESERTION

DESERTION

Trust and Mistrust in Civil Wars

Theodore McLauchlin

CORNELL UNIVERSITY PRESS   ITHACA AND LONDON

Cornell University Press gratefully acknowledges receipt of a grant from the Faculty of Arts and Science, Université de Montréal, which aided in the publication of this book.

Copyright © 2020 by Cornell University

All rights reserved. Except for brief quotations in a review, this book, or parts thereof, must not be reproduced in any form without permission in writing from the publisher. For information, address Cornell University Press, Sage House, 512 East State Street, Ithaca, New York 14850. Visit our website at cornellpress.cornell.edu.

First published 2020 by Cornell University Press

Printed in the United States of America

Library of Congress Cataloging-in-Publication Data

Names: McLauchlin, Theodore, author.
Title: Desertion : trust and mistrust in civil wars / Theodore McLauchlin.
Description: Ithaca [New York] : Cornell University Press, 2020. |
    Includes bibliographical references and index.
Identifiers: LCCN 2020012043 (print) | LCCN 2020012044 (ebook) |
    ISBN 9781501752940 (cloth) | ISBN 9781501752957 (epub) |
    ISBN 9781501752964 (pdf)
Subjects: LCSH: Desertion, Military. | Trust. | Spain—History—Civil War,
    1936–1939—Desertions. | Syria—History—Civil War, 2011—Desertions.
Classification: LCC UB788 .M35 2020 (print) | LCC UB788 (ebook) |
    DDC 946.081/4—dc23
LC record available at https://lccn.loc.gov/2020012043
LC ebook record available at https://lccn.loc.gov/2020012044

To Jen

Contents

Illustrations

Figures

Tables

Acknowledgments

This is a book about desertion and solidarity, and I could not have written it without the solidarity of many people. I am forever grateful to Hudson Meadwell and Steve Saideman for their guidance and wisdom in orienting this whole project.

In Spain, Juan Díez Medrano and the Institut Barcelona d'Estudis Internacionals generously provided me a home base and insightful critique, and Guillermo Mira Delli-Zotti kindly supported a research trip to Salamanca. I owe a great debt to the late Carlos Engel, who oriented me in the study of the Spanish officer corps and generously shared his data with me, the fruit of a life's work. I enjoyed a great deal of help, and patience, from the staff at the Centro Documental de la Memoria Histórica in Salamanca and the Archivo General Militar in Ávila.

Portions of chapter 4 appeared as Theodore McLauchlin, "Desertion and Collective Action in Civil Wars," *International Studies Quarterly* 59, no. 4 (December 2015): 669–679, reproduced by permission of Oxford University Press; other portions appeared as Theodore McLauchlin, "Desertion and Control of the Home Front in Civil Wars," *Journal of Conflict Resolution* 58, no. 8 (December 2014): 1419–1444, reproduced by permission of Sage Publications.

I gratefully acknowledge the support of many different institutions. I received funding from a Canada Graduate Fellowship and a Michael Smith Foreign Study Supplement from the Social Sciences and Humanities Research Council of Canada, a PhD fellowship from the Security and Defence Forum, research travel grants from the McGill-Université de Montréal Institute for European Studies and the Faculty of Arts at McGill, and an Alexander Mackenzie Fellowship and Graduate Excellence Fellowship from the Department of Political Science. Support from the Faculty of Arts and Sciences at Université de Montréal and the Fonds québécois de la recherche supported the latter stages of my research. Juliet Johnson and Jennifer Welsh kindly welcomed me back to McGill for a sabbatical semester.

I had an excellent group of research assistants: Juan Carlos García, Braulio Pareja, Daniel Blanco, Patricia García, and Manuel Talaván in the archives in Salamanca, and Alejandro Ángel Tapias, Julie-Maude Beauchesne, Guillaume de la Rochelle Renaud, Julien Morency-Laflamme, Margaux Reiss, and Rainer Ricardo in Montreal.

Among the many friends and colleagues who have shared their advice and expertise in conversations about this book, I want to single out Laia Balcells, who helped me get oriented in Spain and invited me to contribute my work at several different venues over the years, and whose work provided a constant inspiration. I was extremely fortunate to collaborate with Álvaro La Parra-Pérez on an article. Our work together greatly assisted with preparing chapter 5 and helped to sharpen my thinking about violence against the Spanish officer corps. Aisha Ahmad, Ceren Belge, André Blais, Juan Andrés Blanco Rodríguez, Megan Bradley, Michael Brecher, Gabriel Cardona, Fotini Christia, David Cunningham, Kathleen Gallagher Cunningham, Ruth Dassonneville, Claire Durand, Michael Gabbay, Emily Kalah Gade, Jean-François Godbout, John Hall, Amelia Hoover Green, Juliet Johnson, Keith Krause, Jonathan Leader Maynard, Janet Lewis, Jason Lyall, Zachariah Mampilly, Hudson Meadwell, Frédéric Mérand, Jon Monten, Dipali Mukhopadhyay, Sarah Parkinson, T.V. Paul, Krzysztof Pelc, Chris Phillips, Costantino Pischedda, Will Reno, Andrea Ruggeri, Lee Seymour, Anastasia Shesterinina, Stuart Soroka, Ora Szekely, Michael Weintraub, and Jennifer Welsh offered crucial advice and commentary on different chapters of this book in one venue or another, and the book has greatly benefited from their feedback. I am grateful to the Center for International Peace and Security Studies at McGill, the Chaire de recherche en études électorales at UdeM for inviting me to present some of this research, and to the audiences there and at the International Studies Association and American Political Science Association for searching comments and questions. I am also very grateful to the production team at Cornell University Press, above all to Roger Haydon and Kristen Bettcher. Bill Nelson ably produced the map in chapter 3.

I could not have asked for a better department to work at than Science politique at Université de Montréal. Above all, it has been my honor and privilege to share a home with Lee Seymour and Marie-Joëlle Zahar, dear friends, close collaborators, and sharp scholars. All of the faculty and students embody collegiality, and I am grateful for their generosity of spirit and their willingness to share their expertise.

I was fortunate to be a part of a tremendous cohort in graduate school. Above all, I am supremely lucky to count Ora Szekely among my great friends. McGill was full of wonderful, sustaining comrades-in-arms, and this book owes so much to conversations at Thomson House, the social statistics lab, and Else's. I'm fortunate to have had the friendship and warm welcome of the Kissack family in Barcelona for so much of this research.

I have had many great teachers who put me on my path. Kathi Biggs, Pam Butler, Tom McKendy, and Tom Nicoll showed me I could study and write about history and politics as a vocation, and inspired me to scholarship.

Guy-Philippe Bouchard, Kat Childs, Jen Dickson, Justin Mizzi, Mark Ordonselli, and Ian Ratzer are the best of friends. They have propped up my sanity more times than I care to admit, but they probably already knew that.

My family, every branch of it, has been my rock throughout writing this book. Lynn and Matt McLauchlin, my mother and brother, have always been there for me, whenever I have needed encouragement, love, and moral support. I am lucky to have wonderful in-laws in the Bracewells and Glasers.

It was hearing the voice of my late father, David McLauchlin, over the radio and talking with him about what he had seen as he reported from around the world that awakened my interest in politics at a young age. His example has been a constant companion. Stephen McLauchlin inspires me every day, drinking deeply from the cup of life and wanting badly to learn about everything and help everyone he can.

I don't really know what to say to my wonderful wife, Jen Bracewell. I know this book has been hard to live with, as have I. But there were points where I would not have kept going with this book, if not for her support. Through her patient and perceptive critiques, she helped me think through the ideas behind this book. Ever the archaeologist, she exhorted me to go get data at a time when that was exactly the right piece of advice. I'm finishing my edits during a global pandemic in which we have no idea what is likely to happen, and if I can manage it, it is much thanks to her. Thanking her is not enough, though I do, profusely. I only hope I do the same for her. I owe Jen this, and I dedicate it to her.

Abbreviations

AGMAV	Archivo General Militar, Ávila
CDF	Civil Defense Forces, Sierra Leonean militia group
CDMH	Centro Documental de la Memoria Histórica, Salamanca
CES	Cuerpo de Ejército de Santander, Santander army corps
CNT	Confederación Nacional del Trabajo, anarcho-syndicalist trade union confederation
FAI	Federación Anarquista Ibérica, Anarchist political organization
FMLN	Frente Farabundo Martí para la Liberación Nacional, Salvadoran insurgent group
FSA	Free Syrian Army, Syrian insurgent umbrella label
GIC	Gabinete de Información y Control, internal investigation office in the Spanish Republican armed forces
ISI	Islamic State in Iraq, insurgent group in Iraq
ISIS	Islamic State in Iraq and al-Sham, insurgent group in Iraq and Syria
JN	Jabhat al-Nusra, insurgent group in Syria
JSU	Juventudes Socialistas Unificadas, joint Socialist-Communist youth wing
MAOC	Milicias Antifascistas Obreras y Campesinas, Communist-organized militias
NCO	noncommissioned officer
PCE	Partido Comunista Española, Spanish Communist party
PKK	Partiya Karkerên Kurdistanê, Kurdistan Worker's Party, Kurdish insurgency in Turkey
PLA	People's Liberation Army (Vietnam)
POUM	Partido Obrero de Unificación Marxista, revolutionary Marxist party
PSOE	Partido Socialista Obrero Española, Spanish Socialist party
PYD	Partiya Yekîtiya Demokrat, Democratic Unity Party, Syrian political party
RUF	Revolutionary United Forces, Sierra Leonean insurgent group
SAA	Syrian Arab Army, regime forces in Syria
SDF	Syrian Democratic Forces, armed group in Syria
SIM	Servicio de Investigación Militar, military internal security and counterespionage service

UGT	Unión General de Trabajadores, Socialist trade union federation
VC	Viet Cong
YPG	Yekîneyên Parastina Gel, People's Protection Units, Kurdish armed group in Syria
YPJ	Yekîneyên Parastina Jin, Women's Protection Units, Kurdish armed group in Syria

DESERTION

SLIPPING AWAY

Vicente Pozuelo Escudero was a medical student and a member of the fascist Falange party before the Spanish Civil War began in 1936.[1] The way he recounted it in an interview in 1996 with Pedro Montoliú, the start of the Civil War saw Pozuelo doing military service in Madrid, a fascist in a city the left-wing Republican government still held. Leaving his outfit, Pozuelo managed to avoid joining the Republican army for almost eighteen months, before having to enlist again at the start of 1938 as a medic.

In the army, Pozuelo kept his head down, hiding his right-wing past as much as possible. But eventually his politics caught up with him. He came under suspicion of treason. On April 22, 1938, the brigade's chief medical officer, Siro Villas, approached Pozuelo and told him that men were going to kill him that night.

That evening, Pozuelo walked down to the river near where his unit was posted, as he did every day to bathe. Juan Carrascosa Peñuela, another doctor recently arrived to the unit, followed him. Pozuelo turned around to face Carrascosa. "Look, man. I'm going to desert, right now, because if I don't, they'll kill me tonight. What I can't do is let you stay here. Either you start yelling, or they'll shoot you for letting me get away." But as it turned out, Carrascosa had been thinking about leaving too. The two men slipped out and followed the river to where it met a Nationalist position. A Republican disciplinary patrol fired on them, but, jumping in the river, they alerted the Nationalist forces, who gave them covering fire. Pozuelo and Carrascosa had deserted. They were far from alone. We do not know exactly how many soldiers in the Spanish Republic deserted, but the number may run into the tens of thousands, and several times the desertion rate on the Nationalist side.[2]

This book sets out to explain how armed groups in civil wars are able, or not, to prevent desertion. Sometimes—very often in some wars—combatants leave. They go home, they switch sides, or they flee the war zone altogether. Others stay and fight, despite the hardships of war. How do some armed groups keep their soldiers fighting over long periods of time? Why do other groups fall apart from desertion and defection? Do the successful ones have members who are committed to the cause and trust in each other, working together for a collective goal? Does reliability grow out of the barrel of a gun, out of coercing soldiers?

The Argument in Brief

To answer these questions, this book zooms in on the world of combatants in military units, with their comrades and commanders. Put simply, my argument is that bonds of trust among combatants keep them fighting, mistrust pushes them to leave, and beliefs about political commitments and the motivation to fight shape both. Trust and mistrust depend on what soldiers perceive about others' motivations, both political (in a broad sense) and military. Trust emerges more easily when a group of combatants knows that it has something to achieve together and that others accept the costs of fighting for it. They create norms of cooperation, social rules saying "if others fight, I will too." Trusting that others will indeed do their part, they pool their effort and fight for each other and—in doing so—for the cause too. This represents a powerful obligation, pushing soldiers to stay and fight rather than deserting.

But for many units and armed groups, this picture does not fit. After all, a civil war environment shrouds combatants' motivations in uncertainty. One cannot always assume that soldiers in a unit want to fight. Indeed, soldiers in civil wars often have little commitment to the armies they join. Like Vicente Pozuelo, they may find themselves by geographic accident on territory held by a side they have opposed politically in the past. Many may have only a weak preference for one side or the other and just want the conflict to end. Others may act more for their subfaction than for the whole. Even motivated troops may not be able to well endure the hardships of war. So soldiers often serve with unit-mates who just want to survive until they get home or who want to actively undermine their army. Soldiers—even deeply committed ones—who fear that others will let them down can only wonder what the point is of serving. They have a powerful reason to desert while they can. And some, like Pozuelo and Carrascosa, can join together to flee, not to fight. Hence the decision to fight or to desert depends not just on your own goals and will but on those of everyone around you.

Whether bonds of trust emerge is thus the first central issue of this book. I show how armies build up trust and generate norms of cooperation among groups of combatants. Trust emerges when soldiers can prove to each other that they are motivated. They show this through their actions above all. Years of political activism before the war; joining up voluntarily even when doing so requires difficult training, submission to military discipline, and harsh conditions without much personal gain; proving yourself on the battlefield—all these are costly signals showing the sacrifices someone is willing to make to fight. Hence armies that build on prior political networks and then insist that new recruits prove their motivations are those that are best able to build up trust among combatants. Letting such standards slip undermines trust and can even move strongly motivated loyalists to despair. Mistrust also emerges when soldiers and armies stop using actions to judge someone's commitment and instead rely on stereotypes or subfactional memberships, presuming others to be disloyal whatever the reality may be and using judgments of disloyalty to pursue factional rivalries.

Can coercion work when trust fails? This is the second key issue in this book. Threatening punishment can indeed be effective, especially when it is kept in reserve and applied after an actual attempt to desert. But punishments can also make matters worse. Pozuelo stuck around in an army he did not want to serve because, in part, of the risk of being caught if he tried to leave. But it was the risk of punishment itself—preemptive, presuming that Pozuelo would betray the Republic at some point—that pushed him to get out in the end. Pozuelo's story is unique, but the key point repeats itself often. Where punishment follows a rush to judgment rather than actual preparations or an attempt to desert, it backfires. This is especially likely precisely in armies riven by deep mistrust. Long-standing political conflicts can create stereotypes classifying whole groups of soldiers as suspect, and divide one faction from another in the same army. Here, soldiers fear they will be punished even if they stay, and so they leave. In the end, coercion cannot fully overcome mistrust.

This book therefore develops a *relational* approach to desertion, focused on the links among combatants in an armed group and how they come to deeply trust or mistrust each other. This perspective shows that a group of combatants' capacity to fight together rather than fleeing depends both on their sense of obligation to each other and on the cause they put it toward. It shows that the political, ideological aims of an armed group matter (a point that is far from a consensus in scholarship on civil wars), and shows how: through the trust and mistrust that combatants have in each other as individuals. On the one hand, a common belief in a cause, even an extremely basic and unsophisticated one, helps combatants trust each other. On the other, these same ideologies often designate enemies, and when those enemies are in the armed group, the result is mistrust and division, provoking them to leave. Finally, the approach provides a model of a cohesive armed group, one that recruits patiently, both demanding and allowing that soldiers prove their loyalties through their actions. In turn it proposes explanations for why some armed groups are better able to succeed at this than others, on the basis of how patient they are willing to be, how ideologies play out in them, and the raw material of relationships among combatants that they have to work with.

The Principal Context: Civil War Spain

I develop this account of desertion primarily in the context of the Spanish Civil War (1936–39). My study of Spain, outlined in chapter 3, has two goals in mind. First, this book attempts to clarify the role of several variables, and Spain provides a particularly rich environment to do so: there were many different organizations on both the rebel side and (especially) the Republican side, and their differences, and evolution over time, allow me to examine the impact of different armed group characteristics on desertion. But the Spain case study has a second goal, to understand desertion dynamics in a particularly fascinating civil conflict.[3] I pay special attention to the Republican side, examining the dynamics of its relatively high rate of desertion at various points in the conflict.

In the context of this war, I first demonstrate my two key mechanisms—norms of cooperation and coercion—at the micro level, statistically analyzing individual soldiers' decisions to fight or to flee. I show the influence that soldiers' commitments can have on each other in chapter 4. This chapter takes advantage of the evolution in recruitment over time in the Spanish Republic. It shifted from volunteers to conscripts, soldiers who sent little signal that they really wanted to fight, because they had been forced to do so. This evolution put volunteers and conscripts together in different proportions in different units. I find that soldiers were more likely to desert to the extent that the other soldiers in their units were conscripts (rather than volunteers). Unit-mates mattered just as much as the soldier's own characteristics. I show that this was because groups of volunteers built up norms of cooperation more strongly than groups of conscripts did.

In chapter 5 I turn to coercion, analyzing a critical instance of it in Spain: the execution for disloyalty of over a thousand members of the regular officer corps on the Republican side. The war had started with a failed coup attempt on July 18, 1936, that split the officer corps and cast a shroud of suspicion on the officers who remained on the Republican side. This deep fear drove the executions of many of those officers, often in uncontrolled and local violence. Many officers subsequently deserted to join the Nationalist side. I show that the violence provoked many of these defections, especially in those units where the violence seemed to be driven mostly by the stereotype of traitorous officers, rather than by officers' actual behavior. Coercion can indeed backfire in armies riven by mistrust.

After chapters 4 and 5 demonstrate the operation of trust and mistrust in individual decisions in specific contexts in Spain, the following three chapters zoom out to consider military organization over the course of the whole war. Republican-side desertion had its seeds in the failed coup attempt that began the war. In light of the relational approach to desertion, this event set up future desertion problems in several respects. In addition to the suspicions toward officers, it meant that the Republic needed to build up armies fast. This led many parts of the Republican side to keep recruitment standards low in favor of rapid expansion. In breaking down central authority, the coup attempt empowered many different political organizations, sowing the seeds of rivalry and factionalism, and it wiped away the ability to control violence to really police desertion effectively. As the Republic steadily wore away at these problems in the first year of war, it created new ones in imposing conscription. Thus while some elements of the Republican side found the formula of costly signals that could reduce desertion and build an army, many did not.

In comparison, while the rebel Francoist or Nationalist side mainly used a conscript army, it had several key advantages in preventing desertion. It had a clear central hierarchy and comparatively unimportant factional rivalries. It had no equivalent, within the army at any rate, to the suspicion of officers that reigned on the Republican side. It had elite volunteer forces that demanded sacrifice and thus insisted on costly signals. These forces won the Nationalist side's key victories and reduced the fighting burden on less cohesive forces built on conscription or on less demanding terms of service. From the outset, the Nationalists also had a much more effective coercive apparatus to punish deserters. Ultimately, therefore, the rebels enjoyed important advantages in identifying those who were willing to fight, coercing the rest, and avoiding the dilemmas of suspicion within their armed forces.

There were many reasons the rebels won, and I do not claim to offer an exhaustive explanation for this victory. For example, my account makes little mention of the role of external support, the source of a crucial Nationalist advantage. My argument is mainly focused on explaining desertion, not victory. Even then, I do not claim to provide a full account of the reasons for desertion. Notably, hunger and impending defeat played an important part in the increasing Republican desertion rates as the war wore on, and in any event individual combatants have a wide array of reasons for fighting, and for deserting. But what my argument does do is to show which groups of combatants in the Civil War could generate the trust and norms needed to fight, how political divides played out in the trust and mistrust among ordinary fighters, and how armed groups grappled with how to deter deserters. This is a large part of the puzzle of desertion.

One might think that Spain's Civil War can provide only limited contemporary insights. It was fought over eighty years ago between (eventually) mass conscript armies using conventional tactics. But in many essential regards, the dynamics of loyalty in Spain speak to issues present in civil wars generally. There was the demand to be on one side or another, backed by the threat and the reality of brutal violence. This demand was made on a society where, despite the political passions of the time, many people had mundane and local concerns or were altogether indifferent. To show that the book's approach has value today, chapter 9 applies my approach to the Syrian Civil War, ongoing since 2011. In this chapter I compare across five forces: the regime's Syrian Arab Army, the Free Syrian Army umbrella, Jabhat al-Nusra, Islamic State in Iraq and al-Sham (ISIS), and the Kurdish People's Protection Units and Women's Protection Units. The chapter finds that the forces best able to maintain their cohesion, like their counterparts in Spain's militias, grew out of long-standing armed networks and maintained tight standards for recruitment, thereby building strong norms. The Syrian case has also seen the ambiguous effects of threats of punishment to keep soldiers fighting; these coercive measures have provoked desertion as well as preventing it. The problems of fighting desertion while fighting a civil war, I argue, are neither particularly new nor particularly old.

Wars of Desertion

Indeed, desertion is all around us in today's conflicts. The Iraqi army collapsed in June 2014 in the face of the ISIS assault on Mosul. Later, the rapid decline of ISIS itself, at least in Iraq and Syria, was marked by waves of desertion too. Deserting soldiers from Bashar al-Asad's armies fed the Syrian Civil War, but his core of loyal soldiers and officers has kept his regime in power. In 2011, some Libyan pilots flew their planes to Cyprus or Malta rather than bomb civilians. Governments of the North Atlantic Treaty Organization (NATO) have poured thousands of troops and billions of dollars into Afghanistan, but the desertion rate of their allies in the Afghan National Army remains extremely high and threatens to undermine the whole effort.

Desertion has an important impact on victory and defeat. A century ago, the flight of the czar's troops was central to the success of the Russian Revolution.[4] So it was in Libya in 2011.[5] D. E. H. Russell finds, reviewing fifteen rebellions, that the key predictor of success or failure is the cohesion of the government forces.[6] As for the cohesion of rebel groups, a survey of over eighty insurgencies shows that an important sign of their impending defeat is a crescendo of desertion and side switching.[7] A case in point is the Tamil Tigers, who suffered a wave of defection in advance of their final defeat at the hands of the Sri Lankan government.[8]

The dynamics around desertion also tell us a lot about life during wartime. Trust in one's unit-mates, the sense of participating in a common project, can deeply shape the lived experience of civil war and can fuel collective action after wartime.[9] And as I show in this book, desertion creates large incentives for the threat and use of violence against soldiers and their families. This is an underexplored form of force. The threats made against deserters and the suspicion of the disloyal also lead individual combatants to try to "pass," a vivid drama of their war experience.

Understanding contemporary conflict therefore requires a better understanding of military loyalty. So we need to peek under the hood, at the micro dynamics of military units and individual soldiers' circumstances. Any rebellion, or defense against one, needs to get combatants to fight. But up to now, with some important exceptions, the literature on civil war participation at the micro level has focused mainly on recruitment and not as much on retention.[10] On the flipside, while there is an extensive literature on the fragmentation of armed groups—studying when groups split apart into their component elements, and factions break their alliances with each other—there has been comparatively little work on individuals and small groups leaving their armies.[11] This book seeks to redress that balance.

Alternative Explanations

One of the key alternatives to this book's approach is very simple: some armies cannot meet the basic, mechanical requirements of going on. There is little that is more important to a combatant than the daily conditions of soldiering. Soldiers live with mud, disease, vermin, cold, exhaustion, and hunger. These factors put supply and organization at a premium. An army that cannot supply its soldiers with regular food, fuel, often drugs (including caffeine, nicotine, and alcohol), and medicine, and that does not regularly rotate soldiers out to rest, will face an elevated desertion rate regardless of what else it does. This is most obvious with food: rare meals and poor fare weaken morale terribly. At a certain point, without sufficient nutrition and rest, an army just cannot go on.[12] The same goes for weapons and ammunition.

This powerful argument has two consequences for this book. First, it sets a parameter or scope condition. In an army without food or bullets, trust may simply be irrelevant. But given that an army does solve these basic logistical problems, trust and mistrust can shape whether it holds together or falls apart. Second, the issue of supply furnishes an alternative explanation for desertion that must be disentangled from trust. However, trust also makes it easier for the individual soldier to go on in spite of relatively poor conditions, though again these conditions may need to meet a minimum of tolerability.

A second straightforward alternative rests on the prospects of victory. A succession of losses may induce soldiers to desert, suggesting both that there is no point wasting effort in a lost cause and that it would be unwise to be caught on the wrong side once the opponent wins. At the limit, this argument would suggest that desertion just accompanies defeat, that it does not play an important causal role in making defeat more likely. Both the prospect-of-victory argument and my relational account expect to see more desertion in a losing cause. Combatants will lose their motivation to go on as defeat looms, and this can undermine unit norms as soldiers believe that their fellows despair of going on. But there is a difference: in the relational account, it matters to soldiers whether others in their army are fighting, not just whether they are winning or losing battles. It is not so much the prospect of defeat as the loss of solidarity, the erosion of the norm that one should go on, that enables combatants to desert.[13] This can explain why we see high desertion rates even in some units in close-run or winning causes, like militias on the Republican side in the early part of the Spanish Civil War, when defeat was far from assured. It also can explain why some units fight on doggedly in a losing cause, such as in volunteer units in Republican Spain as time wore on. And it can explain variation among different groups on the same side, which was extensive in the Spanish Civil War.

In addition to these two basic alternatives, the relational perspective on desertion bridges four other perspectives on military cohesion: those that focus respectively on comrades, cause, socialization, and coercion. First, many scholars have argued that the key to keeping soldiers fighting is to surround them with a community, a primary group. Abstract political ideologies do not keep you trudging through the muck under enemy fire. What does is the thought of protecting your buddies. Units with strong social relationships among soldiers—regardless of their politics or how much they supported the cause—would then have low desertion rates. For instance, a major study of the American Civil War finds that socially heterogeneous Union companies had much higher desertion rates than homogeneous ones, arguing that this is because those who resembled each other would be likelier to have strong bonds.[14] This view also has deep roots in American scholarship about the German and American armies during the Second World War, and coheres with the experience of war as many soldiers see it.[15]

But there are problems with this view. Most notably, cohesive primary groups of soldiers may undermine an army as much as support it.[16] Buddies can get together to frag an officer or to desert together.[17] Indeed, in another study of the other side of the American Civil War, North Carolina companies whose members came from the same hometowns held together better than heterogeneous ones at the start of the war (as the theory would predict)—but, by the end, when the Confederacy was losing, they were more likely to fall apart. The same hometown-based social solidarity, in other words, could be put at the service of the armed group or against it.[18] The valence of a primary group—that is, whether a group decides to fight together or shirk together—needs explanation. More generally, a group of combatants may not become comrades if they doubt each other's commitment. The relational approach makes sense of these patterns by seeing the primary group as important but dependent on other soldiers' trust in a common aim and a willingness to fight for it.

A very different account of desertion places grand aims and ideologies front and center. Most prominent, in civil war studies, is the idea that people will tend to fight for the side they identify with: communists against capitalists, Serbs against Bosniaks.[19] More sophisticated analyses examine why some identity or ideological appeals have greater weight at different times and places but still see joining an armed group as, to a great degree, a function of an attachment to a common cause.[20] One survey of combatants in Colombia indicates that strong ideological attachments reduce the likelihood of side switching.[21] Again, this has resonance in international conflict, especially Omer Bartov's argument that ideological ties to Nazism kept German soldiers fighting on the Eastern Front long after their primary groups were destroyed.[22] The general expectation here is straightforward: better-motivated troops should be less likely to desert.

But this account, too, runs into problems. There are too many anomalies—people fighting for the "wrong" side of civil wars, for example—to accept a clear correspondence between one's grand aims and one's decision to fight or leave.[23] Further, soldiers do not make that decision separately from others. It is a rare soldier whose own ideals are enough to carry on fighting regardless of what anyone else does. Relatedly, the objection that the "comrades" approach raises, that ideologies do not matter much in the foxholes, strikes me as generally persuasive. More mundane concerns and the sheer terror of the battlefield will tend to overwhelm abstract political aims. As we will see in the Spanish Civil War, when committed ideologues arrived at the front, some fled in fear, and others left when disgusted with the war effort. But the relational approach to desertion argues that demonstrated commitments to common aims have an important *indirect* impact. Enduring daily hardships and battle depends on trusting one's fellow combatants, and trust in them must come from somewhere. Commitments to fight for an armed group tell combatants something about whom they can trust.

"Cause and comrades" represents a basic debate in military sociology, about whether soldiers are motivated more by ideology or by personal comradeship.[24] However, I follow a synthesis in this literature that suggests that the two sides of the debate are not fully separable.[25] I argue that in order to establish interpersonal trust in a way that supports the unit, it helps to have a basic sense that another's motivations are in line with the group. In this, my approach has much in common with the emphasis in military sociology on "task cohesion": the finding that effective performance in a military unit depends to an important degree on sharing a goal.[26]

A third approach emphasizes processes of socialization and ritual in armed groups.[27] Much of this research reinforces a familiar point: people can be made to identify with a surprisingly wide array of groups. Once someone joins a group, particularly one with numerous and well-enforced common rituals and practices, a physical space of its own, and a sense of opposition to an Other, they are likely to follow along: first as a conscious choice not to rock the boat out of fear of punishment or ostracism for doing so, later as an automatic, unreflective process without much of a decision being taken, and still later out of internalizing the rightness and importance of the group and its values.

At first glance, my approach would seem incompatible with socialization. The latter suggests that combatants' prior commitments are often not especially important; commitments to a cause would be more the product of group solidarity than what produces it. Cooperation with other members of the group, on a strong version of this view, is not really based on trust, not in the sense of evaluating what someone else's motives are. Instead, it is simply because holding to group norms is the done thing—enforced at first, until enforcement is no longer necessary and compliance is fairly automatic. This approach would then hypothesize that strong solidaristic practices, enforcing and ritualizing compliance, would keep combatants fighting regardless of initial adherence to a common aim.

But instead I see these approaches as close complements in important regards. Socialization is undoubtedly an important process in transmitting group norms. However, the question remains which group norms exist in the first place—that is, what it is that soldiers are socialized into doing. As we will see in the Spanish Civil War, units can develop norms of evading and shirking duty instead of fighting, making combat more dangerous and loosening the obligation to continue to fight. Moreover, group norms can face challenges from within. Devorah Manekin shows that even well-socialized combatants bring in competing norms to an armed group, creating a basis to resist and challenge group norms collectively.[28] Compliance with the group, in these conditions, is far from automatic. Socialization also faces challenges from individuals who actively intend to resist being socialized.[29] Finally, armed groups can be divided by social and political characteristics, with combatants treated differently not on the basis of whether they comply but on the basis of social or political markers. Such practices undermine the experience of solidarity and belonging that is central to how ritual and socializing practices fuse individuals together in a collective. In other words, soldiers' degrees of commitment and their mutual trust shape how socialization works. They give a direction to socialization, indicating what soldiers are socialized to do, and mistrust sets limits on socialization's ability to bring a military unit together.

Finally, in contrast to much military sociology, literature on civil wars has often emphasized how armed groups reward fighting and punish shirking.[30] This view emphasizes that war is a miserable slog of privation and risk and it is hard to persuade anyone to endure these hardships for some far-off common goal that they would be about as likely to get even if they did not join up. But offer a sufficient mix of carrots and sticks, and it becomes worthwhile for the individual soldier to fight and to keep on fighting. Minimizing desertion, then, would depend on high payment and on strong coercive penalties for deserting. As noted by many scholars, these are shaky grounds for motivation over the long term, particularly in the chaos of contemporary battlefields where behavior is very hard to observe.[31] Moreover, it is difficult to truly individualize reward and punishment in the military context. After all, war is a collective endeavor. Individual combatants depend on their unit-mates to survive. The question of whether soldiers can trust their unit-mates to have their back must be a key element of any cost-benefit calculation. The focus on coercion also requires an analysis of trust and mistrust because of the risk that an innocent soldier could come under suspicion and suffer a grave penalty despite staying loyal in reality. This risk means that a system of punishments could wind up provoking desertion, not just deterring it. In the Russian Civil War, for example, old-regime officers under suspicion and tight control from the revolutionary regime often realized that Bolshevik justice could be highly arbitrary, and defected.[32] Effective coercion therefore depends on a minimum degree of assurance—enough to assume that you will be relatively safe if you keep fighting.

The relational approach to desertion draws together these four major schools of thought on military loyalty around a new explanation focused on trust and mistrust. My approach argues that cause, comrades, socialization, and coercion are not rival explanations. Rather, the effects of socialization, comradeship, and coercion all depend in part on how soldiers and commanders assess combatants' willingness to fight, including their commitments to a cause. These assessments put trust and mistrust at the heart of desertion.

Implications for Civil War Research

This synthesis also helps advance our understanding of ideologies and armed organizations in civil wars more broadly. To what degree and in what ways do grand causes really animate armed groups and people in them? In civil war research, the pendulum has swung back and forth. Much scholarship in the 1990s made rather sweeping claims about civil wars as contests of easily definable sides (such as considering the Bosnian civil war a clear fight among Croat, Bosniak, and Serb and distinguishing ethnic conflicts in the 1990s from ideological wars during the Cold War).[33] In response, a wave of research in the 2000s and 2010s showed just how many exceptions to these grand narratives there were. To explain armed groups' behavior, this research largely put aside identity and ideology and focused on how these organizations meet the demanding requirements of launching and winning civil wars.[34] Scholars emphasized concrete motivations among individual combatants, like profit, survival, and parochial local interests.[35] However, research on civil wars has recovered its interest in struggles to mobilize followers around an ideological program (including ideologies like nationalism that promote particular identity groups at the expense of others).[36] Notably for this book, Jason Lyall's new study of mass desertion across two hundred years of conventional warfare shows that states that brutally repress citizens along ethnic lines pay for it in high rates of mass desertion and defection in their conventional wars: such regimes alienate whole groups of soldiers, who do not want to fight.[37]

But how are we to make sense of the importance of group goals, ideology, and identity when the concrete concerns of survival, power, and profit are important as well, and when there are many episodes of combatants deserting from "their" side, lining up on the "wrong" side, or pursuing their own agenda in tactical alignment with others? We have a tension in civil war studies between the sense that civil wars are fundamentally political phenomena in which collective aims, identities, and ideologies must matter at some level, and of civil wars as dangerous environments that individuals navigate in order to survive as best as they can.

There is a more productive way out, suggested by another major theoretical development in the past ten years of civil war research—the turn to opening up armed organizations to study their inner workings.[38] These works focus on the micro-level details of how armed groups mobilize, recruit, and maintain support, search for resources to keep their wars going, experience and manage factional cohesion and conflict, and generate norms and rules for members' behavior, including with respect to civilians.[39] This "organizational turn" has not yet taken up individual and small-group desertion in a sustained way, but it offers some vitally important tools.[40] At its heart are relationships among members, and how these relationships link members to the armed group as a whole, and to its politics.[41] For example, armed groups mobilize rapidly and effectively when prior personal relationships become conveyor belts for political messages that appeal to a shared sense of a group under threat.[42]

I build on this kind of argument in this book to suggest, in the conclusion, that an armed group's "grand cause" matters through the relationships among combatants in an armed group. When these combatants demonstrate to each other that they are willing to fight, their collective goals become personalized, and obligations to one's fellow combatant serve the greater cause, while a group of unmotivated unit-mates can drive even a highly committed combatant to desert out of a sense of futility. At the same time, the content of ideologies, the way that they designate friends and foes, can generate relationships of mistrust and push combatants to desert—even those who might otherwise have stayed.[43] Hence, a relational approach focusing on trust and mistrust resolves the tension between the political and apolitical views of civil wars.

This provides a mechanism to help explain the broad trend of the importance of collective motivations. But it also helps explain exceptions. The book's approach shows that committed fighters can desert when others in their units do not want to fight, and that the unmotivated can be made to keep fighting out of penalties and socialization. It also shows another way that grand ideologies and narratives influence civil conflicts: these ideologies come with stereotypes about who is loyal and who is disloyal, and these stereotypes can provoke desertions among fighters who are on the "wrong" side. In this way, it shows that ideologies can operate as self-fulfilling prophecies; such fighters may have carried on loyally as further exceptions to expectations, but for an armed group's decision to act on the stereotypes.

Such an understanding has practical ramifications, which I explore in the conclusion. The approach gives analysts tools for understanding contemporary conflicts, which the analysis of Syria in chapter 9 helps demonstrate. It suggests which characteristics help armed groups stay together and where these characteristics come from. Observers looking at armed groups as a whole can thus gain some insights into where cohesion problems come from. But this approach also suggests that policies that focus on individual combatants, such as Disarmament, Demobilization, and Reintegration programs, amnesties, and deradicalization, cannot assume too much about any individual's motivations and must take account of the relationships these combatants had in their armed group. Relationships of trust and mistrust shape desertion decisions and then carry on after life in the armed group. Civil wars are ultimately both political and social activities: they are about political objectives and the everyday relationships among those who fight in them.

TRUST, MISTRUST, AND DESERTION IN CIVIL WARS

From time to time, Viet Cong (VC) companies in South Vietnam developed serious morale and motivation problems, posing a major risk of desertion and defection. The VC would then try to isolate the problem unit and reform it. Henderson describes how this worked:

> The unit was situated in a remote area deep in VC territory, if possible. Fighters from the same village and friends prior to joining the PLA [People's Liberation Army, the Viet Cong's army] were kept apart to prevent desertion together or the emergence of old norms. Sentries were posted. No inter-unit visits were permitted above squad level, and the mail was heavily censored. Within this strictly controlled environment the cadres, removed from the responsibility of conducting combat operations, moved among the three-man-cells concentrating on reestablishing comradely relations and operating the informants system.[1]

So, on the one hand, the VC tried to spur trust and cooperation among combatants ("comradely relations"). On the other, it tried to cut off cooperative relationships that could undermine the VC itself. At the same time, it was not always easy to know if combatants could be trusted. One VC defector told RAND Corporation interviewers of the lengths he went to in order to hide his intentions:

> I knew quite well that my cell leader watched over me at the request of my squad leader. In order to dissipate their suspicion, for a long while I had been trying to show myself as quite indignant about desertion and

always made insulting remarks or criticisms about deserters. Only when they became less suspicious of me could I be given the change [*sic*] of going on assignment. And that was the opportunity for me to run away.[2]

Here is a dilemma, then: the armed group needs trust and cooperation to motivate its soldiers to fight for each other. But if soldiers might be looking for their chance to desert, putting up a false front of enthusiasm and conviction, where can trust and cooperation come from?

I put these questions at the heart of my approach to desertion. A crucial way of keeping soldiers fighting is through a norm of cooperation in a military unit, a social rule saying that each will fight if others do. Such a norm is based on an obligation to do one's part and on the trust that others will too. This kind of trust shows up most in units where most combatants clearly demonstrate their commitments. But in some units, combatants cannot rely on each other the same way. They fear their compatriots will let them down because they will not endure fighting or secretly support the other side. In these units, more combatants shirk and desert. Even committed soldiers come to doubt that their sacrifices are worthwhile, and some give up.

Much then rests on trust, but is coercion an alternative? Can an armed group rely simply on the threat of punishment to keep combatants fighting, even if trust is not in the cards? Coercion can indeed be a powerful tool. Note how the VC isolated problematic units and kept them under surveillance. But even coercion does not work very well if mistrust is severe enough. In deeply mistrustful armed groups that use factional memberships or stereotypes to assess soldiers' loyalties, it is easy to see coercion as arbitrary persecution. Punishments then provoke desertions and defections that they are supposed to prevent.

These issues of trust and mistrust can occur in both civil and international conflicts, but I argue that they weigh especially heavily in the former. This book is about desertion in civil wars in particular. Kalyvas defines these as "armed combat within the boundaries of a recognized sovereign entity between parties subject to a common authority at the outset of the hostilities," though I add to this definition two provisos about the armed groups involved: they are organized enough to maintain a distinction between members and nonmembers (unlike many riots, for example) and they publicly pursue a political agenda.[3] I argue that these conflicts' political divisions set them apart from international wars. There is a greater risk that a combatant actually prefers the other side, particularly in civil conflicts with highly mobilized populations.[4] Also, the armies of civil wars are often fairly new organizations, forming from the ground up or from splinters of previous organizations, from alliances of various social actors and prior armed groups.[5] All of this can raise especially acute questions of what it is that soldiers are fighting for. Of course, there is often suspicion of disloyalty or weak commitment to the cause in armies fighting international conflicts, such as among American troops in Vietnam, Polish troops in the Imperial German Army, or aristocratic officers in the armies of the French Revolution.[6] The distinction between civil and international wars may be more of degree than of kind. But the political level of mistrust is likely to be especially acute in civil conflicts.[7]

At some level, though, fighting is fighting. Some basic elements of military life matter greatly to desertion in civil as well as in international wars, and intersect directly with the concerns about trust and mistrust in the foreground of this book. For one thing, the collective character of conflict applies equally to each. Further, the issue of trust in other combatants is not just about perceived commitment to a common political cause but also about whether they are able and willing to engage in combat and in the slog of daily soldiering, politics aside. Trust also draws on social ties, which matter to both civil and international wars (indeed, it was the Second World War that made such ties central to military sociology). And armies in both international and civil wars have tried to employ coercion as a strategy to stop desertion (though I believe that, in civil wars, stereotypes of disloyalty can be sharper and can therefore cause coercion to backfire more readily).[8] I therefore draw on scholarship about both international and civil wars. However, I argue that in the particularly political and spontaneously organized character of civil conflicts, the question of trust in the commitments of others becomes central and shapes how all of these other factors work.

The book's theoretical approach operates at two different levels. At the micro level of interpersonal relationships in a unit, it identifies recurring mechanisms (costly signals, social ties, stereotypes, norms, and coercion) shaping the process of desertion and its prevention. Mechanisms are little bits of theory, building blocks for larger explanations.[9] Figure 2.1 summarizes this argument at a micro level. This chapter works backward through the micro-level argument, from the basic circumstances of the decision to desert, through trust and norms, to variation in motivations and different ways of assessing them; it then takes on coercion as a way of making up for a lack of trust.

The approach also lets analysts compare across whole military units and armed groups, suggesting what practices and characteristics help generate trust and reduce desertion. Armed groups that build on long-standing networks, recruit volunteers, and demand that those recruits prove their commitment tend to keep their soldiers fighting. Those that take anyone struggle to generate trust and often have to rely on coercion. And groups that are riven by factionalism and stereotypes of disloyalty will suffer from desertion problems. What is worse,

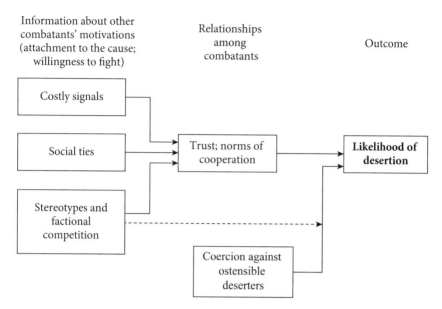

FIGURE 2.1.   The relational approach, at a micro level.

coercion will not help them much. The end of the chapter lays out the hypotheses at this level.

I do not claim that deserters are just less committed to the cause than soldiers who fight on. Grand causes often seem far away from the front, and even from one rank back, where soldiers often take the decision to desert. Soldiers tend to care more about the day-to-day of hardship and the risks posed by combat. Instead, commitments to a cause have potent indirect, second-order effects on desertion. "The cause" works, when it does, through the ties that soldiers have to each other.

This approach is also not a comprehensive view of the causes of desertion. Basic considerations like having enough food, actually being paid what one is promised, and the sense that the cause is lost and it is pointless to continue will always be important for desertion rates. Trust and norms of cooperation can help combatants get through difficult times, to be sure, but when supplies are cut off or there is a string of defeats, we can expect desertion rates to increase. My approach does not much take up supply or defeat, important though they may be. Instead it hopes to illuminate the social and political dimensions of decisions to fight or to desert.

The Decision to Desert

Desertion is leaving an armed group entirely, before an agreed term of service expires. I focus here on the decisions of individuals and small groups to stay or to leave, rather than faction leaders' decisions to break away from existing alliances to found a new armed group or switch sides. Desertion includes both what might be called desertion proper (leaving the fighting entirely) and defection (switching sides to a different armed group). There are important differences between the two. Armed groups often see defection as unpardonable but forgive desertion proper in order to bring fighters back into the fold. Different deserters may be more inclined toward one or the other; soldiers who join to profit from war might be more inclined to defect to find a better deal than to leave the fighting altogether, while those with political motivations who find the fight to be futile would do the reverse.[10] But despite these differences, it makes sense to theorize both desertion and defection together. At different moments in a conflict, the easy way out for a combatant may change. In the ordinary course of things, going back to civilian life might be easiest, but as the other side piles up victories or offers an amnesty program, side switching may make more sense. Lumping desertion and defection together lets me ignore these differences. I can focus on the more basic issue of why combatants leave and how to get them to stay, paying less attention to where they leave *to*. Also, critical aspects of my approach to desertion are similar for both desertion proper and defection. Trust, for example, is the faith both that other combatants will fight and not head for home, and that they will not sell out to the enemy. Last, at the level of data, it can be hard to distinguish between the two because an armed group that records a desertion often has little idea of where the deserter went. So I bring the distinction between desertion and defection into focus only when necessary, focusing instead on the decision to leave or to stay.

This decision is distinct from other important and connected issues, like joining up and fighting on the battlefield. John Lynn distinguishes very usefully among initial motivation (the reasons to join up), sustaining motivation (reasons to remain in the armed group rather than deserting or defecting), and combat motivation (the reasons to fight once in combat).[11] This book is concerned with the second decision. Unlike the decision to join up or not, the decision to stay or to leave an armed group is strongly affected by being in the armed group itself— subject to military surveillance, able to take a weapon and valuable information (which makes desertion a greater risk for the armed group than draft dodging, for example), under the influence of other soldiers, and with less input from civilians.[12]

The decision to stay or to leave the group is also not the same as what to do during combat, which has preoccupied military sociologists the most. Combat motivation is about the will to fight and to act together in the teeth of the terror and disorder of the battlefield, not giving in to the paralysis of fear or the instinct to save oneself.[13] In contrast, the decision to desert is very often not taken in combat at all. Whatever the war, combatants have long periods of rest, and for Lynn this is where the decision to desert is typically taken: "The soldier must exercise, train, march, and endure, but there is still time to talk things over."[14] Deserters often lay plans and pick their moments. For example, deserters from the Syrian armed forces in the civil war ongoing since 2011 depended on networks of family and friends to help them get out of the army and to rebel units or out of the country, and they had to wait until everything was ready.[15] Some soldiers even have the time and space to leave notes for their ex-comrades, explaining their reasons.[16] Many soldiers desert simply by failing to return to the unit after a period of leave.

That said, the decision to fight or not in a battle and the decision to stay or desert are linked. Sometimes, desertion is a spur-of-the-moment decision, after a unit disintegrates in the face of an onslaught. In other cases, deserters look to the chaos of combat as the cover they need to leave. Most importantly, after they have seen combat and seen how they and their unit-mates react to it, soldiers may well decide that they cannot face another battle, and so desert. This means that combat motivation and sustaining motivation are very likely correlated: if combat terrifies you to paralysis, you may become more likely to get out so you do not go through it again. It also means that how well a unit performs in battle—its ability to hold together and fight—can have an important influence on the decision to desert, for the risk and the terror are all the greater if one's unit-mates are paralyzed too.

Deserting, then, is a choice about which soldiers can deliberate—within the limits of human rationality, of course, but at least in relatively cold blood. The approach I develop here may therefore be called soft-rationalist. It is based on individual combatants seeking their own goals (though these vary greatly from combatant to combatant, and very often include the success of the armed group itself), and with a basic capacity to figure out how to act on them, within a social world with social relationships. It is not based on soldiers as calculating machines or isolated automata, but instead explicitly brings in information shortcuts, mutual obligation, following the crowd, trust, mistrust, and fear.

Trust and Norms of Cooperation

In this decision to desert or to fight, a soldier's relationships with others make a major difference. As Siniša Malešević argues, "All warfare is inevitably a social event."[17] Relationships with others can induce people to fight and to sacrifice themselves rather than desert.

Central to these relationships are norms of cooperation. These are social conventions that say *if enough others contribute, so will I*.[18] Norms of cooperation are integral to participation in both civil and international conflicts. Individuals can feel obliged to participate because others—even others that they do not know or in other places—are doing so.[19] For Elisabeth Wood, for example, El Salvador's campesinos supported and joined the Frente Farabundo Martí para la Liberación Nacional (FMLN) insurgency of the 1980s because together they could accomplish something—above all, a more just distribution of land—but many of them had to contribute if they were to accomplish it.[20]

Even if the collective goal is a long way off, soldiers in military units often develop very concrete norms in everyday life—specific obligations to each other and to the immediate group. Joining a military unit means joining a community whose members have to be able to rely on each other to do their jobs. If a combatant takes the first opportunity to hide or desert when the confusion of the battlefield or a home leave lets them slip away, the efforts of the remaining soldiers are all the more futile. The goal fades a little, whether it is defending a hometown, taking the next ridge, or imagining a different society. And if a combatant cannot be trusted to run risks to pressure another flank, provide covering fire, place an improvised explosive device, or ambush a patrol, it imperils the lives of others.

The collective character of war is a feature of both civil and international conflicts, dominating both the pioneering studies of combat motivation in the Second World War and Costa and Kahn's crucial analysis of desertion in the American Civil War.[21] Summarizing their argument, Costa and Kahn quote a veteran of several battles: "I myself am as big a coward as eny could be . . . but me the ball [bullet] before the coward when all my friends and comrades are going forward."[22] Mutual obligation is therefore central to scholarly understandings of soldiers' combat motivations.[23] This sense of obligation by itself is enough to push many soldiers, but when combatants waver, norms also establish collective penalties. Notions of avoiding shame, particularly playing on highly gendered ideas of what it is to be a man, appear in many armies.[24]

But not all military units develop strong norms. Why some and not others? Critical to this kind of reciprocal action is trust. I adopt a basic, broad definition of trust as the willingness to "accept vulnerability based upon positive expectations of the intentions or behavior of another."[25] It is a willingness to take on a risk about the future: the person I trust may let me down. I do not believe they will, but they still might.[26] For me to embark on the hardships of war together with a group of others is to make myself vulnerable to them. They have the power to make my fighting productive (in working toward a common aim) or futile, and more or less dangerous while I do it. I trust them if I believe they will fight too. This belief underpins exactly the kind of costly, reciprocal action that military service exemplifies.[27]

And the norm in question is indeed reciprocal. In other words, people wind up contributing or not, fighting or deserting, depending on what others do. While some rare individuals might believe that a sense of obligation to an ideal or to a collectivity requires them to fight regardless of what anyone else does, the majority of us balance our ethical obligations to others with a sense of self-preservation and a desire not to waste our efforts on pointless crusades. Norms of cooperation, in this sense, are a way of solving the classical collective action problem (that each member of a group wants to achieve a common goal but also wants to avoid paying the high personal cost that comes with making a contribution).[28] But this dynamic depends crucially on one's expectations of others.[29] Each combatant wants to know whether others will hold up their end of the bargain. In a unit where combatants believe that everyone will do their share, the obligation is very powerful: "they would do the same for me."

Not that every member of a group of combatants has to be strongly committed, and not that following the group is always (or even primarily) a matter of rational deliberation. Instead, socialization processes can transmit group norms to ordinary members. In social life, most people are fairly willing to conform to a group's expectations once in it. When we join a group that is strongly defined around a particular kind of goal, the behavior of others in that group can have a big impact on each of us. We look to others to get a sense of the values of the group and to develop an idea of what is appropriate behavior.[30] If there are initially unmotivated troops serving in such a unit, they are likely to fight too, despite their initial lack of motivation. At first, the committed majority can enforce the norm of cooperation and punish stragglers with ostracism and isolation.[31] Over time, uncommitted troops may be socialized into strongly held norms of the group, conforming because that is just what is done, and eventually changing their beliefs and values in line with what others want from them.[32]

However, these socialization processes have limits. Mutual obligation is precisely mutual. Hence, the presence of soldiers believed to be unmotivated, uncommitted and unlikely to reciprocate has effects on the rest. Fewer soldiers are willing to risk their lives for the success of the armed group. After all, there is less confidence that one's own efforts will really help produce a common good. The risks of combat increase for everyone, since each has less confidence that others will do their jobs. Fewer combatants will spontaneously push their wavering fellow combatants, upholding the norms of the group. With norms weakened, inertia and routine are no longer such strong elements keeping a combatant fighting. If others will not do their part, why should I? Is it really my part anymore?

Moreover, if uncommitted soldiers see that there are enough others like them, they can collectively resist some group norms.[33] In Wesbrook's words, they can develop a kind of "counterideology," such that "the non-obligated soldier does not see himself as dishonorable; rather, the counterideology makes him believe that his resistance or escape is right and proper."[34] These combatants can help each other out in *not* fighting—for example, to look the other way at shirking in combat or to hatch a plot to desert or defect together. Norms of cooperation have therefore resulted in groups of soldiers cooperating to resist the armed group in various ways. Wesbrook developed this idea in an international context—American troops in Vietnam. In that war, solidarity among groups of U.S. service personnel was sometimes turned against the unit and against the army.[35] Most notoriously, soldiers occasionally banded together to assassinate their officers.[36] But as we shall see, civil wars carry an especially high chance of this kind of counterideology given the strong possibility that combatants actually support the other side.

Willingness to Fight and Commitment to a Common Aim

In order to trust their fellows, combatants need to believe two things about them: that they are willing to fight and that they share some common goals. First, soldiers vary in their willingness to abide soldiering itself, leaving aside politics or grand causes. Some endure the boredom and hardship of daily military life, the submission to orders, and the terror of combat better than others. People join up for lots of different reasons, not all of which lend themselves well to soldiering. Surveys and interviews with ex-combatants in conflicts like those in Sierra Leone and Colombia find numerous different self-reported reasons for joining armed groups in the first place, ranging from community defense to profit to adventure.[37] Some join because their societies tell them that military service with honor is part of what it means to be a member (especially a male member) of their ethnic group.[38] Others join for a wage or to escape dangers in civilian life.[39] Such a combatant may be little inclined to take risks compared with, for example, an adventurer or someone looking to prove himself or herself.[40]

Soldiers also vary in their combat motivation. This is a problem common to civil and international war, with much written about the latter in particular. There are a rare few, such as the almost mythical figures of Alvin York, Audie Murphy, or Léo Major, from the two World Wars, who seem capable of an extreme willingness to endure fire and act with courage, in turn inspiring others.[41] There is a more general variation too. Major Lionel Wigram, chief instructor of the British infantry battle school at Chelwood Gate, noted in 1943 that "every platoon can be analysed as follows: six gutful men who will go anywhere and do anything, twelve 'sheep' who will follow a short distance behind if they are well led and from four to six ineffectual men."[42] In strikingly similar language, a VC fighter suggested that even a "normal unit" in good shape has many combatants who would rather not be there: it "must have at least 50 per cent of the men enthusiastic, 30 per cent middle-of-the-road, and 20 per cent unenthusiastic ones."[43]

The second dimension of commitment is that soldiers vary in the value they place on the armed group's military success. In civil conflicts, an armed group's ideology typically proposes a broader social group on behalf of which it claims to fight, and a political program to put in place.[44] People whose personal ideologies align with those of an armed group are more likely to join up.[45] However, ideology does not have to be very sophisticated to be effective. Sophisticated ideologues, well versed in the details of their political program, are of course rare.[46] But it is common enough for people to see themselves as part of one social group rather than another, and to react strongly when the group seems under threat.[47] This is all an ideology really proposes, to most people.[48] So, for example, in Abkhazia in 1992–93, when people framed the arrival of Georgian troops as a threat to the community, they were likely to stay and fight.[49] And combatants need not agree with the armed group on everything—just enough to see objectives mostly align. Armed groups can offer many different reasons to support their cause. For example, soldiers in the American Civil War, especially in the Southern Confederacy, often identified with their state above all. This helped mobilize recruits but also meant that soldiers often resented having to defend other states.[50]

Other collective goods can be highly concrete and immediate rather than abstract. In Sierra Leone, for instance, village self-defense militias provided an opportunity to protect a community not only against the rebel Revolutionary United Front but also against abusive government soldiers.[51] In El Salvador, the FMLN's success was the key factor directly permitting the redistribution of land.[52]

Soldiers vary dramatically in the value they place on collective success. This is true even in international conflicts; a national ideology can have a very different degree of influence on different individuals.[53] In some cases, members of persecuted and powerless groups may be little inclined to sacrifice much in an international war.[54] But the question of commitment to aims likely comes up more frequently and more deeply in civil conflicts than in international ones. As Laia Balcells emphasizes, civil wars are sites of intense and competitive political mobilization.[55] The stakes of a civil war can divide societies greatly between supporters of different sides. Many will instead be in the middle, without a strong preference for or identification with one or the other.[56] And even a single broad side can in fact be an uneasy alliance of competing factions with competing mobilization projects. The risks, then, are betrayal, apathy, and factionalism.

If people do not especially care about a group's success or would prefer to see it lose, how do they come to join it in the first place? First, there is payment: Sendero Luminoso in Peru attracted both peasant ideologues committed to land reform and opportunists out to enrich themselves in the drug trade.[57] Others may be forced to fight. About one-third of a sample of African rebel groups recruited combatants coercively, for instance.[58] The pressure to pass as a loyalist may be a major factor. People living in territory where an armed group is active and recruiting might support that group strongly, or indeed secretly oppose it and strongly support the other side. For a leftist in Nationalist Spain or an opponent of the Islamic State in Iraq and al-Sham (ISIS) under its thumb, it can be very difficult to cross the lines, and they may be under considerable pressure—from overt coercion to social norms—to serve a side they would rather see lose. It is to a large degree up to recruitment conditions whether someone who has little commitment to an armed group, or even is opposed to it, joins it anyway.

Civil wars also often raise the issue of factionalism. Combatants within an armed group may come from multiple different political groupings in alliance with each other. The examples are numerous.[59] The civil war in Bosnia-Herzegovina included frequent shifts in alliances among various Muslim-, Serb-, and Croat-identified organizations.[60] Uprisings in Palestine and in Iraqi Kurdistan have seen behavior among factions ranging from relative unity under umbrella organizations to open violence.[61] As in international relations, allies may (temporarily or otherwise) share the aim of defeating a common foe but conflict about much else.[62] So, alongside seeking battlefield success, members of different factions may seek to promote their own faction's particular interests at the expense of others. For example, they may try to gain preferred access to military supply and payment, to secure the promotion of friends within the military hierarchy, or to denounce rivals. They may have competing ideas about how to run the war, and have to divide burdens among themselves. Factions are frequently concerned about being exploited by each other. In Bosnia, for example, the crumbling of the alliance between the Croatian Defence Council and the mainly Muslim Army of Bosnia-Herzegovina in 1993 came with mutual accusations of betrayal to the Serbs.[63] Hence, factionalism can present additional aims that interfere with the common aim of overall military success.

These variations in two dimensions of commitment—to endure soldiering, and to do so in order to help the armed group win—may affect the individual soldier's decision to desert directly. Combatants with stronger political motivations and a greater willingness to endure combat may be less likely to desert than neutral or opposed fighters or those who suffer terror in combat and privations outside of it.[64] However, this direct explanation is secondary in my account. Instead, the heart of the relational approach is that commitment's major effects are indirect and second order, manifested in the mutual effects of groups of combatants on each other. "They would do the same for me" expresses both a profound obligation and a profound trust. Not every group of soldiers enjoys this trust.

The Problem of Information about Motivations

If many combatants may not be willing to endure fighting for the sake of a common aim, the problem of trust among combatants is a problem of knowing who is willing and who is not. Soldiers who have little motivation to fight or interest in victory generally have good reason to hide these facts. It helps them avoid suspicion (allowing them to shirk or desert more easily) and avoid punishment. It can therefore be hard to know for sure what someone's real motives are.

It is possible to pretend to have more combat motivation than one really does. Because combat is a property of all conflict, this observation comes from both civil and international war. It got easier to feign fighting while shirking in reality once modern firepower induced armies to abandon close-order formations with prescribed, coordinated sequences of actions for musket fire that could be easily observed.[65] Charles Ardant du Picq was already noting the problem in 1880:

> The soldier is unknown to his comrades; he is lost in smoke, separated, floating in one direction or another, or fighting alone. Unity is no longer ensured by mutual surveillance. He falls, disappears, and who is to say it was from a bullet or the fear of going forward? The ancient soldier was never hit by an invisible weapon and could not fall so.[66]

The problem continued through the world wars. Just after D-Day, for example, at Carentan in Normandy, American Lieutenant Colonel Robert Cole had difficulty getting his troops to charge. Only twenty-one men followed him when he blew the whistle, the others claiming not to have known the signal. As Anthony King notes, it was hard to know whether they were telling the truth: "Whether feigned or not, other soldiers pleaded ignorance: 'I heard someone yell something about a f—— whistle.' His men made a credible but not wholly convincing case for their non-participation."[67] And this problem continues to plague guerrilla war, with its dispersion of forces, hiding among civilians, and quick, hit-and-run strikes. As Jeremy Weinstein argues, a rebel unit that returns from a raid on a police post with no weapons may have actually raided it and found none, or may never have tried to complete its mission at all.[68]

It is also possible to pretend to be committed to a common cause when one is not—a particularly pressing issue in civil wars. A soldier would have to tread carefully before revealing disaffection for the cause to other soldiers and military leaders with guns desperately trying to win a war. In Timur Kuran's words, soldiers falsify their preferences.[69] Fascinating testimony to this point come from Koehler, Ohl, and Albrecht's interviews with defectors from the Syrian armed forces. The monitoring of soldiers' loyalties was intense, particularly of the Sunni majority who might be prone to side with rebels. The result, as one defector described it, was that in witnessing regime atrocities, "as long as you are within the military, you cannot show any reaction to this. From the inside, however, you are burning."[70] One defector reported that one day his commander was present while he was watching television footage from his hometown of Baniyas. "The officer reportedly asked him if he knew these people, and the soldier felt he had to conform, exclaiming: 'Yes! This person is a terrorist! He's a criminal!'"[71] Sunni officers interviewed by Hicham Bou Nassif confirm this view, talking of "the imperative of 'putting on a permanent mask' in the presence of Alawis,"[72] who are generally considered regime supporters. In short, armed groups face a basic trust problem. There may be many combatants whose real motivations stay hidden. China's People's Liberation Army defined the problem as one of distinguishing "beets" from "radishes": those who were red all the way through, and those who were red only on the outside.[73]

How, then, does a soldier know that a unit-mate will actually rise from cover to shoot, patrol where he is supposed to, and not take advantage of the confusion of the battlefield to run away? How does a commander or an intelligence officer know that a soldier will not pass key secrets to the enemy or defect at the first opportunity, taking other soldiers with him? I distinguish among three sources of information that have three very different relationships to a combatant's actual likely behavior. *Costly signals* show directly, through deeds rather than words, that a combatant is committed. *Social ties* are important, but indirect. Their effect depends on what information they convey. Finally, *stereotypes* and *factional ties* often generate inaccurate assessments of disloyalty because they are based on characteristics and not actions. At worst, there can be very little relationship between the combatant's commitment and the belief in it.

Costly Signals

The best source of information is simple: prove it. Soldiers must show through their actions that they are willing to fight for the armed group. A productive way to think about this process of "proving it" is through costly signals. Someone sends a costly signal of their preferences when they do an act that only someone with that preference would do, because it would simply be too costly for anyone else.[74] For example, did you support the cause when it was easy or when you had few good alternatives? Genuine supporters would, but so might those who are only weakly committed or who support the other side. On the other hand, did you support the cause when it was hard and you could easily have refused? Doing so indicates that your support is much less circumstantial, and you are much more likely to carry on supporting the group in the future.

I focus on four key methods of signaling. The first is the use of prewar political networks, which speaks to the specifically political dimension of commitment more than to soldiering as an activity. Activists who come to know each other in political networks before the war learn about others' commitment to the cause and can more easily trust them, a principal reason why these networks often underpin insurgencies.[75] In Kashmir's Jamaat-e-Islami, for example, activist networks intertwined political with social ties and developed a highly committed "backbone" of cadre, who "emerged out of [a] continued process of disciplined training for years together."[76] Activists show each other that they are committed enough to a cause to work for it even when in the political wilderness, and to suffer great risks for it. However, the political character of these ties among activists is important and distinct from purely social ties. The latter, as I show below, can convey lots of different information.

Activism, however, does not necessarily signal that someone is willing to fight in a war for the cause: to endure battle, to shoot, to kill, to take on an even greater risk of death. New wartime signals—recruitment, training, and combat experiences—speak to this willingness to fight. They can also, however, potentially speak to political commitments; showing the willingness to fight may show just how much the cause matters to a combatant.

The conditions of recruitment show what a combatant is willing to sign up for. Jeremy Weinstein's pathbreaking work focuses on material incentives: well-funded armed groups like Mozambique's Renamo attract "consumers" who look for short-run profit from joining a rebellion. In contrast, Uganda's National Resistance Army, which started up with very limited resources, attracted strongly motivated recruits, because to join up one had to be willing to endure hardship and privation for little obvious reward.[77]

Payment can be considered just one aspect of a broader calculation of what recruits are getting out of military service compared with what they have to put in. For many recruits, there is not much of a choice at all. Conscription means that the fact that one is part of an armed group does not indicate very much willingness to fight at all—not when the alternative is draft evasion and running the risk of harsh penalties if caught. Volunteers at least take the sacrifices of war on themselves. But among volunteers, terms of service can vary greatly. Pay can be a part of this, but even then, a high wage does not necessarily indicate lax volunteers out for an easy way to profit. An army can demand a lot from its recruits, impose strict discipline, and insist that soldiers obey orders that force them to put their bodies at risk, all while forgoing material comforts. Voluntarily taking on these obligations is a powerful signal because it says, "I am willing to put myself in a situation where someone can demand a great deal from me and I will have to obey."

A further moment for signaling is in training. Enduring a grueling training regimen proves to other combatants a willingness to endure and to do the soldier's share. Training with a group and then fighting together creates the confidence that those specific other soldiers will do their part; they have all been through it together before. It can also create a credential among soldiers one does not know.[78]

Performance on the battlefield is, of course, another key way of demonstrating reliability or lack thereof. Many soldiers and writers about war suggest that nothing really prepares one for combat.[79] So the battlefield is a place to learn about others, and indeed about one's own capacities and limits.[80]

Some armed groups will be better able to impose some of these signals than others. Notably, these factors may differ generally between rebel groups and states. In general, because rebels typically start from a position of weakness and seek to overturn an existing order, joining a rebel group may entail more sacrifice and thus say more about one's commitment to a particular political cause than joining a state army does. Rebels are also likelier to build on prewar political networks, though states often do so too, for example through ruling parties and their militias.[81] On the other hand, state armies may maintain more institutionalized training programs and may often have greater battlefield experience, though this is far from universal.

Hence I expect that units where combatants signal their commitment, by building on preexisting political networks, joining up freely and voluntarily submitting to discipline, undergoing rigorous training, and enduring first combats, are more likely to develop stronger trust and norms of cooperation among combatants, and to suffer lower desertion rates, than other units. Crucially, recalling the dynamic of trust and norms developed earlier, I expect the effect here to be social. The same soldier, regardless of his or her own motivations and the signals he or she sends, should be less likely to desert when serving among soldiers who have signaled their commitment, and more likely to desert when serving among those who do not. In a unit full of troops who prove their commitments, it is not only the committed who fight; in a unit full of the indifferent, it is not only the indifferent who desert. Hence, the approach's first micro-level hypothesis is as follows:

H1. The greater the share of combatants in a unit who send costly signals of their willingness to fight for the armed group, the likelier any member of that unit is to stay in the unit rather than desert.

Costly signals thus have two distinctive features. Through *actions*, not characteristics, combatants prove their commitment to fight for the armed group; and they thereby create ties with *content*, directed toward that common goal. Other sources of information—social ties, stereotypes, and factional loyalties—do not share these features.

Social Ties

Social ties among combatants can help them learn about each other's motivations, but the effects are much more ambiguous than with costly signals. Some prominent approaches to cohesion stress the importance of social ties and similarity. Network theory holds that knowing someone grants access to information about their preferences; this is how networks can overcome some problems of collective action.[82] People who do not know each other but who are socially similar, sharing a job, a hometown or a region of origin, or a language, tend to find it easier to communicate and cooperate and believe that they have values in common.[83] Hence Costa and Kahn find that Union volunteers in the American Civil War were less likely to desert the more socially homogenous their companies were. Union soldiers, they argue, fought ultimately for each other; they were "loyal to men who looked like themselves."[84] In contrast, socially heterogeneous units became areas in which stereotypes about motivation and loyalty were more likely to emerge, such as prejudice against Irish soldiers in Union companies.[85]

But in contrast to costly signals, social homogeneity does not always help reduce desertion. Since people vary in motivation, sharing a hometown or an occupation with another soldier may only mean that one soldier knows (or can find out relatively easily) that a unit-mate is indifferent or indeed actually supports the other side and is just in the armed group out of fear or opportunism. This would hardly help build trust. Worse for the armed group, if combatants' social connections and homogeneity allow them to identify others who, like them, do not want to fight, they can draw on those ties to desert together, not just to fight together. Purely social commonalities among combatants in armed groups may reduce desertion rates only where combatants generally have a commitment to fighting, with social ties acting an aid to finding out this preference and generating trust. In contrast to the finding about the Union side noted above, as the Confederacy was losing, North Carolina units had *higher* desertion rates the more homogenous they were, with soldiers despairing of victory and relying on their social networks to help each other desert.[86]

I therefore expect a contingent relationship. Social homogeneity should reduce desertion rates in units where combatants are generally fairly committed to the armed group and its aims. (Here, costly signals provide evidence of this.) Homogeneity should have little effect, and can even increase desertion rates, in units where combatants are uncommitted.

> H2. *The more socially homogeneous the military unit, the less likely any soldier is to desert, provided soldiers in that unit are generally committed to fight for the armed group, as evidenced by sending a (somewhat) costly signal of that commitment.*[87]

Stereotypes and Factionalism

In contrast to signals based on actions, combatants and officers often use stereotypes about loyalties. They can seize on an attribute to judge someone's loyalty or motivation and extend it out as a general method of assessment. In times of civil strife, armed groups and other political actors mobilize groups around identities, telling people which side they and others *should* be on—that the working class is for the communists, Sunnis support the rebels, leftists are for the regime, and so on. Mobilization makes these identities salient, in other words. But this also means that people who do not share these identities (say, peasants, Kurds, liberals) may be suspected of apathy, and people identified with groups mobilized by the other side (the bourgeoisie, Alawites, conservatives) come under suspicion for treason. Mistrusted, fearing denunciation or abandonment in combat, a soldier under suspicion is more likely to desert.

Probably the most common set of stereotypes has to do with ethnic or communal identity. State armies have frequently relied on what Cynthia Enloe calls "ethnic state security maps": more or less systematic assessments of who is loyal and who is not on the basis of ethnic identity.[88] Armed groups can employ lots of other markers for stereotypes, however. Class identity is another major division— for example, during the French Revolution and the Russian Civil War. During the latter, as Kalyvas notes, "the Whites sometimes determined who was a Bolshevik by looking for callused hands."[89] Beyond large-scale social divides, military life itself provides further bases for stereotypical judgments. Elite, handpicked units like Presidential Guards may develop reputations as through-and-through loyalists.[90] In rebel armies, certain generations of recruits are sometimes seen as associated with particular sets of loyalties or motivations.[91]

It is difficult to generalize about which stereotypes matter. In one conflict, ethnicity might be more pertinent, while in another, actors might more frequently employ social class. Indeed, alignments and stereotypes may be highly localized within conflicts.[92] For example, while the Syrian Civil War generally pitted Sunnis against Alawis in Homs, it sharply divided the Sunni community in Aleppo, such that sectarian identity could much more easily be used as an indicator of support in the former than in the latter.[93] The likeliest path for analysis is a back-and-forth process in which people make political choices that are simplified into stereotypes that then shape further choices. Across societies, beliefs on the order of "Alawites support the regime" or "peasants are for the Viet Cong" or "the Imperial Guard will always back the Shah" can become widespread shorthands for understanding political alignments.[94] Actual instances of disloyalty are likely to reinforce the sense that members of a given group are generally disloyal. But it should be clear that these judgments are frequently mistaken.

> H3. Soldiers who are stereotyped as disloyal are more likely to desert than they would be in the absence of the stereotype.

One important basis for mistrust deserves special mention because of the frequency with which it divides armed groups: factional alignments. Combatants can come to believe, or to fear, that others are more interested in the faction's interests than in defeating an opponent. Combatants may fear that they will be let down by unit-mates who are members of a different faction, looking to promote their faction's interests at the expense of the success of the unit. They may come to conclude that mistrust in their unit is at such a pitch that they are at risk in combat. Hence, units that are more divided among rival factions may struggle to generate norms of cooperation among their soldiers, and so suffer more desertion, regardless of soldiers' revealed commitments to fighting and their social homogeneity.

> H4. Soldiers are likelier to desert when their units are divided by factional competition.

Coercion as an Alternative to Trust?

Thus far, the book's approach rests on how to develop trust and norms of cooperation within armed groups. But when these norms are not strong enough to keep soldiers fighting, can coercion fill in? Frederick the Great of Prussia, for example, said that his soldiers simply needed to "fear their officers more than any danger."[95] In principle, coercion does not depend on what the soldier's commitments are. If the choice is either to be executed for sure or to fight for a side one does not believe in among other soldiers who will not much help, it is safe to assume most would choose the latter. The difficulty, however, is in making soldiers' incentives as clear as that.

Coercing soldiers to fight is a recurring feature in armies in civil and international wars.[96] Tight surveillance is a fairly common practice, especially in contexts in which desertion or defection seems likely. In Bahrain, leading up to the 2011 Arab uprisings, there were apparently nine to fifteen intelligence personnel within each unit, and these personnel used soldiers' families as a coercive instrument. According to interviews by Albrecht and Ohl, "If a soldier stepped out of line, he would receive a phone call from his own family advising him to modify his behavior."[97] Joanne Richards notes intense surveillance in the militias of the Eastern Congo.[98]

Is this coercive control effective? Scholars are skeptical.[99] Some argue that fear of punishment cannot be an explanation for combat motivation, because concerns for immediate survival on the battlefield should be more important than the risk of possible punishment after the fact, particularly as battlefield surveillance has become so much more difficult than it was in Frederick the Great's time.[100] Frederick's armies used easily observed lines of musketmen, helping officers see who was shirking, who was about to leave.[101] Tactics have changed radically since the eighteenth century, putting a premium on greater autonomy for soldiers, who often operate independently of any immediate oversight.[102]

Digging within armies, however, some studies suggest that soldiers are less likely to desert if they cannot minimize their likelihood of capture. Lyall finds in process-tracing analyses that blocking detachments do reduce desertion in the short run, including from the battlefield.[103] Nor does punishment need to be so immediate; the fear of later capture and punishment can weigh heavily. It appears that soldiers are more likely to desert if they have better opportunities to evade capture. For example, mountainous terrain like the Ozarks and Appalachians became destinations of choice for deserters in the American Civil War, as did Mexico and the border states—in short, areas under less state control.[104] This pattern linking rough terrain to desertion has repeated in Santander province in the Spanish Civil War (in my own work), and in upland Southeast Asia.[105] Richards has found that in militias in the eastern Democratic Republic of Congo, the ability to evade capture is critical to desertion, so that desertion is more likely when a combatant can find a United Nations (UN) safe haven or another armed group to shelter them.[106] The credibility of threats can make a great difference.

However, effective coercion depends not just on the threat. The flipside of deterrence is, as always, assurance: in this case, assuring combatants that they will *not* be punished if they stay and fight.[107] The risk, ultimately, is that armies jump the gun, punishing soldiers for desertion preemptively and mistakenly. Soldiers who fear this have a clear incentive to get out, in order to be safe. Ultimately, coercive tactics can backfire.[108] Jason Lyall has similarly argued that coercive tactics (specifically blocking detachments) reduce desertion but also reduce morale and spur internal conflicts and resistance.[109] I take this argument a step further: coercive tactics are often not very good even at the intended aim. They may not just deter desertion but provoke it.

Provocation essentially comes from the risk of arbitrary punishment. One reason why coercion may be arbitrary is institutional—a lack of restraint on authority. If you can be sent to the brig or the gallows on the whim of an officer, a security agent, or a local power holder, then there is a high risk of an arbitrary penalty. In other words, coercive power is especially risky if it is fragmented and held in many hands.

Beyond institutional characteristics, though, the risk of provocation turns on the same dynamics of mistrust we have already seen, on the problem of evaluating combatants' motivations. Officers and security services often try to predict who will desert, in order to decide whom to keep an eye on. To an extent, this is a rational response to constraints in resources. Commanders and security officers cannot observe everyone all the time. So they develop working theories of the kind of person who typically supports the other side, and keep an eye on behaviors like keeping to oneself or talking furtively with another soldier, or appearing disgruntled or distant. Doing so helps decide whom to monitor, so that if that combatant does try to desert, it can be detected quickly.

But, crucially, predicting who is likely to try to desert can slide into presuming guilt. Combatants stereotyped as supporters of the adversary have obvious reasons to fear punishment. It might be all too easily believed that, say, an aristocrat in Russia supported the Whites or that a Tamil soldier in Sri Lanka supported the Tigers. Such a soldier could easily become the victim of a malicious denunciation—a rumor of a plot to desert, for example, a stray comment misinterpreted, a furtive conversation seized on as evidence of disloyalty. In addition, in factionalized environments where multiple groups come together for the common aim of defeating an opponent, their other disagreements can present serious problems of mistrust as well: one faction might fear that efforts at controlling desertion coercively will really just be a cover for a factional rival exercising violence arbitrarily against it. Rather than sticking around, then, the safest course of action may be to get out.

I want to stress, though, that even if the use of punishments for desertion in an army can backfire and prompt many soldiers to leave, this does not necessarily mean that coercion is wholly ineffective. Even if the likelihood of a penalty is high if the soldier stays, it might be even higher if the soldier leaves. If the army can make sure that it can effectively monitor its soldiers and their families, then even a slim chance of survival would be better than a guarantee of death, and even severely oppressed soldiers might stay—a brutal predicament. But this scenario means soldiers itching to leave, if they can, in order to escape the danger of continuing to serve. Such soldiers would naturally look for lapses in surveillance to get their chance to slip away.

In sum, then, stereotypes and factionalism increase the pressure on the coercive apparatus and make it work considerably less effectively, because these threats will often provoke soldiers to leave. Whether these punishments absolutely backfire, provoking more desertions than they prevent, is essentially a matter of the balance between the severity of the stereotype and the willingness to punish preemptively (on the one hand) and the capacity to catch and punish deserters if they really try to desert (on the other). This balance is hard to predict. The best way to test the combined effect at a micro level is as two separate and concurrent hypotheses highlighting factors that can affect a potential deserter at the same time, with countervailing effects:

> H5a. Provocation effect: An increase in the soldier's perception of the likelihood of punishment **without** an attempt to desert should **increase** the soldier's likelihood of desertion.

This perceived likelihood should be greater if the soldier is part of a group stereotyped as disloyal or a member of a weak rival political faction; if the soldier witnesses or hears of punishments to members of a stereotyped group of which he or she is a member that seem disproportionate to actual attempts to desert; and if coercive power is fragmented, held in many hands with little oversight.

> H5b. Deterrent effect: An increase in the soldier's perception of the likelihood of punishment **with** an attempt to desert should **decrease** the soldier's likelihood of desertion.

This perceived likelihood should be greater with increases to the armed group's capacity for surveillance and punishment.

Taken together, these hypotheses also mean that punishing ostensible deserters has a weaker effect on soldiers stereotyped as disloyal or members of weak rival political factions. For these soldiers, coercive tactics may even, on balance, provoke more desertion than they deter. Such soldiers are likelier than others to fear that they will be punished on trumped-up charges. In this way, mistrust undercuts coercive measures and may even make them counterproductive.

Throughout the book I make reference to both the deterrent and provocation effects. However, as noted, there is a pretty well-established link between the capacity to find and punish deserters and a decrease in the likelihood of desertion, found in existing systematic studies including my own. (Notably, this work tends to focus on the army's capacity to find and catch deserters *after the fact*, such as its control over areas where deserters might hide—which is consistent with H5b.) But the provocation effect in H5a needs a systematic demonstration. I provide one in chapter 5.

Hypotheses at the Macro Level

Thus far, I have developed the book's approach at a micro level, exploring the key dynamics around trust and norms of cooperation within groups of soldiers. I have outlined hypotheses about soldiers' behavior. However, the hypotheses can also scale up to whole military units and their overall rates of desertion. Armed groups have different policies of recruitment, training, military discipline, and material rewards, and thus vary in the signals they require from their combatants. They are more or less riven by internal stereotypes and factional competition, undermining trust to greater or lesser degrees. And they have different degrees of coercive capacity to try to make up for a lack of trust. It is therefore possible to use this variation to predict overall levels of desertion in an armed group. Of course, there will be important variations within units from time to time—occasional uses of stereotypes to justify violence, for example; some groups of soldiers who have social ties while the bulk do not; lapses in coercive capacity; or some combatants who are pressed into service despite a general policy of voluntarism. These hypotheses are thus for general assessment.

Table 2.1 sums up the implications of the relational approach to desertion at the level of the military unit—that is, in terms of how overall characteristics of a

TABLE 2.1.   Military unit characteristics and hypothesized overall desertion rates

		THREAT OF VIOLENCE WITHIN ARMED GROUP		
		HIGH; AT MOST OCCASIONALLY STEREOTYPED OR FACTIONALIZED	LOW	HIGH; SYSTEMATI-CALLY STEREOTYPED OR FACTIONALIZED
Information about motivations	Clear and positive (costly signals, social ties, weak stereotypes, and little factionalism)	Strong norms; effective coercion	Strong norms; ineffective coercion	Coercion backfires
	Unclear or negative (no costly signals; factionalism or stereotypes)	Weak norms; effective coercion	Weak norms; ineffective coercion	

Note: The darker the cell, the greater the hypothesized desertion rate. Text of the cell indicates mechanisms that should be observed.

unit shape the overall desertion rate. It produces hypotheses about which groups should have higher or lower desertion rates, other things being equal, as well as about the mechanisms underlying these desertion rates that we should observe. It combines an overall assessment of the unit characteristics that produce information about motivations (i.e., costly signals, social ties, stereotypes, and factionalism) with characteristics of the use of penalties for desertion. The latter includes an assessment both of the capacity to inflict a punishment and of the pattern of the *use* of this violence, whether along factional lines or stereotypes (or apparently so). In the chapters that follow, I analyze hypotheses at both levels. The next chapter lays out my strategy for doing so.

STUDYING DESERTION IN THE SPANISH CIVIL WAR

This book's approach to trust and desertion operates at two levels. The macro level is about which armed groups and military units have higher and lower desertion rates, linking them to broad unit characteristics. The micro level traces out how these conditions facilitate or impede trust among combatants, and hence bolster or weaken norms of cooperation, and ultimately impel soldiers to fight or to desert. It also explains who within armed groups is likely to desert.

The book's research follows this macro/micro setup. Over the course of the next five chapters, I examine desertion in the Spanish Civil War at each level. I take advantage of how widely different factions in this war differed in their military practices. At the micro level, I use statistical analysis of individuals' decisions to desert, and use process tracing based on primary and secondary sources to show the development of trust and mistrust and the decision to desert. At the macro level, I conduct comparisons across armed groups, using variation both within and between the Republican and Nationalist sides.

After analyzing desertion patterns intensively in the case of Spain, I turn to Syria in chapter 9. This conflict, often compared to the Spanish war in its bloodiness and complexity and in the fraught problem of international intervention, allows me to see whether the relational approach to desertion travels outside Spain. I leave it to that chapter to introduce the Syrian war, but for the remainder of this chapter I introduce the Spanish conflict and describe my strategy for using the complexity of this conflict to test the relational approach to desertion.

Why the Spanish Case?

Spain's civil war offers critical opportunities to test and explore the relational approach to desertion. Within the same country, facing the same opponent, fighting a war in the same way, there were many different armed groups that did things quite differently. Some built on prewar political networks and some did not; some recruited voluntarily and imposed strict discipline, others insisted on very little from their combatants, and others conscripted. Some units were torn apart by factionalism while others were relatively unified. Some experienced intense mistrust of whole classes of combatant and others less so. This lets me isolate the impact of trust and mistrust, getting away from other issues like the military challenge posed by the opponent, the style of warfighting, available military and surveillance technology, or other concerns that plausibly affect desertion rates. This means in turn that I accept that these other factors may play a role in desertion rates (otherwise it would not make a difference whether I controlled for them); my goal, however, is to test the importance of trust and mistrust.

Some contextual factors assist this focus on trust and mistrust, but also raise some questions of applicability or external validity. Spain is a classic case of a conventional (as opposed to guerrilla) war. The two armies were in separate zones of control and fought along clear front lines.[1] This means that soldiers had to respond above all to what was going on within their own armed group. In contrast, guerrillas continually navigate the group and life outside it, swimming in the sea of the people and interacting with state security forces constantly, with or without fighting them.[2] In guerrilla wars, then, the use of violence and inducements by the other side may become critical variables in deciding to stay in the group or desert or defect. Further, the armies that fought the Spanish war were very often mobile, relatively distinct from civilian life.[3] Taken together, these factors enable me to focus on trust within the militias and armies of the Civil War without additional complicating factors. The flipside, of course, is a limit to how applicable the model is outside. Studies of desertion in guerrilla wars, for example, may have to include a stronger analysis of the interaction between the two sides or the influence of civilian networks, in addition to these internal dynamics.

Spain's Civil War is especially insightful because of the critical role of political mobilization, infighting, and enmity. The Civil War was fought along broad lines that had existed for years in Spanish politics, and along which political parties, unions, the church, and groups within the armed forces had mobilized civilians and soldiers for politics.[4] These conditions, argues Laia Balcells, shaped whom people saw as their comrades and enemies. Balcells shows how these issues drove the use of violence behind the lines, as political actors sought to eliminate their opponents when the conditions of local competition warranted it.[5] In a similar way, I argue that these highly mobilized prewar identities gave rise to the dynamics of trust and mistrust within armed groups, and hence to desertion patterns. Comrades who had struggled alongside each other in politics for years, for example, could trust each other intensely; and they could just as intensely *mis*trust members of other factions, those who fit the profile of their opponents, or the comparatively politically inactive many. Indeed, this was the war that gave us the phrase "fifth column" to describe hidden enemy forces behind the lines. This gives me key sources of variation, allowing me to compare groups of true comrades with units riven by mistrust. But it also makes the Spanish Civil War a most likely case for an approach that focuses on trust and mistrust. This suggests that, in other settings, the dynamics I show in Spain may be less sharply drawn: on the one hand, prewar activist networks may not have such intense commitments, and on the other, factionalism and stereotypes may be less of an issue.

Finally, as a well-studied historical case, the Spanish Civil War offers data availability advantages. I had access to official records relevant to desertion and defection that I would not necessarily have had with a later war, subject to information embargoes. Interviews and survey research, it is true, can certainly help make up for this in a contemporary setting and can allow researchers to ask probing questions.[6] But these methods also face the challenges—manageable but still present—of access and of the sensitivity of answering questions about one's loyalties in a conflict. Nor can they easily examine the loyalties of the dead, notably those who died while (ostensibly) trying to desert.

The Roots of War

The Spanish Civil War began with an attempted military coup by right-wing officers against the Popular Front government of the Second Spanish Republic on July 18, 1936. Beginning a day earlier in Spain's Moroccan colonies and proceeding throughout the country, rebel officers attempted to raise their military garrisons, with mixed success. Small extant civilian militias on both the rebel (or Nationalist) side and on the loyalist (or Republican) joined with soldiers and officers. Different actors on each side then organized new militias on a large scale. Over time— relatively easily on the Nationalist side, much more arduously on the Republican— each side converted its armed force into a unified conscript army and called up many draft classes. The character and organization of the opposing forces helped shape the patterns of desertion on each side and ultimately on the outcome of the war. Military organization was certainly not, however, the only factor leading to a Nationalist victory. Notably, Italy and Germany supplied the Nationalists with personnel and military supplies that far outstripped the Soviet contribution to the Republic.[7] But of the other factors influencing the outcome, military organization was highly important, and desertion a central part of that story.

The coup attempt of July 18, 1936, had its roots in the political conflicts that had dominated the short life of the Spanish Second Republic.[8] Founded in April 1931 out of the ashes of Miguel Primo de Rivera's dictatorship (1923–30) and the abdication of King Alfonso XIII following Republican-dominated local elections, the Second Republic was beset by intense political opposition, escalating violence, and ultimately civil war.

The liberal-left Republicans who formed the first Republican government (1931–33), with support from the moderates in the socialist Partido Socialista Obrera Española (PSOE), embarked on an ambitious reform program. They pushed for land reform, labor rights, secularization in public life and especially in education, civil status and the rights of women, and reductions in the privileges of the clergy and in the size and social power of the officer corps. Various conservative groups opposed these reforms: wealthy landowners and industrialists, conservative smallholding farmers across the North, the Catholic Church and much of the highly religious public at large, and a large part of the officer corps, though the armed forces were divided among Republican and reactionary groups.[9]

The right wing was not wholly unified. There were differences in strategy, above all over whether to work within Republican institutions or to try to overthrow them. There were disputes about what system should replace the Republic, such as among Alfonsists seeking to restore King Alfonso's monarchy; Carlists who supported both a dynasty that had been ousted in the nineteenth century and an intensely Catholic, conservative revolution; and the Falange party, which sought to replace these old institutions with a fascist system. However, in the interim, the Right was united in seeking to block the Left's attempts at reform whenever possible. Their parliamentary groups obstructed legislation, and when laws did get passed they encountered resistance from entrenched local power brokers such as landowners and detachments of the Civil Guard, the feared paramilitary police.

At the same time as the Right was blocking the government's efforts at reform, much of the power on the Left was held outside the state, and increasingly against it. The large anarcho-syndicalist union confederation, the Confederación Nacional del Trabajo (CNT), organized strikes to push for faster change and ultimately for a workers' revolution. Within the CNT's major rival, the Socialist Party-affiliated Unión General de Trabajadores (UGT), the revolutionary wing gained in appeal as well, with the moderates who supported the government delegitimized by the Republic's failures. Increasingly, then, the government was caught in a bind: many on the Left were mistrustful of centrist politicians and dissatisfied by what they saw as bourgeois, not true, democracy.

The 1933 elections produced a counterrevolutionary interregnum, "two black years" when a right-wing government rolled back the Republic's reforms. Doing so provoked a revolutionary uprising in October 1934 in Asturias and Catalonia, but the regime crushed it. But when the Popular Front reemerged to win the elections of February 15, 1936, the stage was set for a further violent confrontation. Military officers began planning a rising. Street battles broke out frequently over the following months between cells, still small in number, organized by the UGT, CNT, and the small, tightly organized Soviet-aligned Partido Comunista Española (PCE) on the Left, and by the Falange on the Right. The conflict crested in mid-July. The murder of a prominent Republican officer in Madrid, Lieutenant José Castillo, on July 12, was followed the next day by the revenge killing of the conservative parliamentarian José Calvo Sotelo. Days later, on July 18, 1936, right-wing officers launched their long-planned coup attempt. It started—a day too soon because of miscommunication—in the units stationed in Morocco, which quickly got behind the revolt. It was then followed the next day by attempted risings in garrisons throughout the whole of peninsular Spain, with mixed success (figure 3.1).

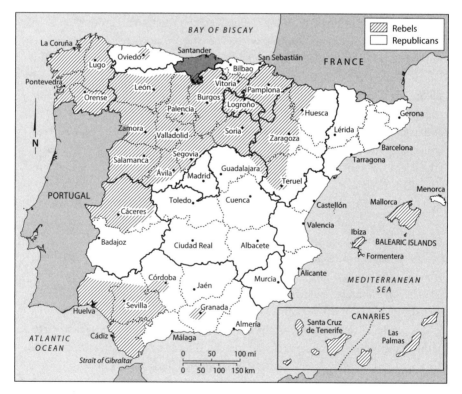

FIGURE 3.1.   Spain, end of July 1936, with Santander highlighted. Adapted from Paul Preston, *The Spanish Holocaust* (New York: W. W. Norton, 2012).

Militias and Armies in Spain

The outcome of the coup attempt depended on many unknowns, prominent among them the decisiveness and hesitation of the coup plotters and the preferences of the officers that they sought to bring onside. For example, the behavior of the Civil and Assault Guards was decisive in many locations, including the key cities of Madrid, Barcelona, and Valencia.[10]

The rising counted tens of thousands of officers and men, and shattered the government security forces. About half of the officer corps remained on Republican territory, but less than half of these officers actually ended up serving the Republic over the long haul; the rest either joined the rising, defected later, or were imprisoned or executed.[11] As for enlisted men, on July 18, the government immediately released soldiers from the duty of obeying their officers in order to stem what was still just a coup attempt, and many soldiers simply left. Again, about half of the army's enlisted men were in Republican territory, but thousands were no longer available to be ordered.[12] The various quasi-military police forces, the Civil Guard, the Assault Guards, and the Carabineers (customs police), all lost thousands to the rising.[13] In this process the Republic lost not only numbers but also the coherence of its military hierarchy: confusion reigned in the chain of command as many of its links were now missing.

The coup thus left a void, and unions and left-wing political parties were ready to fill it. They, and some loyalist officers, had anticipated a military rising more clearly than much of the government had, and had laid plans to resist it, coordinating with friendly officers for arms and training. They quickly formed nuclei of resistance to the coup attempt, backstopping the soldiers and other security personnel who remained loyal to the regime and helping to put down the rising in some areas. But the initial groups, a few thousand strong, would clearly not be enough to fight a war against the bulk of the Spanish military, alongside a deeply weakened regular army whose real strength was unclear. The government therefore decided to arm workers' militias. Indeed, union locals affiliated with both the CNT and the UGT, as well as armed groups organized by different political parties, had already seized many arms caches at the outset of the conflict while the government hesitated. Now with the government's approval to arm, these militias expanded rapidly. They confronted Nationalist advances in Aragón, Andalucía, Asturias, the Basque Country, and the central front on the approaches to Madrid.

The many different militias developed very different practices of recruitment and command. The Republic could not count on uniform standards in the militias, and had immense difficulty coordinating and organizing these forces for military operations. Militia members often looked to their unions and political parties for direction and orders, and these different political tendencies eyed each other with considerable suspicion. At the same time, the Republic confronted a revolution behind the lines: with the power vacuum extending to the local level, workers' committees overthrew local governments, expropriated property, and ran violent patrols and checkpoints.

The weaknesses of the militia system, the threat of revolution, and the encouragement and assistance of the Soviet Union prompted the Republic to reorganize its army from the fall of 1936 through the spring of 1937. In a protracted and contested process, it enacted three basic changes. First, the Republic imposed standard rules of military discipline on militias, incorporating them into a regular military hierarchy, the new Popular Army of the Republic. Those who did not accept this militarization could leave. Thus the Republic banned the lax practices that had been common, and militias converged on the regular, militarized model that some had already adopted. Second, at the same time, the Republican government steadily called up draft classes, thus adding far more conscripts over time to the volunteers who had fought in the militias. Finally, it imposed centralized control over the home front in Spain, reimposing a monopoly on violence. But this process sometimes met intense resistance, most notably among anarchists and the communist but anti-Soviet Partido Obrero de la Unificación Marxista (POUM), who fought active street battles against Republican forces in May 1937 in Barcelona. Still, in the end, it was a centralized, hierarchical, regular, largely conscript army, backed by a more tightly controlled home front, that fought the losing war against Franco's forces over the following two years until April 1939.

The rebel forces themselves were not nearly so disorganized as the Republic's. True, they were heterogeneous: the units of the regular conscript army whose garrisons had joined the coup attempt; the elite forces of the Army of Africa; and volunteer militias raised by the fascist Falange party and the extremely conservative, monarchist Carlists. These groups did not always apply the same methods of recruitment or standards of discipline. Franco relied above all on the Army of Africa and its elite subsections, the Spanish Foreign Legion and the Moroccan Regulares, which marched quickly through southern Spain, and the Carlists, who led the advance toward Madrid from the north. These forces provided the rebel side with a critical advantage over the Republic. The regular conscript army and the Falange militias were considerably less effective, and there were some tensions among the different political tendencies on the Nationalist side. But Franco had an unquestioned power over the Nationalist side from an early stage, drawing on a combination of acceptance for strongman rule and local order, a relatively intact chain of command, and the imbalance of power in the hands of the military leadership. Franco maintained a solid grip on this heterogeneous army as it and its German and Italian allies ground out a victory over three bloody years.

Micro-level Analyses: Comparing Soldiers in Armed Groups

The variety and evolution of armies in the Spanish Civil War offer several good moments to study trust, mistrust, and desertion. The first task is to show that the book's approach does a good job explaining individual soldiers' behavior. To do this, I need systematic records of desertions as well as characteristics of both individuals and their military units. This was not always well done: in the midst of civil war, armies did not always invest to the same degree in recording information, and records are not always well preserved. I found that an effective strategy, then, was to focus on times and places within the war when there was both variation in my key variables (in order to make strong comparisons) and good data availability.

The Republic's shift from volunteer militias to a conscript force over the course of late 1936 and early 1937 allows me to analyze how soldiers behaved when serving among conscripts versus volunteers, who send very different signals of their motivations to fight. Differences across units also let me examine how social ties and political factionalism within these units affected individual soldiers. I pursue this analysis in chapter 4, focusing on the Cuerpo de Ejército de Santander (CES), a component of the Popular Army of the Republic in Santander province (highlighted in figure 3.1), whose records are unusually intact and accessible. The chapter bears out the relational approach to desertion: combatants were much more likely to desert when serving among conscripts than among volunteers, particularly when this voluntarism was reinforced by social ties. They were also more likely to desert in units divided among the key union confederations, the UGT and CNT.

As for coercion and mistrust, several previous studies have already shown that the ability to conduct surveillance and impose penalties can deter individuals from deserting—including my own past work on mountainous terrain and desertion in the Spanish Civil War.[14] What really needs to be shown is therefore not the deterrent effect but its flipside, the provocation effect, in circumstances of deep mistrust. To demonstrate this effect, I turn in chapter 5 to the officer corps. Already before the war the officer corps was feared and loathed by many on the Left, and the feeling was mutual. The coup attempt of July 18 made matters much worse, even for the officers who remained: there was deep, and often justified, fear that they were hidden rebel supporters who would defect or otherwise sabotage the Republic if given the chance. The result was widespread violence directed against officers, including imprisonment and execution. Indeed, well over a thousand officers were executed over the course of the war, particularly in its early months. By the lights of Hypothesis 5a, outlined in the previous chapter, these circumstances should have led many officers to believe that they were likely to be punished even if they did not try to desert or defect, which should have provoked them to leave. The most vulnerable officers, in particular, should have defected. I find that those whose professional networks suffered surprisingly high execution rates—surprising given little participation in the coup attempt—were especially likely to defect, and that this included many who would have most likely remained loyal otherwise. This violence emerged due to mistrust, but mistrust undermined its ability to deter.

Mechanisms like norms of cooperation and the provocation effect of coercion are supposed to be able to explain individual behavior in lots of different settings. There is not space in a book like this to provide another micro-level analysis that could do this systematically. But at the end of each of these chapters, I discuss how the mechanisms I identify may apply elsewhere, and provide examples suggesting that they have traction beyond Spain.

Macro-level Analyses: Comparing across Armed Groups

After chapters 4 and 5 establish that combatants' desertion decisions followed mechanisms of trust and mistrust, I scale up to the level of units and armies, using the variation and the changes in Spain that we have seen as a basis for three comparisons: across units on the same side; over time on the Republican side, since major changes permit this; and between the Republican and rebel sides. I set up the chapters so as to exploit each of these axes of comparison, in order to maximize the leverage that I can get out of the case.

In chapter 6, I turn to the initial period in the Spanish Republic, in the summer of 1936. The militias of this period were all voluntary but varied widely in their approaches to organizing and fighting. Those that built on long-standing networks of activists were well placed to develop strong norms and keep fighting because their members knew each other's motivations well. In addition, the degree of discipline that militias imposed was the key difference among them, and became a crucial factor for the signals that combatants sent. Joining demanding militias sent a clear signal of a soldier's willingness to fight, and these forces developed strong norms. But others developed norms of lax behavior and fell apart more easily. Overlaid on these signals, however, were factors of mistrust. Competition among factions during this period meant that when militias were thrown together at the front, they frequently worked very poorly together, alienating some fighters and prompting them to desert. And these elements of trust and mistrust were especially important because the Republic had little ability to find deserting militiamen and induce them to return to the front or punish them. The shattering of the regular forces of public order meant that it was often not difficult for a deserter to evade.

From these heterogeneous volunteer militias, the Republic's army shifted over late 1936 and early 1937 toward the regular Popular Army of the Republic. Chapter 7 analyzes this over-time shift and compares across the resulting forces, which still varied in composition. The conscripts who ended up as the large majority of these forces sent no signal of commitment. Volunteers, however, sent a stronger signal than the militia had: with the choice to accept the imposition of military discipline or to resign, militia members who carried on fighting showed not only an active willingness to remain, but to do so under tougher conditions. As my approach expects, I find that it was very difficult to build up norms of cooperation among groups of conscripts, that it was much easier to do so among groups of volunteers, and that volunteer units became more cohesive than they had been under the militia period.

The greater centralized coercive capacity in the Republic did eventually intimidate many prospective deserters. This compensated to some degree for the shift to a conscript army. Even so, this coercive capacity was undermined, at first, by

TABLE 3.1. Military unit characteristics and hypothesized overall desertion rates—Spain

		THREAT OF VIOLENCE WITHIN ARMED GROUP		
		HIGH; AT MOST OCCASIONALLY STEREOTYPED OR FACTIONALIZED	LOW	HIGH; SYSTEMATICALLY STEREOTYPED OR FACTIONALIZED
Information about motivations	Clear and positive	Popular Army volunteer units (7)	Fifth Regiment and some other Republican militias (6)	
		Legion (early) (8)		
		Regulares (8)		
		Carlist forces (8)		
	Unclear or negative	Popular Army conscript units (7)	Most Republican militias (6)	Officers under Republic (6)
		Nationalist conscript units (8)		POUM and CNT units during militarization (7)
		Falange militias (8)		
		Legion (later) (8)		

Note: Units are placed according to the independent variables. Numbers indicate chapters in which the unit is discussed.

the mistrust that factionalism engendered. In line with my approach, factional competition made it harder to cooperate. However, the increase in coercive capacity in the Republic allows me to examine a further claim in this chapter: that mistrust undermines coercion, and specifically that factionalism should prompt fears that coercion can be used in an arbitrary way, to target one's political opponents. This is confirmed in the widespread desertion among the opponents of the increasingly powerful Communist Party as militarization was imposed on them; the Republic's new coercive measures governing soldiers and military units were seen, often fairly, as simply a cover for political persecution.

Chapter 8 then turns to the rebel side. Nationalist forces experienced fewer desertions than their opponent. This is not to say that they achieved a wholly cohesive army; indeed, the Nationalists experienced challenges similar to those of the Republic, but in a much reduced degree. In terms of costly signals, key Nationalist volunteer forces—the Legion, the Regulares, and the Carlist militias—were typically subject to strict discipline from an early stage. Voluntary recruits therefore demonstrated a clear willingness to fight in these units. However, there were some exceptions to strict discipline among civilian militias organized by the Falange. And like the Republicans from militarization onward, much of the Nationalist force was conscripted. I take advantage of this variation to compare across elements of the rebel forces, showing that variation in recruitment standards corresponded to variation in norms and desertion rates. Coercive control was maintained rigorously and consistently across Nationalist forces, and so those who did not want to fight often had little choice. At the same time, even as it brutally repressed civilians, the Nationalist side, built as it was on valorizing military strength, did not employ violence against a class of soldiers to the same degree as in the officer corps on the Republican side. However, important exceptions to this pattern did weaken the deterrent effect of Nationalist coercion. Similarly, the Nationalists suffered less from factional competition, such that the state's central coercive power did not have the provocative effect it did in the Republic.

Ultimately, then, the Republic's desertion problem emerged from the challenges it faced from the very beginning of the war. It was difficult to maintain trust among combatants when the shattering of the army led to so many different practices of recruitment and mobilization; when a powerful adversary created pressure to recruit widely; when rival factions competed within the ranks even as they fought; and when the coup attempt left it with few tools of surveillance and monitoring but widespread fear of officers' disloyalty. The Republic had to fight an uphill battle against desertion.

COOPERATION AND SOLDIERS' DECISIONS

How do combatants in a unit come to be motivated to fight for each other? This chapter takes up this question and begins the book's empirical work. I statistically test the hypotheses about trust and norms of cooperation that were outlined in chapter 2. Specifically, I examine how the composition of military units affected desertion rates in Republican forces in Santander province in northern Spain in 1937, a point of transition from a volunteer to a conscript army. Studying the Cuerpo de Ejército de Santander at this moment allows me to examine the impact of an influx of conscripts. I show how the resulting mix of conscripts and volunteers in companies affected the individual soldiers in them.

The chapter shows that it was not just that these new, "reluctant warriors" were, as individuals, more likely to desert than the committed volunteers.[1] They also influenced each other. The more volunteers in a soldier's unit, the less likely that soldier was to desert; the more conscripts, the more likely. Indeed, the share of conscripts mattered more than whether that soldier was a volunteer or a draftee. In other words, a soldier deserted partly because he did not want to fight, but equally because nobody else in the unit did.

The chapter's main finding reframes an important debate about why soldiers keep on fighting against the odds. Some say that it is no more or less than having highly motivated, committed combatants, others that it is about organizing them in cohesive groups, never mind ideology. I find that it is both, in combination. Individual motivations are not enough. Even a relatively committed combatant may desert if he or she does not trust his or her fellow soldiers; even a lukewarm combatant might keep fighting given enough pressure from a generally unified military unit. But armies cannot just dispense with whether their soldiers have a basic commitment to fight by putting them with their buddies. The cohesion of a unit does not mean much if the soldiers in it share a basic sense that it is worthless to fight. But put motivated fighters together so that they can push each other, and they will fight tenaciously.

The Setting: Santander Province, Spain

The point of the chapter is to test whether norms of cooperation among soldiers shape desertion. Doing so requires variation across units, with norms stronger in one unit and weaker in another, and soldiers sending stronger signals of their commitment in the former than in the latter. But I also want the external conditions the units face to be fairly similar. So it makes sense to look at the critical months of the transition from a volunteer to a conscript army: here, in a single force, with more conscripts coming in and new units of conscripts emerging alongside volunteer ones, I have the variation that I need to zero in on norms of cooperation.

The transition occurred across the Republic at different points, but this chapter focuses on Santander province (now Cantabria), between Asturias to the west and the Basque Country to the east on Spain's northern coast (see figure 3.1). Santander province has the right records at the right time: monthly lists of deserters by battalion, systematic reports of individual desertions, monthly company rosters, and over thirty-two thousand individual soldiers' files with information about their conscription status, hometowns, employment history, political affiliations, and service records. The desertion records in particular are relatively rich, many produced between the fall of Bilbao in June 1937 and the fall of Santander two months later; this moment of relative quiet after a major defeat provided the motive and the opportunity for a major investigation into desertion.[2]

In capturing the period of military change in Santander, this chapter is broadly representative of Republican Spain as a whole, with some limits. The course of the war effort in Santander reflected the general pattern of the Republic in some respects, but not others.[3] Cut off by the Nationalist zone from the bulk of the Republic, Santander developed an autonomous government and armed force, as did the Basque Country and Asturias next door. Despite this, Santander's war effort looked a good deal like the Republic's. Beginning with militias set up by unions and political parties as well as the rump military and security forces, it followed the Republic's directives and gradually developed a regular conscripted army, the Cuerpo de Ejército de Santander (CES). Santander's formal political forces also closely mirrored those of the Republic in general in the period 1936–37, with a socialist-dominated government; an uneasy partnership with the weaker but still highly active anarcho-syndicalist union confederation, the Confederación Nacional del Trabajo (CNT); and the small but rising Communist Party whose increasing political strength raised suspicions among the other factions. As elsewhere, political power fragmented among local committees at first, and it was a long and difficult process to reassert it at the center. In some ways, therefore, Santander province was the Republic in miniature.

However, in one important respect Santander clearly differed from much of the Republic: the prewar strength of conservative political forces. Unusually for a province held by the Republic, it had returned a right-wing majority in the elections of February 1936.[4] Unions were less active here than elsewhere, certainly much less than the key union centers of Madrid, Barcelona, and Asturias. The right-wing leanings of much of the population may introduce a bias. As we shall see, the militias in Santander had greater difficulty recruiting voluntarily than in other provinces. Further, the typical conscript, as an ordinary adult male member of the population at large, may have been more likely to harbor an identification with the Right than elsewhere. Hence, groups of conscripts may have had a greater demoralizing effect than elsewhere in Spain, so it is worth noting that the effect may not be as pronounced elsewhere.

Local Republican forces held on to Santander during the coup attempt through tactical ingenuity, a disorganized local group of coup plotters, and a commander who temporized without committing initially.[5] After the coup attempt, a stable (if porous) front was quickly set up on Santander's mountainous southern frontier, which remained much quieter than the Asturias and Basque Country fronts. Santander's militias patrolled this border and fought in the two neighboring regions. The various militias were gradually brought under the single command and organizational structure of the CES, and the draft began in earnest. In the fall of 1936, the Republic attempted offensives across the whole northern front to relieve the siege of Madrid, but they failed; Santander's contribution to the attack was a particular fiasco, prompting the first major desertion problems in the CES. The northern front was stabilized until April 1937, when the Nationalist forces, with their Italian and German allies, carried on with the conquest of the Basque Country and Santander troops conducted another failed attack toward a key highway to the southeast; desertion again plagued this offensive. Bilbao, capital of the Basque Country, then fell at the end of June. At this point it was clear that it was only a matter of time before Santander faced a Nationalist invasion. This began in mid-August and was over within two weeks: the CES's resistance collapsed in the face of the assault. Some CES forces remained in Asturias to fight on until October; others took to guerrilla warfare, which lasted sporadically until the late 1950s; but most surrendered.

Military Units in Santander

The development of the CES saw shifting patterns of recruitment and military organization, which I use to study the impact of military unit composition on desertion. Initially, the Republic counted on improvised groups of volunteers supplemented by the remnants of the army and public security personnel. At the outset of the military rising on July 18, 1936, workers and militias assembled for a show of Popular Front strength at key points of the province's major towns.[6] From that point on, the Popular Front forces proceeded to organize new units. The militia volunteers had nuclei of recruitment centering on particular geographic locations and particular political and union organizations.[7] Units sometimes drew on political and geographic ties at the same time; for example, the anarchist leader Francisco Fervenza formed an anarchist militia unit mostly from outlying neighborhoods of Santander city.[8] But this geographic and political concentration was not wholly strict; members of different unions served in the first column that formed in Santander.[9] However, there was less popular enthusiasm and voluntarism here than in neighboring Asturias or the Basque Country, and by September 5, 1936, there were only 1,470 combatants registered in the province.[10]

As elsewhere in the Republic, in Santander the Popular Front leadership attempted to retain central control of the new political and military forces that had emerged.[11] But Santander also experienced some of the same problems that plagued the Republic during the summer and fall of 1936 (see chapter 6), notably problems of coordination among the various independent militias.[12] In addition, the relatively small force raised in the province suggested a need for conscription.

The Santander government therefore shifted toward a centralized, regularly organized, partially conscripted army corps. It formed a Militias Secretariat on August 12 and a Commissariat of War a few weeks later; the latter was given sole authority in the organization of the Republic's military effort in the province. It divided up the militias into columns and began to keep more thorough records of numbers of men and arms.[13]

Beyond such administrative procedures, the army attempted to centralize military operations.[14] It also attempted to impose common disciplinary rules, as in the rest of the Republic. However, commanders differed in their implementation of military discipline. Some, such as Eloy Fernández Navamuel, commander of the Corps' Third Division as of November 1936, insisted on typical military discipline, including such standard military procedures as the salute, whereas others, like Fervenza, eschewed the privileges of rank and, for example, wore the same uniform as their men.[15]

Conscription accompanied this shift to a regular military: in line with the rest of the Republic, the local government called up men aged twenty-two through twenty-five in October 1936, and added further draft classes throughout the spring, entrusting the implementation and enforcement of conscription to local government and Popular Front committees.[16] A soldier who resisted the draft could be forced into a disciplinary battalion, his family detained, and his goods seized.[17] Through forced recruitment, and because conscription encouraged individuals to join up as volunteers before they would be required to join up as conscripts, the CES expanded rapidly, to over twenty thousand by December 1936.[18]

In sum, over the course of late 1936 and 1937, the composition of the CES changed drastically. It shifted from a group of militias organized by unions and parties at the local level to a centrally organized army with many conscripts, now placed into more heterogeneous units from different factions. These shifts in the CES are visible in the dataset of companies that I analyze later in the chapter. The average share of conscripts in a company increased from 34 percent in January 1937 to 61 percent by July. Both the creation of new units and the replacement of volunteers by conscripts led to this increase. With the shift away from the militias also came an increase in the average geographic and political heterogeneity of the units, by 11 percent and 17 percent respectively, from January to July.

Testing Trust and Desertion

The shift from volunteer to conscript army meant that there were many soldiers who had been essentially forced to join, whereas previously many volunteers had shown a willingness to run the risks of war even when they did not have to. As we will see across the Republic in chapter 7, when conscription began and the militias were militarized, volunteers faced a choice: either resign or accept the militarization order, knowing that if they chose to remain, they could not resign afterward.[19] Any volunteer who remained after this rule change, therefore, freely committed to military discipline. Conscripts had no such free choice. Volunteers therefore had signed on to service that they knew would be hard. Conscripts joined only when there were specific penalties for not joining. This gives me a way to get at a central concept of this book: the signals that combatants send to each other of their basic willingness to fight. In other contexts, there could certainly be other costly signals, such as training or the degree of discipline imposed. In Santander in this period, though, the key difference is between conscripts and volunteers.

According to the relational approach, it is not just that conscripts are more likely to desert than volunteers; crucially, they influence others. So the approach expects to find, above all, that the higher the share of conscripts in their unit (rather than volunteers), the more likely soldiers should be to desert, because groups of volunteers can build up trust and norms of cooperation among themselves much more easily than groups of conscripts can. This is how I test the book's Hypothesis 1, as outlined in chapter 2.

This draws attention to the *content* of the relationships among soldiers—that is, whether they have a link that suggests to each other that they want to fight. This focus on content is a key difference between my approach and some past work on cohesion that stresses that the social, interpersonal ties among soldiers keep them fighting—notably, ties based on their social similarity.[20] My relational approach suggests that these ties can either help soldiers solidify their trust that others are going to fight, help them learn that others are actually uncommitted to fighting, or indeed help soldiers band tighter to desert together. Thus, social commonalities among combatants in armed groups should reduce desertion rates only where combatants generally have an interest in fighting. What we should see in Santander, according to the book's Hypothesis 2, is that social homogeneity should correlate with lower desertion rates in volunteer but not conscript units.

In addition to signals and social ties, factional ties may divide combatants even if they all agree on defeating the enemy. With factionalism comes the problem that combatants may try to promote the interests of their faction at the expense of the armed group as a whole. In turn, interfactional mistrust may push some individuals to desert. As predicted by the book's Hypothesis 4, units that are polarized among rival factions should therefore suffer more desertion, regardless of their members' revealed commitments to fighting and social homogeneity.

To test these three hypotheses about group-level influences on the decision of the individual to desert, I employ a multilevel model combining characteristics of a combatant's company (including changes over time in composition) with those of the individual. My data gathering began by randomly selecting thirty-four of the forty-three infantry battalions in Santander province (this was the largest number of battalions that was feasible to study, given my time and resource constraints), and then randomly selecting one of the five companies from each of these battalions. The CES began systematically keeping lists of soldiers from each company in January 1937. I recorded all soldiers present on the lists at two-month intervals, from January through August 1937. I then matched the names on the lists to the soldiers' individual files and to monthly deserter lists and individual reports of desertion. This ultimately yielded a sample of 3,945 soldiers in thirty-four companies, organized into 111 company-periods.

The dependent variable is binary, indicating whether the army recorded the soldier in question as having deserted or disappeared in a given two-month period. The sources include lists of deserters, broken down by battalion, that the CES published each month; entries indicating that a soldier had deserted on the battalion's monthly roster; and entries in each soldier's file. I included soldiers whom the army listed as disappeared because of recording problems. Official reports tended to record battlefield and mass desertions—known as *desbandada* or disbandment—as "disappeared" rather than deserted, while individual desertions in quiet sectors would more often receive an actual individualized report. Partly this was because desertion was harder to confirm in the chaos of combat, and because officers were reluctant to report bad news; indeed, in some cases, commanders had to be reminded of the order to report desertions.[21] And, of course, a disappearance would be easier to explain in combat than outside it.

The data support this interpretation. Statistically, the rate of disappearance across companies varied much more than that of desertion strictly defined as recorded by the army. While the average two-month rate of desertion (strictly defined) was 1.2 percent with a standard deviation of 2.3 percent, the average rate of disappearance reports was 1.0 percent with a standard deviation of 3.9 percent. As much as 30 percent of one company—the Second Company of Battalion 139—disappeared in a single two-month period. This is consistent with reporting a wave of disappearances in isolated moments, and reporting desertions at other times. These waves seem to have to do with battles. Across companies, disappearance rates have a positive correlation with death rates (.15), injury rates (.13), and overall casualty rates (.20); this last is statistically significant ($p < .05$). In contrast, desertion strictly defined has a negative correlation to death rates (−.08) and overall casualty rates (−.03) and a weaker positive relationship to injury rates (.08). Primary sources also show the army dealing with this misreporting problem. For example, on July 3, 1937, the army issued a list of thirty-seven soldiers from Battalion 124 and reported them as disappeared. However, the investigation section of the General Staff issued a note on August 10, 1937, expressing skepticism that this many soldiers could have disappeared simultaneously. The army later reproduced this same list of soldiers, with "disappeared" changed to "deserters."[22] Ultimately, it looks as though "disappearance" was frequently a cover for desertion—particularly mass desertion. Thus, it seems sensible to treat disappearance as desertion.

The soldiers' files contained information on the soldiers' volunteer status (specifically *miliciano o soldado*, meaning "militiaman" or "soldier"), age, number of children, marital status, occupation, place of residence, parents' names and place of residence, rank, and some details of the military career. These files provided the key data for my analysis. I constructed each company's conscription rate as the number of conscripts divided by the total number of soldiers whose conscription status was indicated. I treated members of the military who had already been serving on July 18, 1936, as conscripts, because the conscription variable is meant to capture whether an individual indicated the willingness to join a common cause in the first days of the war.

Next, I look at social homogeneity in much the same way as Dora Costa and Matthew Kahn, in their analysis of desertion in the American Civil War.[23] I measured heterogeneity, as they do, in terms of place of origin, occupational category, and age. For place of origin, I constructed indices that measure the probability that any two randomly selected soldiers in a company come from the same county of the eleven making up Santander province (or from the same province, for soldiers from outside Santander). I did the same with seven occupational categories, ranging from unskilled laborers and yeomen farmers to resource workers and an economic elite of professionals, merchants, and students. I measured age heterogeneity as the coefficient of variation (standard deviation divided by the mean) of age within the company in question. Finally, to simplify the analyses, I aggregated the three measures of heterogeneity into a single index.

The key test of factionalism involves competition between the two major union confederations, the Unión General de Trabajadores (UGT) and the CNT. These confederations enjoyed considerable power in the Republic. In Santander, they organized the first militias, determined whether people could work, and provided exemptions from military service. Moreover, the UGT and CNT competed keenly for members.[24] I constructed an index of companies' polarization based on combatants' affiliation to the UGT and CNT. This polarization index equals one if a company is equally divided between these two confederations, and is lower the more it is unified.[25]

In order to distinguish from the individual propensity of conscripts to desert, I controlled for whether the combatant in question was himself a volunteer or a conscript. If conscripts desert more often but do not induce their unit-mates to desert, we should expect the individual-level conscription variable to correlate with desertion but the company-level conscription rate not to. I also controlled for whether the combatant had an affiliation to a union or political party. Members of volunteer units were more likely to have such affiliations. Memberships helped individuals gain access to jobs, exemption from service, and influential local allies, potentially giving soldiers less individual reason to want to desert. Finally, I controlled for the time since the soldier entered the army to take account of the possibility that a soldier could become more or less likely to desert over time.[26]

The results of this analysis are indicated in table 4.1. It shows how the predicted probability of desertion changes as different variables change, averaging across all of the soldiers in the dataset. As is intuitive, the results suggest that conscripts were more likely to desert than volunteers, and soldiers with left-wing affiliations were more likely to desert than the unaffiliated. But it also shows that it is critical to go beyond this individual level to assess group influences on individual soldiers. In particular, the figure shows the large effect of serving among

TABLE 4.1.   How predicted probability of desertion changes by different variables

VARIABLE	SHIFT	CHANGE IN PREDICTED PROBABILITY OF DESERTION IN ANY GIVEN TWO-MONTH PERIOD (95% CONFIDENCE INTERVAL)
Conscript	Volunteer to conscript	0.5%
		(−0.02% 1.0%)
Union or party affiliation	Unaffiliated to affiliated	−1.0%
		(−1.6% −0.5%)
Company conscription rate*	All-volunteer to all-conscript	2.8%
		(0.5% 5.1%)
Company social heterogeneity*	5th to 95th percentile	0.3%
		(−0.04% 0.5%)
Company union polarization	5th to 95th percentile	2.2%
		(0.1% 4.2%)

Source: Derived from Model 1, appendix, table A.2.

Note: Time since entry into army is omitted for space.

*Company conscription rate and social heterogeneity are interacted in the model that produces these estimates. The marginal effect of each is calculated holding the other at its mean. I explore the interaction effects below.

conscripts: at companies with mean social heterogeneity, the shift from an all-volunteer to an all-conscript unit is associated with a larger change in predicted probability of desertion than either of these other two individual characteristics.

To further illustrate how important the environment of the company is, figure 4.1 gives the predicted probability of desertion for volunteers and conscripts in volunteer and conscript *companies*. The result clearly suggests that a volunteer in a conscript company is substantially more likely to desert than a conscript in a volunteer company. In other words, even a volunteer might desert if everyone around him was drafted; and even a conscript might stay loyal if everyone around him was a volunteer. Conscripts were influenced by volunteers around them to stay. Volunteers were influenced by conscripts in their units to leave.

The company-level conscription rate also interacts in an important way with the company's social heterogeneity, as expected. Figure 4.2 illustrates how the effect of social heterogeneity varies by the conscription rate. In volunteer companies—indeed, in companies whose percentage of conscripts was 75% or less—social heterogeneity had a meaningful effect on desertion. In conscript companies, however, it had no relationship. This illustrates that social ties among combatants are insufficient to keep them cohesive. They did not matter in conscript companies in Santander, where desertion rates were consistently high.

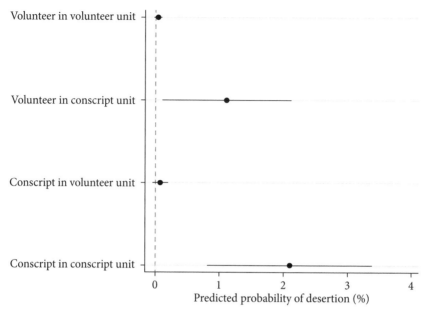

FIGURE 4.1. Company and individual influences on desertion: predicted probability of desertion in a two-month period.

It is also important to stress that social homogeneity and heterogeneity did matter for volunteer companies. Just signaling one's preferences through volunteering was not, it seems, a basis for complete trust; this trust could certainly be reinforced through social ties. Indeed, there is very little difference between conscript and volunteer companies at very high levels of social heterogeneity. While homogenous volunteer companies had uniformly low desertion rates, highly diverse volunteer companies could have similar desertion rates to conscript companies. Social ties were apparently important for volunteers to establish trust among each other. In other words, voluntarism was not a signal that could cut across all social differences in Santander.

Could supply issues and especially food explain the relationship between conscription and desertion? It is true that the CES suffered from hunger and that its rations were cut over time, and Solar attributes elevated desertion rates to this problem among other factors.[27] Clearly this hunger was not so severe or widespread as to completely incapacitate the army and make desertion the only option; many still stayed and the desertion rate varied widely. But there may have been favoritism with food and other supplies. Especially later in the war than the period under study here, there were continuous accusations that the well-connected received special treatment in access to supplies and notably to food.[28]

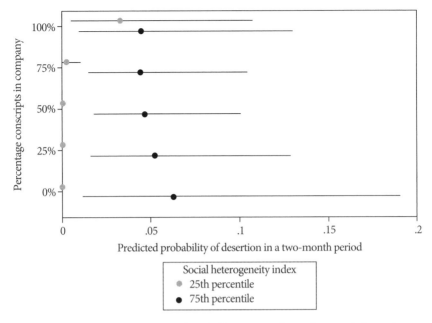

FIGURE 4.2. Interaction effect of social heterogeneity and conscription rate on desertion.

It could be, then, that soldiers were likelier to desert when serving among conscripts not because of a lack of interpersonal trust, as I argue here, but because they were too hungry to go on. I lack direct data on the unit-by-unit distribution of food or other necessities, and if corruption were an issue, such data would be difficult to credit anyway.

However, illness provides a way into this issue. Presumably, soldiers would be more likely to fall ill or sustain noncombat injuries when faced with supply problems of different kinds, such as food, adequate clothing, and first aid supplies. I therefore examined hospital admissions in May–June 1937. At this point, medical reports are especially complete in soldiers' files, and the overall relationship between conscription and desertion is strong for more socially homogenous companies (the coefficient estimates, not shown here, are very similar to those of the full sample). If conscript companies faced chronic supply shortages, we should expect to see this reflected in a higher rate of hospitalization. I therefore took the set of companies with low social heterogeneity (below the mean), which is where the conscription-desertion rate holds up. Within this set, I examined hospitalizations in the four companies with the lowest conscription rates (9%, 53%, 71%, and 74%) and zero desertions, against four randomly chosen companies with high conscription rates (above 95%) and relatively high desertion rates (excluding two companies with desertion rates less than 2%; the overall mean was 2.3%). In this sample there is no evidence that conscript companies faced higher disease rates. The mean disease rate, defined strictly to exclude injuries and include only disease (fever, influenza, and bronchitis were most common) and psychological difficulties, was 7.5 percent among low-conscription companies but 5.9 percent among high-conscription companies.[29] A preliminary test, then, gives no reason to suppose that life was systematically more miserable in conscript companies than outside.

How Conscription Affected Trust and Desertion: Qualitative Evidence

The quantitative results bear out the book's Hypotheses 1, 2, and 4: individual soldiers are more likely to desert when serving among others who do not send a clear signal of their commitment, social ties are no help in this situation, and factional divides make matters worse. In addition, histories of the war in Santander province, local oral histories, and archival material such as reports and orders within the CES bear out the point that the influx of conscripts and political factionalism undermined trust within units, and this mistrust played a central role in desertion.

In line with Hypothesis 1, conscripts had difficulty mustering much enthusiasm to fight, and some conscript units developed norms of refusal. "When we were ordered to advance, some fainted, others shot themselves in the hand," recalled one soldier in Battalion 105, whose fellows were almost all conscripts.[30] The army command clearly thought that the presence of volunteer veterans would help prevent desertion. On May 8, 1937, the chief of operations sent a message to the division commanders noting cases of desertion and abandonment of positions. It referred specifically to an incident two days prior, when "a small post of conscripts abandoned their position. . . . Having studied the causes, it is believed that the crime arises from insuperable fear, since, just before it occurred, an enemy battalion arrived." They were ordered, therefore, to transfer twenty-five veterans "of demonstrated valor and loyalty" to conscript units and to transfer twenty-five conscripts out. The order also underlined that these soldiers were not to undertake a "purification" mission but instead to "sustain the platoon's morale" by demonstrating "their enthusiasm for the cause of the freedom of Spain"—suggesting an awareness that active mistrust could make matters worse, and that the thing to do was to focus instead on creating norms that would push the wavering to fight.[31] Ten days later, a follow-up message noted that there were still cases of desertion, though their numbers were "not alarming." The division commanders were therefore instructed to direct their officers, noncommissioned officers (NCOs), and reliable veterans to remain in close contact with troops at all times to keep an eye on morale.[32] In another case, in May 1937, the chief of operations requested that Battalion 138, which had been detached from its brigade, be returned to it. The battalion had suffered a high rate of desertion (in my data, its Second Company had one of the highest bimonthly rates of desertion, 11.3%, in May and June 1937), and according to the chief of operations, "this loss would be neutralized in part [if the battalion were] under the orders of commanders they knew and with companions who on different occasions had suffered the same burdens."[33] In short, CES command seems certainly to have believed in the importance of serving alongside known, trusted comrades.

In addition, the process of conscription brought into the CES a variety of individuals of suspect political loyalties. To be sure, this had been a problem early on in the war in volunteer units, with rightists passing themselves off as loyal Popular Front supporters, including through getting hold of union membership cards.[34] The committed Falangist Francisco Rivero recounts that he was able to join the Popular Front in Escalante since, as a highway engineer, he had skills in some demand. He was able to use his position to gain safe-conducts to travel the province, organizing a clandestine network for the transportation of right-wing civilians to Nationalist territory.[35] Some volunteer units had trouble keeping out right-wing "volunteers" aiming to get to the front to defect to the Nationalists.[36]

Though these cases of hidden right-wingers certainly occurred under voluntary recruitment, the growth in the armed forces in the autumn of 1936, and particularly the use of conscription, intensified and generalized this fear of the political loyalties of soldiers. Local Popular Front committees reported on the political pasts of members of each draft class. Soldiers could be denounced for having done propaganda for right-wing political parties in past elections, membership in Falangist syndicates before the war, having worn Carlist political paraphernalia, or having been ousted from a left-wing union in the past.[37] Letters from a local union or Popular Front committee could be damning indications of disaffected political opinions, on evidence such as having leafleted for right-wing parties in the February 1936 election.[38]

Dubious political commitments posed very difficult dilemmas for the armed forces, undermining the ability of a cooperative, mutually supporting set of norms to emerge in military units. Political commissars, appointed at the battalion and company levels and appearing on battalion rosters in these positions starting in March 1937, had to supervise the political attitudes of the men in their units. Their instructions captured the dilemmas of maintaining cooperation and control. Keeping military discipline was highlighted as "the most important and most difficult" task of the commissar. To maintain such discipline, the document went on, commissars needed to keep a positive, cooperative relationship among the troops. The document explicitly contrasted the difference between "our discipline and fascist discipline," highlighting the cooperative, persuasive nature of the former. However, some situations required authoritative action; commissars were tasked with "knowing the moment to impose oneself over all." Commissars also needed to keep a close watch on soldiers' political loyalties, isolating agents provocateurs within the unit and "seeking out secret collaborators in the heart of the unit who would maintain vigilance over any suspicious elements."[39]

These were hardly ideal circumstances for cooperation. Soldiers frequently found that they had to be careful about their words lest fellow soldiers denounce them, and they sometimes decided to leave when the climate of rumor became too problematic. For example, one soldier in Battalion 134 was denounced by other soldiers, who said he celebrated Nationalist victories and insulted his compatriots. In his trial for desertion, he attested that these rumors drove him to leave.[40] Another told unit-mates that the war was lost if Bilbao were to fall; a fellow soldier alerted the company commander, who, on the basis of this and other incidents, ordered him detained, whereupon he tried to defect to the enemy lines.[41] These cases of desertion brought on by suspicions of disloyalty hint at a confirmation of the book's Hypothesis 3, that soldiers stereotyped as deserters are more likely to desert. Unfortunately, there is no way of testing this systematically; there is the possibility that these two soldiers would have attempted to desert anyway.

Such problems of cooperation, emerging from dubious political commitments, could reach a crisis point. Francisco Fervenza, commanding the Twelfth Brigade, faced serious tensions with militiamen accusing conscripts of being secret right-wingers, including sinister hints of getting rid of those conscripts. Fervenza gathered all two thousand men of the brigade in a field and announced that he would shoot any man who killed another in the unit. Those who attempted to defect would be tried and, if found guilty, executed, but this justice dealt with acts and not thoughts: "Never can someone be guilty just because of his way of thinking. Never!" Subsequently, according to Gutiérrez Flores and Gudín de la Lama, several right-wing soldiers in his unit were actually decorated for valor.[42] But such an approach was relatively uncommon.

The change from volunteer to conscript units also affected how groups of soldiers from similar backgrounds came to trust each other, and how they used that trust, confirming Hypothesis 2 and the mechanism behind it. One soldier from Battalion 125, who went with others from Liébana county to Santander city to volunteer at the start of the war, remembers: "In Battalion 125 we were mostly Lebaniégos [i.e., from Liébana], fighting to defend our own."[43] However, especially as conscription brought in more uncommitted soldiers, connections between soldiers could allow them to learn that they had little interest in fighting. For example, in the 133rd Battalion (mostly conscripts in my dataset), one soldier denounced a former coworker as a rightist.[44] These connections could also increase the propensity for desertion, by allowing soldiers who did not want to fight to find allies in their plans to desert. There were several plots among soldiers to desert together, and these plots rested on trust. Reports of the detention of prospective deserters sometimes noted that the deserters had attempted to bring others in on a plot to leave together, but were then betrayed to a commanding officer.[45] Connections among soldiers, therefore, could sometimes facilitate the success of these plots. Friendship and family ties could indicate problematic motives. For example, cousins of deserters would be detained on suspicion of deserting themselves.[46] The head of the Engineers' Battalion wrote the following, explaining why he wanted to sideline the aide to the commander of the Engineers' unit at Reinosa (who had defected): "As is logical, a man who has won the confidence of a deserter and spy cannot win our confidence."[47] Groups of soldiers from the same hometown became sources of suspicion. For example, the head of Battalion 131 wrote to the head of the General Staff on June 24, 1937, reporting that on April 19 many soldiers joined his battalion, asking to serve together since they were from the same hometown. He believed that this may have been a plot to desert all together.[48]

Political rivalries fed the army's trust problems still further, demonstrating the mistrust that underpins Hypothesis 4. Factions attempted to defend their members, clouding soldiers' loyalties. For example, when a soldier in the 136th Battalion came under suspicion after his brother defected, a letter from an unknown source informed the battalion's information officer that the soldier was to be trusted, as a staunch loyalist from "our party."[49] In a high-level example of political competition, communists attempted to assassinate Eloy Fernández Navamuel, a senior officer, claiming that he was a Nationalist. The anarchist camp then recruited Fernández and provided him an armed guard.[50] Thus two factions competed over this officer with little regard for how to use him most effectively against the common Nationalist adversary. Finally, factions kept track of commissars' political affiliations in order to ensure their influence within military units.[51] In such circumstances, it was not easy for a combatant to trust that a compatriot had the best interests of the overall cause in mind.

Thus, with the influx of conscripts into the CES came fundamental changes in the dynamics of military units. The initial enthusiasm of the small number of volunteers from the early days was now joined by the forced service of the uncommitted. Suspicion of these recruits undermined the ability of soldiers to trust each other. The occasional infectious enthusiasm of a group of volunteers from the same place or union all joining together to fight against fascism now had a counterpart in networks of deserters helping each other out instead. Factional rivalries overlaid on these shifts, further undermining trust in the CES.

The findings presented in this chapter, in general, confirm the importance of trust in a shared commitment to the faction's goals. Such a shared commitment is considerably more likely among volunteers than among conscripts, and the higher the proportion of conscripts in a soldier's company, the higher the likelihood of his desertion. I also established that—at least as far as illness goes—this relationship does not appear to be due to conditions being any more miserable in these conscript companies. However, I also found the conscription-desertion effect to depend to an important degree on social homogeneity: the most heterogeneous volunteer companies still had a high rate of desertion. In addition, I found that factionalism spurred higher desertion rates, as soldiers in politically polarized units were more likely to desert. Social heterogeneity, in contrast, has an association with desertion that is contingent on the proportion of conscripts in the unit. Social homogeneity is associated with lower desertion rates only where there is a large proportion of volunteers, not where there is a large proportion of conscripts. In the latter scenario, it appears that social homogeneity is no help in keeping soldiers fighting together. Social ties may even, from time to time, facilitate deserting together. These findings add clear support for an approach to desertion based on trust in a commitment to fight for the armed group, and norms of cooperation.

Other major approaches to desertion get partial support here, but each produces expectations that are not borne out. Individual, personal motivations and commitments did make a difference: on average, as individuals, volunteers and soldiers with political affiliations were less likely to desert than conscripts and the unaffiliated. But this theoretical approach would presume that such individual commitments are enough. They are not. Instead, motivations and voluntarism had in Santander a crucial interpersonal character: for example, a volunteer serving among conscripts was more likely to desert than a conscript serving among volunteers. Staying in the army was plainly an act of collective will, not just individual will.

Such a collective will would seem to tell strongly in favor of a social cohesion approach, and social ties clearly made a difference, reducing desertion rates among volunteers considerably. Indeed, highly diverse volunteer units were just as prone to desertion as conscript units; it was when more volunteers came from the same counties and had the same ages and occupations that they really hung together well. But social homogeneity had a weaker relationship with desertion the more conscripts there were, and it had no effect in all-conscript units. If social ties alone were enough to create a collective will that could underpin military service, one would expect their impact to be felt across the board instead. The result here reinforces the idea that political linkages provide an all-important direction to social ties.

The political character of collective action here raises a key question about how well these findings travel to the supposedly apolitical conflicts that the world has seen since the 1990s. The Spanish Civil War has entered popular myth as a conflict of idealists and ideologues. In contrast, conflicts in the 1990s and 2000s—as in Somalia, Bosnia, Sierra Leone, South Sudan, or the Democratic Republic of the Congo—were often characterized as not being "about" really anything at all, other than naked self-interest from looting natural resources and committing acts of violent extortion, or parochial ethnic interests.[52] We can wonder, then, whether commitments to fight for a common aim would be as important in such conflicts. On the one hand, it is clear in this chapter and in substantial scholarship that many fought for the Republic who had very little interest in being there at all.[53] And on the other, post–Cold War conflicts have a political character that outside observers often miss.[54]

We might therefore wonder whether this chapter's findings travel—for example, whether volunteer fighters in other civil wars are really committed to a common cause and therefore likely to sustain each other's willingness to fight, bolstered by community ties. To investigate this, Margaux Reiss and I examined desertion patterns in Sierra Leone on the basis of ex-combatant surveys, and found that in fact this chapter's hypotheses hold up very well. In the Revolutionary United Forces (RUF), which included a mix of volunteers and abductees, a higher share of abductees in a unit led to a dramatic increase in the likelihood that a combatant would desert. In reverse, in the Civil Defense Forces (CDF), almost all made up of volunteers, not only was the overall desertion rate much smaller than in the RUF, but additional signals of a willingness to fight made a difference too: the more fighters in a unit were trained, the less likely any member of that unit was to desert. Finally, social ties within units had opposite effects, associated with lower desertion rates in the volunteer CDF and with higher rates in the RUF (though this last analysis is not statistically significant in the case of the CDF).[55]

Indeed, the Republic's army is far from the only force to have to grapple with how to mix combatants with very different degrees of motivation. As wars drag on, armed groups sometimes turn to coercive recruitment, just as the Spanish Republic did. Kristine Eck finds a common pattern among rebel groups, like Renamo in Mozambique, the Liberation Tigers of Tamil Eelam in Sri Lanka, or the Lord's Resistance Army in Uganda: they generally start by recruiting volunteers but sometimes shift to forced recruitment when shocks to their financing or military conditions leave them desperate, with short time horizons. They then take on the long-run risk from an unmotivated body of troops in order to get a short-run, rapid increase in manpower.[56] For example, the Communist Party of

Nepal-Maoist shifted from voluntary recruitment based on indoctrination to conscription after about 2002, as it changed from guerrilla tactics to open, conventional warfare, requiring a much larger force capable of absorbing more casualties.[57] On the state side, conscription is actually less common overall in countries experiencing civil wars than in countries at internal peace, perhaps because of the difficulty of enforcing it in weak and divided states or because of concerns about loyalty in divided societies.[58] However, in some of the most prominent and violent cases of civil conflict, notably conventional civil wars, incumbents did impose or expand conscription in the middle of the war itself: these include wars in Russia, China, and Syria.[59]

While the lack of commitment of conscripts is a well-known problem, here I want to highlight the particular challenges that come from mistrust. As in Spain, different recruiting techniques in a single army sometimes mean that well-motivated combatants who demonstrate a commitment to the cause fight alongside the much less committed. The result is not only that there are uncommitted troops who might desert but also that new trust problems are created among old-guard, highly committed troops. They may begin to wonder about the usefulness of fighting and the risks they incur. In the Fuerzas Armadas Revolucionarias de Colombia, for example, expanded recruitment beginning in the 1990s brought in many combatants with little ideological preparation, provoking mistrust among more long-standing recruits.[60] Veterans may become demoralized because of their mistrust of others, and not just because of a change in their own beliefs or motivation.

Thus, the ability to rely on trust and norms of cooperation is a luxury that not every armed group enjoys. This raises the question of whether they can instead use coercion. In the next chapter, I turn to an in-depth analysis of this alternative, the use of negative sanctions.

COERCION AND SOLDIERS' DECISIONS

The previous chapter established the critical influence that soldiers in a unit have on each other's decisions to desert. Soldiers who signal a strong motivation to fight generate trust, and trust in turn keeps soldiers fighting. But without this trust, can an armed group prevent desertion just by threatening deserters with punishment? This chapter demonstrates that coercion is a double-edged sword. Severe mistrust against groups of combatants can feed violence that is not connected to actual instances of disloyalty. This kind of violence backfires, provoking rather than preventing desertion. Fearing that they will fall victim to such violence, members of the group are more likely to desert.

The goal of this chapter, like that of the previous one, is to establish a critical mechanism of desertion at a micro level, among individual combatants in military units. I focus here on professional military officers in the Spanish Republic, whose reputation for disloyalty creates an excellent terrain to test my key hypotheses about stereotypes and coercion. Long seen as an adversary of the Left and hostile to the Republic, the officer corps' reputation only worsened with the coup attempt of July 18, 1936. The officers who remained lay under a dark cloud of fear: Did they sympathize with Franco? Had they simply remained because the rising had been defeated in their garrisons? Would they rebel too, given the chance? In this climate, Republican-side military authorities, militias, and vigilantes kept officers under close scrutiny and executed upward of one thousand. Many of the punished officers really had tried to join the coup or were about to. But many other punishments, including executions, had nothing to do with the coup plot. The provocation effect outlined in Hypothesis 5a should hold here. Laboring under a stereotype, officers witnessed violence against their comrades that was often out of proportion to actual disloyal behavior and meted out by many different local actors with little accountability. Hence many officers should have been provoked to defect. As I show in this chapter, they were.

Above all, I show in this chapter that violence provoked defection where it was unexpected and disproportionate to the problem of disloyalty—in other words, where violence was likely to be experienced as disconnected to officers' actual behavior, and therefore targeting officers because they were officers. I look at relatively close groups of officers, those serving in the same corps (infantry, artillery, and so on) and in the same province. In groups where many officers had participated in the coup attempt, the killing of officers had little effect on defection. If anything, it may have made remaining officers slightly less likely to defect. But in groups where few officers participated at the outset, executions very clearly provoked defection. They could make an officer up to twice as likely to switch sides.

There are two main reasons for turning my attention to the officer corps. These officers experienced high levels of both mistrust and punishment. Since officers came under intense suspicion for disloyalty, this is an extreme case for my approach to mistrust and coercion: this is not a small degree of mistrust, which might be expected to have marginal effects on desertion, outweighed by the deterrence effect. Second, there is a remarkable dataset about the Spanish officer corps and its participation in the war, prepared by the late Carlos Engel.

However, this should also be a relatively easy case for the provocation effect. The context made desertion an especially attractive option for officers under suspicion. Officers had a relatively safe destination—Franco's rebel forces, who valorized the officer corps (this is a major reason why I focus on defection in particular in this chapter). At the same time, the Republican government suffered severe disorganization at the outset of the war, and so an officer who feared for his life could hope to have an opportunity at some point to get away. It is possible that, as the deterrent effect outlined in Hypothesis 5b in chapter 2 suggests, greater capacity to monitor and conduct surveillance to capture and punish actual defectors could have kept some of these officers loyal in spite of their fear of persecution. Hence if mistrust undermines coercion anywhere in civil wars, and punishments against ostensible deserters can actually provoke more desertion, it should be visible here. The corollary is that it may be that mistrust does not always have such dramatic effects. The point of this chapter, however, is to demonstrate that the mistrust-coercion connection exists.

Officers under Fire in Republican Spain: Suspicion and Violence

The coup attempt of July 18, 1936, on top of years of conflict between the Left and the security forces, put officers under deep suspicion. In the Civil War, the risk was clear: many officers may have remained on the government's side not out of any preference but merely because, in their garrison, the rising had failed. Several incidents during and immediately after the coup attempt confirm the difficulty of identifying loyal officers from rebels. Rightist officers would trick some of their leftist subordinates by shouting "Long Live the Republic!" before taking advantage of an opportunity to defect.[1] On the second day of the rising, a boy in Oviedo, the capital of Asturias, "saw lorry-loads of civil guards approaching. They were giving the clenched fist salute and shouting '¡Viva la República!'"[2] However, this was apparently trickery. The garrison commander in Oviedo, Antonio Aranda Mata, put up an appearance of loyalty long enough to ensure that the left-wing militia columns departed the city, and then took it over with the help of most of the same Civil Guards.[3]

Desertions by Nationalist officers continued and indeed persisted. In a prominent incident, on July 29, Civil Guard members of a column from Valencia fought the militia they were supposed to join, and over four hundred defected to the Nationalists at Teruel.[4] María Martínez Fernández, the wife of a Civil Guard, says that her husband's unit had been planning on defecting entirely, "with their lieutenant at their head," if called to the front, but early on they were left well behind the lines. Eventually ordered up in September 1936, her husband was able to defect during the Battle of Brunete, southwest of Madrid, in July 1937.[5] It was clear to many, therefore, that members of the army and paramilitary police had interests that were quite different from those of most of the volunteer militiamen. Many *did* want to desert and fight for the Nationalist cause.

The officers who remained on the Republican side came under intense suspicion. Many were dismissed from their posts, and many others were shot. On the basis of Carlos Engel's data on the Spanish officer corps, it appears that of the 4,732 officers in the main services and paramilitary police who were on Republican territory and who did not immediately and successfully join the coup attempt, local authorities on the Republican side, militias, and other gunmen shot and killed 1,145: 24 percent.[6] Engel's data come largely from Nationalist sources, even if they are largely corroborated by cross-checking with widely used analyses (see below). This suggests that the number may be inflated compared with reality, and in any case it certainly should not be considered the number of executions that can be attributed to Republican authorities as opposed to private actors with a variety of motivations.[7] But even accounting for some inflation, this would be a very high rate of execution.

Execution in the Republic had many authors. They included the regular agents of military justice, punishing officers for mutiny. But as we saw in chapter 3, power had fragmented in the coup attempt. Agents of the Republic rebelled and left administrative chaos. Local committees seized power in many places across Spain. These committees ordered and enacted executions in many places. Unions and parties, and many individuals who simply took weapons at the start of the war in the general disorder, formed armed patrols behind the lines.[8] These patrols committed numerous extrajudicial killings justified as targeting "fascists," defined loosely.[9] These killings took different forms with different euphemisms. *Paseos* meant taking an individual "for a walk" and shooting him or her. *Sacas* involved raiding prisons, removing prisoners, and killing them. The most notorious massacre on the Republican side was a *saca* in November 1936. Agents of the local Madrid government and of the Communist Party took two thousand inmates at the Model Prison in Madrid, removed them to Paracuellos de Jarama, and shot them, burying them in a mass grave.[10]

Importantly, it is difficult to tell how much of this violence was really directed at preventing defection, whether by eliminating the disloyal or by deterring the rest. Much of it clearly had these aims. Many of the Republican-side officer casualties had tried to defect and were caught and shot. Most simply, according to Paul Preston, killings frequently targeted those who actually participated in the coup attempt, as "the usual punishment for mutiny." This included, for example, General Joaquín Fanjul and Colonel Tomás Fernández de la Quintana, tried on August 15, 1936, found guilty, and executed the next day.[11] Many other coup participants were executed summarily, without trial.

Other executions targeted soldiers and officers presumed to be disloyal, even if they were not caught in the act. Local left-wing forces looked to different signals from soldiers to determine where their loyalties lay. This put them on a knife's edge. For example, at Caspe, Catalonia, a young libertarian saw a group of Civil Guards wearing red neckerchiefs. "One of the guards came up to me. 'Ah, my friend, when you see a civil guard without one of these round his neck, shoot him. Only those wearing them are on the republic's side.'"[12] On October 8, 1936, retired officers in Madrid were called on to assemble, and faced a dilemma: If they did not go and were captured, they were likely to be shot. But if they went, they might be presumed disloyal anyway since they had not already been fighting for the Republic, and could be imprisoned in any case. According to Martínez Reverte, "The majority who presented themselves ended up in the Model Prison. And the majority of them were executed at Paracuellos."[13]

Indeed, it could be extremely difficult for an officer under suspicion to know what signals to send, since protestations of loyalty were often considered cheap talk. The case of Colonel José Villalba, the chief of the garrison at Barbastro in Huesca province, illustrates this nicely. Villalba had been in contact with both the coup plotters and Republicans before siding with the latter because they had a stronger presence within his garrison. He came under the suspicion of local militias immediately, because he was known to have supported Spain's colonial wars in Africa, a touchpoint of political conflict before the war.[14] Later, Juan García Oliver, the delegate for war of the anarcho-syndicalist Confederación Nacional del Trabajo (CNT) in Catalonia, considered Villalba the most qualified candidate for the job of overall commander of the militias operating in Aragón. But he did not fully trust Villalba's politics. García Oliver relates his strategy for dealing with this dilemma:

> I made a decision. I would call Col. Villalba and ask him bluntly his opinion of the war. If he responded that he had always been a leftist and republican, I would order him imprisoned on the *Uruguay* [a prison ship in Barcelona harbor] to be tried for treason. But if with complete frankness he answered that he did not understand politics, but was just a professional officer, then . . . we would present him as Chief of Operations of the Aragón Front.[15]

Villalba apparently passed this test, but he could be forgiven for thinking it somewhat Kafkaesque.

The government assessed loyalties as a central, conscious policy as well. Within the War Ministry, an effort began, under Captain Eleuterio Díaz Tendero at the Gabinete de Información y Control (GIC), to classify the Republic's remaining officers as Republican, indifferent, or fascist. These designations were then used to promote officers or to imprison them; the latter became especially vulnerable to execution.[16] Among prisoners in Madrid (among whom were hundreds of officers), as Franco's forces got closer in early November 1936, a further effort at classification took place, distinguishing in a matter of hours among "Fascists and dangerous elements," the less dangerous, and those without responsibilities; the first were to be subject to "immediate execution, disguising our responsibility."[17]

Beyond the efforts at individual targeting, officers were sometimes targeted as a category to reduce the risk of defections. Santiago Carrillo, a communist youth leader implicated in the massacre of prisoners at Paracuellos, noted that unlike other possible defectors to the Nationalists, officers represented the danger of creating new military corps if they went over. He was especially concerned if the hundreds of officers taken prisoner for presumed Nationalist leanings were liberated.[18] Carrillo always denied any direct responsibility for the massacre, a denial now generally discredited.[19] However, he later reflected on Republican-side efforts to terrorize the rebel-sympathizing fifth column into submission that "war is war. . . . When the battle started, all Republican forces were in agreement, even if it was recognized that they might be innocent victims. It is what in the wars of this century the military have called *collateral damage*."[20]

If strategy accounted for some executions, revenge led to others, often with little distinction between loyal and disloyal officers. When militias besieged the Montaña Barracks in Madrid at the beginning of the war, trapped Republican officers who wanted to surrender raised the white flag, but Nationalist officers carried on firing at the assembled workers anyway. The militia members thought that the white flag had been pure trickery, and killed many pro-Republican officers in taking revenge.[21] The sense of vengeance and mistrust carried on after the siege. On July 20, Manuel Carabaño, a fifteen-year-old anarchist, "saw a group of men in shirt-sleeves who were trying to hide the fact that they were officers by crying '¡Viva la República!' A group of militiamen surrounded them shouting 'Fascists!'" They were then executed.[22] The general hatred of officers also gave cover for other agendas, personal and political.[23]

More broadly, revolutionary forces on the Left targeted officers as a broader political project, of eliminating long-standing opponents. After the executions of General Fanjul and Colonel Fernández de la Quintana, mentioned above, "the anarcho-syndicalist newspaper *CNT* thundered: 'the shooting of these military traitors symbolizes the death of an entire class. What a pity that this is no more than a metaphor!'"[24] Certainly the long-running hostility toward the armed forces on the Left, born among other reasons from the brutal repression of strikes in the prewar period, meant that a blow against the officer corps was welcome in some quarters, coup or no coup; the coup attempt itself may have helped justify it.[25]

In sum, some executioners chose victims on the basis of their actual behavior; others targeted officers as a class without regard for their actions. To find out how prevalent these links were, Álvaro La Parra-Pérez and I analyzed Carlos Engel's data on Republican-side executions.[26] We find that there was certainly evidence for executions following directly on behavior: the profile of executed officers and coup participants was similar in important respects, such as short tenure in service and slower career progress under the Republic. But we also find that this varied from place to place. First, where more information was available about loyalties, executions apparently followed actual disloyalty more closely. Loyalties were better known in provinces where many officers joined the coup attempt right at the outset of the war. Here, remaining and fighting for the Republic sent a clearer message that one was committed to the Republic winning, because it meant re-

fusing to follow the herd. In contrast, in provinces where very few officers joined
the coup and it fizzled out quickly, many of those who remained would likely just
have been following the local trend. It would be hard to tell whether they really
supported the Republic. Correspondingly, we find that predictors of coup participation do a better job of predicting executions in the former than in the latter. In other words, in provinces with low participation in the coup, there were
more executions that seem to have little to do with whether the officer was a likely
defector. Second, provinces where the union confederations, the CNT and Unión
General de Trabajadores (UGT), had more followers also seemed to exhibit more
arbitrary violence, as local union committees with an interest in targeting officers as a class took power. In sum, officers were victimized both because of their
behavior and for simply being officers. The stereotype of disloyalty drove violence
more often in provinces where officers had not had as much of a chance to prove
their loyalty in the coup attempt, and where unions were in the ascendant. In a
climate of intense suspicion of officers, violence against them sometimes targeted
the really disloyal, and sometimes went far beyond. This is exactly the kind of violence that should trigger the provocation effect.

At the same time, there were limits to the ability to target officers who were
actually planning to defect. As noted above, there were several notorious cases of
officers continuing to leave at the start of the war, and successfully doing so. The
artillery officer Antonio Cordón was involved in the GIC effort, and notes its lack
of staffing and resources:

> The Ministry [of War] operated with the bare minimum personnel: the
> majority of officers who served in each department had disappeared;
> among the few that stayed, someone vanished each day either because
> he voluntarily left . . . or because it was discovered that he belonged to
> the UME [Unión Militar Española, a conservative, semi-clandestine mil-
> itary organization] or to Falange [the Spanish fascist political party]
> and if he stayed at the Ministry it would be to serve rebel interests and,
> naturally, he was arrested.[27]

Hence, for Cordón, the GIC often lacked the information it needed, such as when
it attempted to assess how many officers remained: "We lost time uselessly, most
of the time not knowing whom to contact for the information we wanted." He
estimates that the standard claim that only 20 percent of the officers were loyal
was too high: they were unable to detect the other disloyal officers.[28] This means
that an officer seeking to leave could perhaps find his chance to do so.

Consequences of Violence

This purge left the officer corps in even worse shape than after the coup. The fact that violence and dismissals often targeted the innocent directly removed many officers from the Republic's disposal who were actually loyal.[29] For example, in Barcelona, the loyalty of the Civil Guards was crucial in defeating the rising, but the government still dismissed 40 percent of its officers.[30]

These direct effects would have been bad enough for the Republic, but did the punishment of the ostensibly disloyal provoke others to leave also? Testimony from various Republican officers suggests that some of their comrades, who would have otherwise remained loyal, defected out of fear. Major Jaime Solera, "a self-styled liberal democrat without political affiliation," was serving as a staff officer at the war ministry in Madrid when the war broke out, and carried on serving the legally constituted government, as he saw his duty to be. He further believed that "the majority of officers in Madrid . . . shared his view." However, given the public's suspicion of all army officers, Solera claims, "many officers were not only in terrible danger of their lives, they were killed. Living in fear, they tried to escape."[31] Jesús Pérez Salas says that in the militia units from Catalonia, officers were under constant suspicion and could be killed "for the slightest hint of a lack of enthusiasm," ultimately giving those officers a strong reason to try to defect.[32]

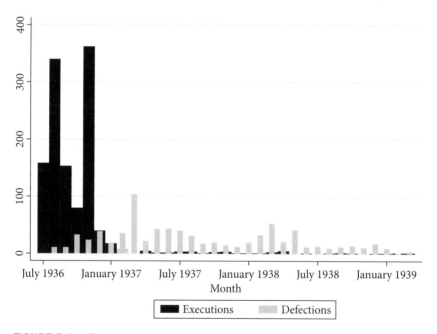

FIGURE 5.1. Executions and defections of officers in the Republic.

Thus, several sources claim that officers who would not otherwise have tried to desert did so in response to violence. Moreover, the wave of violence was followed by side switching throughout 1937 and 1938 (figure 5.1). Did violence against officers generally produce more of these desertions? The logic is intuitive.

But there is reason to believe the opposite—that violence would not affect defection, or may even help control it through deterrence. In Spain, the issue stands in the middle of a politicized historiographic debate.[33] The claims that violence provoked officers into defection often come from career officers who served the Republic, like Solera and Pérez Salas, or from Nationalist historians like Ramón Salas Larrazábal. They had a clear motivation to valorize officers and to condemn antagonistic left-wing forces. In contrast, accounts by left-wing political figures like that of Julio Álvarez del Vayo, the socialist minister of foreign affairs during the war, often claim that very few officers remained loyal and that their defections had little to do with the circumstances of the war.[34] (It is worth a reminder that Cordón—an artillery officer—makes a similar claim.)[35] It is certainly possible, in line with left-wing claims, that the officers who defected would simply have changed sides in the absence of violence, or that violence against officers followed an attempt to desert rather than provoking it. Moreover, even if some officers' defections followed killings of other officers, it is possible that those who defected were likely to defect anyhow, and that violence, if it had any effect at all, simply sped up their plans.

This historiographic debate connects with broader theoretical issues. Accounts of civil conflicts talk as though they pit one group against another, suggesting that their loyalties can be read from their identities—Hindu Tamils versus Buddhist Sinhalese, Catholics versus Protestants, peasants against landowners, communists against capitalists. It is tempting to talk about the Spanish Civil War as ranging the officer corps (alongside other right-wing groups) against the arrayed forces of the Left. Some antagonists in the Spanish Civil War, both Nationalists and Republicans, made such claims themselves. In this reading, officer defection is easy to understand: officers joined the side that was always "theirs," especially so for right-wing officers. But if, in contrast, violence provoked officers to leave, then Franco's was not necessarily "their" side at all. They might have stayed and fought for the Republic if they had not been presumed disloyal. Grand claims of what a civil war is about hide the circumstantial character of people's decisions about which side to join. And at the same time, when conflict actors themselves make these claims, they may act like self-fulfilling prophecies, underwriting violence that pushes people to join the side that they are supposed to.

The theoretical stakes are therefore important not just for understanding desertion and defection but for understanding loyalties and narratives in civil wars. I turn now to a systematic analysis, aiming to establish whether the mechanisms linking violence to defection, and claimed in multiple anecdotal accounts, occurred on a general scale.

As chapter 2 argued, bringing mistrust into the picture sets up two major alternative possibilities for the impact of violence on defection. On the one hand, violence may have coercive, deterrent effects (Hypothesis 5b). On the other, in circumstances of deep mistrust, it may have a provocation effect (Hypothesis 5a). The question is which it will have and when. The historical accounts suggest that the provocation effect occurred when officers felt that executions had no relationship to any real disloyal behavior. This would make them fear they would be next. Some executions may have seemed quite justified—it was, after all, the standard penalty for treason, and there really was a coup attempt—while others would not. In an extreme case, an officer who had witnessed a fellow officer joining the rising or passing secrets to the Francoists before being caught and captured may see that officer's execution as a terrible tragedy but would still be deterred by it. In a contrasting extreme case, an officer who witnessed a show trial of a comrade he knew to have never attempted any kind of treason but who made the wrong enemy would likely be both disgusted on behalf of his friend and fearful of the consequences. But this implies knowing the victims well, and this was far from always the case, even in the officer corps; and with the months of plotting before the war, it would have been difficult for an officer to be sure what any given fellow officer had really tried to do. Crucially, as well, my data cannot distinguish whether any given victim of violence had really tried to defect.

One critical way of assessing the meaning of executions was through whether they were in proportion to the strength of the coup attempt. Potential defectors may not know exactly who was guilty and innocent, but have a general sense of how far disloyal behavior had gone, and thus a basic sense of whether the violent response could have been linked to that disloyal behavior. Where there is little overt challenge, it may be much easier to see subsequent violence as excessive and unjustified, and therefore apt to target anyone regardless of their previous actions. Officers writing about the period focus on excessive violence, well beyond what was necessary to put down the revolt. Major Solera's disgust emerges in part from his belief that the majority of officers in Madrid were simply loyal to the legally constituted authorities. A wave of violence in places and units where there had been little participation in the coup would seem particularly unjustified and excessive. In contrast, a heavy toll of violence in places and units that had seen a high degree of coup participation may simply be seen as logical, if tragic—relatively likely to have targeted officers who had actually tried to defect, and therefore likely to deter any future defection.

Hypotheses 5a and 5b, the provocation and deterrence effects, therefore translate into the following hypotheses for this chapter:

Hypothesis 5a (provocation effect): Among groups of officers with a **low** initial participation in the coup attempt, the more executions of officers, the **higher** the likelihood of subsequent defection.

Hypothesis 5b (deterrence effect): Among groups of officers with a **high** initial participation in the coup attempt, the more executions of officers, the **lower** the likelihood of subsequent defection.

Data and Methods

The data for this chapter are largely the work of Carlos Engel Masoliver (1927–2015), a chemist and amateur historian. Engel compiled a database of the entire officer corps at the outset of the war, using official bulletins from the Republican and Nationalist sides and a huge secondary literature to record what happened to them during the war. He kindly made the database available to me in 2013. The data are perpetually incomplete: Engel continually added information as he found it. But it is a remarkably rich resource of immense scope. Engel arrived at a judgment of whether each officer ultimately sided with the Republicans or the Nationalists and compiled this list into a book.[36] I go deeper into his dataset than this, seeking to piece together how and when different officers ultimately arrived on the Nationalist side.

There are different ways in which one might define which executions would drive desertions—for example, the impact of executions in the same place or in the same service corps (infantry, artillery, cavalry, engineers, general staff, transport, and aviation; Civil Guard, Assault Guard, and Carabineers). I build from the assumption that an officer would pay particular attention to what is going on in his immediate network—that is, in the same corps and in the same province. He would know these officers better than anyone, and indeed accounts of unjust executions, such as that by Martín Blázquez, focus on officers they knew personally.[37] An officer would also have firsthand experience of what happened in this group during the coup attempt—who rose and who stayed loyal. This would therefore be the context within which he would judge whether executions were unjust and arbitrary. And such executions would make him worry that he could be a target, whether he remained loyal or not. Hence, I examine whether defection is more likely in province-corps groups (groups of officers serving in the same province and in the same corps) with high rates of execution, particularly when these executions seem disproportionate to actual disloyalty (i.e., with a low rate of initial coup participation).

The defections I analyze here are those that occurred after the initial wave of coup participation. This is because I want to examine how officers who stayed at first reacted to conditions on the Republican side. Several scenarios produced a coding of defection. First, some officers were listed in official bulletins as being removed from the Republican rolls for reasons consistent with desertion (like desertion listed explicitly, absence, disappearance, failure to present, and—the largest category—whereabouts unknown); I coded these as defectors when there is no earlier Nationalist-side record for the officer in question (i.e., he was not already on the Nationalist side at the outset of the war). In the case of "whereabouts unknown," the date had to be after the beginning of December 1936 to qualify, since earlier records seem simply to be an exercise in keeping track of the mass of officers who had left in the coup attempt in July. While it is true that many of these reasons, like absence or disappearance, do not clearly mean desertion, as noted in chapter 4, many desertions were misrecorded as disappearances in order to mask the full extent of the problem. Second, other officers generated records (like announcements of promotions or postings), first on the Republican side and then on the Nationalist side, indicating that they switched sides during the conflict rather than right at the outset. Third, on the basis of a large secondary reading, Engel directly included notes of officers' defections after the initial rising in his dataset.

For executions, Engel's data include the date, place, and manner of death; those coded as shot on the Republican side (*fusilamiento*) have a record of the officer's family receiving a pension accorded by the postwar Franco regime. The regime therefore attributed the shooting to the Republican side—a problematic empirical basis given that the regime would have had an interest in inflating the scope of Republican killings. In order to confirm the validity of Engel's estimates, for a project examining the origins of executions, La Parra-Pérez and I cross-checked Engel's execution codings against publicly available and widely used lists of victims for Catalonia and Madrid and noted a high rate of reliability (80% in Barcelona, 95% in Madrid).[38]

This violence, according to the hypotheses outlined above, should have different effects depending on initial coup participation. There is no way of knowing the full extent of attempted coup participation, because we do not know who among the executed officers actually tried to defect. But we can tell who successfully joined the coup at the outset of the conflict, on the basis of who made it to the Nationalist side. I coded as a successful coup participant any officer who never produced a record on the Republican side *and* who joined the Nationalist side at some point— who produced a record of a deployment, promotion, or medal on the Nationalist side, was killed in action on the Nationalist side, or who was in the Nationalist army at the end of the war without generating any explicit record before this.

In all these analyses, it is critical to control for a propensity to defect in the first place. After all, it could simply be that killings of officers prompted defections only among those officers who were already thinking about it and who feared being detected. We cannot have a perfect indicator of a propensity to defect, of course. There were many surprising defections, like that of General Miguel Cabanellas, reputed to be a Republican, and other surprisingly loyal officers, like Colonel José Miaja, a member of the UME, the right-wing military network that provided much of the organization of the coup plot.[39] But La Parra-Pérez identifies several variables that are correlated with an individual's propensity to join the coup attempt.[40] The first is age; younger officers were more likely to rebel.[41] The conspiracy targeted combat officers, who were likely to be younger. The fascist Falange party, with an ideology of rejuvenation, recruited among young officers as well; and youth might also be an indicator of a willingness to take risks, especially if officers had fewer family obligations. Second, officers who had had relatively slow career progress under the Republic had professional and pecuniary motives to rebel. I use La Parra-Pérez's measure of career progress since the founding of the Republic in 1931, which is based on advancing in both rank and in one's position in the seniority list within a rank, and is thus a fine-grained measure that captures not only promotions but how close an officer is to the next promotion. La Parra-Pérez compiled this on the basis of the officers' yearbooks from 1931 to 1936. I include variables for the officer's rank in 1936 (controlling for other factors, officers were slightly more likely to defect the more senior they were), for whether they were posted to a unit and were unit leaders (leaders and posted officers had lower defection rates).

Finally, in the analyses that follow, I analyze the impact of executions only on *subsequent* defection rather than, for example, comparing the overall execution rate over the whole war with the overall defection rate. This is to guard against the possibility of a wave of executions responding to defections. Hence, I have one observation per officer for each quarter year, provided the officer was on the Republican side at the beginning of that quarter. The dependent variable, then, is binary—whether he defected in that quarter. This is assessed by the date associated with any report of the officer's defection (for example, the date on a Republican report of his having abandoned his post), or, failing that, the earliest date on which he has a record of some kind from the Nationalist side. I included only those province-corps groups that had at least ten officers at the start of every period. I analyze binary cross-section time-series logit models with a multilevel structure—officers within province-corps quarters (to capture the time-varying executions variable) within a province-corps (to capture the time-invariant rate of successful coup participation).

The critical measure of the independent variable is the cumulative percentage executed, which increases over time as executions continue. Thus, if 5 percent of a province-corps is executed in the first quarter and 7 percent in the second, the cumulative percentage is 5 percent in the second quarter and 12 percent in the third. The cumulative measure allows that past violence leaves a legacy on the officer's decision. The reason is that, as we saw above, suspicion of military personnel meant that there was considerable reluctance on the Republican side to permit groups of officers to get to the front initially, but officers who apparently had the intention of defecting from early on bided their time until later. The statistics of violence show that it was concentrated in the summer and fall of 1936; this measure therefore assumes that such violence could have long legacies.

Results: Violence and Defection

Results from several different statistical analyses are given in the appendix, in table A.4. Figure 5.2 uses simulations based on these analyses to give the predicted probability that a given officer with typical characteristics on key variables—mean age, rank, and career progress; not a leader; and posted to a unit—would defect in a given quarter. It focuses on how that probability changes as the rate of violence in a unit changes, from the 5th percentile (0% executed) to the 95th (35% executed).

The first analysis, in the top panel of figure 5.2 (corresponding to table A.4, model 1), estimates the overall relationship of violence to subsequent defection in the Republican officer corps. It shows no statistically significant difference in the propensity to defect. However, the hypotheses for this chapter suggest that in

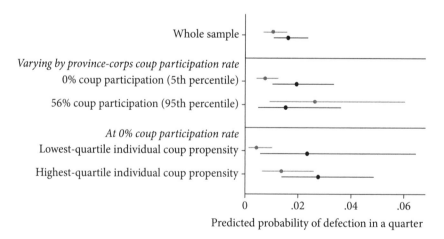

FIGURE 5.2. Results: predicted probability of defection in a given quarter. Derived from estimates in Models 1–3, table A.6, appendix.

some units, the deterrent effect should prevail, while in others the provocation effect should.

The second panel therefore includes these hypothesis tests. It is based on a model in which the unit's coup participation rate is interacted with the rate of violence (table A.4, model 2). I first give the relationship between violence and defection for a hypothetical unit in which no one successfully joined the coup at the outset, and then one at which 56 percent did (the 95th percentile of successful coup participation). The provocation effect is borne out: more unexpected executions, more defection. In province-corps with low initial coup participation, officers are more likely to defect as their comrades are shot. In any given quarter, the effect is not large, from 0.75 percent to 2 percent predicted probability of defection. But this adds up over time. Over the ten quarters of the war (after the first quarter), it would increase the probability of defection from 7.3 percent to 18.3 percent. This is a substantial increase—a probability over twice as large as with a low cumulative execution rate.

In contrast, Hypothesis 5b, for a deterrent effect, receives less support. In units with high coup participation, violence had a negative relationship with defection. But this relationship is not statistically significant. In other words, it is not clear that, even in high-participation units, Republican violence successfully deterred officers from defecting. Of course, deterring some from defecting is not the same thing as punishing a defection in progress. Since we do not know whether any given executed officer had been trying to defect, it is possible that many executions successfully targeted those who actually tried to do so, hence punishing the crime even if that punishment did not change anyone else's calculations. Indeed, my analysis with La Parra-Pérez suggests that it was in these high-coup-participation contexts that executions were actually relatively well targeted. But it is not clear that this violence actually successfully intimidated anyone else.

While this analysis indicates that a provocation effect occurred where the theory expected it to, is it possible that the only officers who were "provoked" were those who stood a good chance of defecting anyway? In other words, were a statistically substantial number of Republican loyalists actually pushed toward defection through violence? Most concerning for this analysis, it is possible that the apparent provocation effect is just a statistical artifact; it could be that there is a positive relationship between violence and defection because the violence focused on those units where there were many hidden rightists, waiting for their chance to leave.

To assess this, in the third panel of figure 5.2 I report the results of two further analyses (table A.4, models 3 and 4). These look at the same violence-defection relationship and simulate a 0 percent coup participation scenario. But this time, I split the sample by the officer's personal, individual-level likelihood of participating in the coup. To generate this, I took the whole sample of the Spanish officer corps that was not executed during the war (because, again, we do not know with certainty whether executed officers had really tried to defect). I then modeled the officer's likelihood of ultimately ending up on the Nationalist side as a function of key individual characteristics. These included the officer's age, rank, career progress under the Republic, service branch, whether the officer was posted to a unit or inactive, whether the officer was a unit leader, and—to capture the effect of following the herd—whether the officer was serving in territory that initially fell to the Nationalists at the outset of the conflict. I then used this model to predict the coup propensity of each officer who remained with the Republicans at the outset. In other words, it estimates what we would think a given officer's likelihood of joining the Nationalists would be, if we abstracted from violence. I then examined separate models for both the lowest quartile of officers on the Republican side and for the highest quartile.

Here, I report the results of simulations that examine the relationship between violence and defection in a unit with low coup participation—that is, where the provocation effect was found. The results suggest that the provocation effect occurred just as much among the least likely defectors as among the most. The Republican army may have lost many loyalists to violence.

I note that the results do *not* hold up when considering violence and initial coup participation at the level of the whole province rather than the province-corps (table A.4, model 5). In other words, officers are not responding to executions of officers in other corps in the same place, but only to those of other officers both in the same corps and in the same place. I think the province-corps frame is justifiable in the sense that officers would be particularly concerned by the experiences of fellow officers they know and work with and have direct relationships with, especially considering that there was wide variation among corps in coup participation, such that an engineer (a corps with relatively low participation) might not see the execution of cavalrymen in the same province (who had a very high coup participation rate) as terribly surprising or problematic.

On the whole, the results are clear: if perceptions of officers' disloyalty drove violence against them, then violence often backfired. Punishments for these ostensibly disloyal soldiers, especially in groups where few had rebelled in the first place, often provoked others in the group to leave.

Coercive punishments, then, are not just a second-best for mistrustful armies, a replacement for trust that can keep soldiers fighting regardless. This chapter finds that mistrust can reach a point at which not even threats work, for there is no assurance that complying with the threat is better. This is a very difficult situation for armies. And it is, I argue, a phenomenon likely to be found above all in civil conflicts. The live possibility that members of one's own army not only do not want to be there but would actively prefer to fight for the opponent is at the heart of the severe distrust I consider here. It is this possibility that legitimizes the preemptive, widespread use of punishment and violence within a side of a conflict, under the logic that one must at all costs prevent and deter defection.

Relatedly, this chapter offers clear evidence that defection and desertion are not just about finding your way to the side you were always supposed to be on; that is, it was not just that typical Franco supporters defected. Many officers who were unlikely to defect, if one considers their personal characteristics, did so anyway, and this appears to be linked to violence in their units. Hence defection, in my view, is part of a process that is endogenous to the war itself. But my argument does not replace an easy ideological story with an apolitical one that reduces loyalty and disloyalty to motives of material self-interest. Rather, the ideological environment of the armed group, including ideas about who is loyal and disloyal, shapes the individual's decision.

The notion that officers were for Franco, and were the enemies of the Republic, acted not just as a claim about reality but also as a kind of self-fulfilling prophecy. It motivated and legitimized attacks on officers regardless of their loyalties, and thereby pushed officers into Franco's camp through provocation. This reflects an important impact of ideologies in civil conflicts: they define identities, indicating who is fighting whom, and thereby shape individuals' incentives.[42] In this case, a prevailing approach in the Republic, built up over years of social conflict and the brutal military repression of uprisings, notably in Asturias and Catalonia in 1934, identified the officer corps with the Right. But this association was cemented in the Civil War, as Martínez Reverte argues.[43] The Spanish armed forces *had* been quite divided at the outset. This is one of the reasons the Civil War occurred: the coup attempt of July 18, 1936, failed not only because workers' militias resisted it but also because *officers* did as well. But the rebellion separated them. Nationalist officers shot those officers on their territory who resisted. The officers who stayed loyal on the Republican side were out after the war: the Franco regime drove them into exile, imprisoned them, executed them, and cashiered them from the military. But during the war, the Republican side had already gone some distance to reinforcing the link between the officer corps and the Nationalists. Seeking to combat officers' disloyalty, it helped drive officers into Nationalist hands. For Martínez Reverte, "the coup plotters' message contained an overriding claim . . . that it was the only Spain and the rebel army the only Army. Paradoxically, this identification had more success among the rebellion's enemies than among its friends. The friends knew what divided them. The enemies immediately identified the Army with the rebellion."[44] Civil wars are rife with claims about what the war is "about" and about who is fighting whom. This chapter describes a way in which these claims make themselves true. There are pressures on people to support "their" side, but they are not automatic, and violence is one of the ways they come about.

In chapter 4, examining how mistrust undermines norms of cooperation in armies, we saw that mistrust in groups of soldiers can make otherwise loyal, committed soldiers decide to desert when they serve among uncommitted soldiers. In this chapter, something very similar occurred—the defection of combatants the Republic could have kept, because mistrust pervaded the force in which they served. But stereotypes lead to a key difference. The defection of officers was in line with the stereotype of the disloyal officer. In the case of volunteers who deserted, however, their desertion went against type. The defection of officers who might have remained loyal ultimately reinforced a polarization of identities. It seemed only to confirm the stereotype of officers' disloyalty. In this way, the identities associated with sides of a civil war came to seem accurate through an endogenous process in which behavior and stereotype reinforced each other.

The polarization this chapter describes probably does not often reach the extent that it did in Spain. Years of suspicion; the coup attempt; the fact that the coup attempt left thousands of officers on the Republican side, so that they posed a particularly troubling threat of disloyalty; the revolutionary justifications for arbitrary justice; the brutality of Nationalist tactics that prompted revenge; a Nationalist side that valorized the officer and hence some hope of good treatment if one were to defect; weak monitoring and surveillance that may have reduced the ability to detect an *actual* attempt to defect—there were many factors that combined to produce arbitrary killing, plenty of reasons for officers to fear they would be next, and plenty of incentives to defect under these circumstances.

But the processes described here are not unique. Fear of violence within the armed group may be a driver of desertion that goes well beyond this case. In Colombia, Rachel Schmidt's interviews with ex-combatants from the Fuerzas Armadas Revolucionarias de Colombia and the Ejército de Liberación Nacional confirm this; several of her interviewees cited attacks by other combatants or fear of the same as a reason for leaving.[45] This extends to the arbitrary imposition of "justice" within an armed group. For example, in the Revolutionary United Forces (RUF) in Sierra Leone, Zoe Marks has found that executions were meted out in line with the personal interests and favoritism of the commander. While there were systems of People's Courts and courts martial within the RUF, they were often too overwhelmed to provide anything like due process. Commanders would often target "expendable" recruits for punishments for various crimes in order to make an example of them.[46] To see how this impacted desertion rates in the RUF, Margaux Reiss and I analyzed a survey of ex-combatants gathered by Macartan Humphreys and Jeremy Weinstein, and found that combatants who reported that they would have been punished by the faction for desertion were *more* likely to desert than those who said they would not have been, and the actual punishment rate of deserters within their units had, if anything, a *positive* relationship with desertion. These effects were especially pronounced among abductees into the RUF, who had particular reasons for feeling vulnerable in the group.[47]

The expressly political axis of violence on the Republican side in Spain also has broader ramifications. Fratricide within armed groups in civil wars is more common than is often recognized. I know of no data on purges within rebel groups, but on the state side, elite purges happen in about 13.4 percent of civil war years in authoritarian regimes, more often than outside of civil wars.[48] And such measures are often directed against whole classes of soldiers, reflecting existing dynamics of political mobilization.

In several cases, they appear to have driven defections. In France, from 1792 to 1799, the revolutionary regime enacted almost one thousand punishments against its 1,378 generals, including numerous executions. Officers of aristocratic background fell particularly often, but all officers were under suspicion, especially after several high-profile defections.[49] Dismissal or death could come from remarks deemed counterrevolutionary or from the wrong sorts of friendships and enmities.[50] Georges Six argues that the arbitrary treatment during the revolutionary period was one of several important drivers of the unprecedented rate of desertion among generals.[51] In the Russian Civil War of 1918–21, Leon Trotsky conscripted former czarist officers into the Red Army. Around a third of them later defected, largely in 1918 and 1919. True, Andrei Ganin argues that the officers preferred the White side generally, and that the solidification of the Bolshevik repressive apparatus helped reduce the number of defections over time. However, he also argues that the new Soviet regime's repression, notably in the summer of 1918, drove potentially loyal officers to switch sides too.[52] This appears to be above all the case when revolutionary violence targeted officers in a blanket fashion in spite of Trotsky's insistence that the old officers were vital for the Red Army.[53] The Taliban regime of mid-1990s Afghanistan brought in about sixteen hundred members of the old communist regime's forces but later purged many of them. According to Antonio Giustozzi, "Even many of those who were not purged left of their own initiative. The specialists however were living in a climate of fear, as many Taliban were opposed to their presence. Jokes such as 'when we control all of Afghanistan, we'll hang you like Najib' [Najibullah Ahmadzai, president of Afghanistan 1987–92] were sometimes heard."[54] And after a failed coup against President Pierre Nkurunziza of Burundi in 2015, the regime started assassinating officers belonging to rival factions in the armed forces, which had been integrated with former rebels after the civil war of 1994–2008. Many officers and soldiers subsequently deserted—for example, refusing to return home from postings abroad. These officers notably formed and assisted new rebel groups that launched attacks from 2014 through 2016.[55] Officers may be especially vulnerable to the dynamics that this chapter outlines, in part because their disloyalty can be especially damaging to an army.[56]

But the rank and file can likewise suffer greatly from the use of stereotypes to identify loyalties and assign punishments. One such categorization is social class, used prominently during the Russian Civil War. Mirroring the tension about the recruitment of former czarist officers, Red Army officials felt that they faced a dilemma in drafting peasants: the vast majority of the population, necessary for a mass army but not obviously aligned with the industrial proletariat at the center of communist doctrine. While the Red Army shifted its rhetoric and categorizations to include poor peasants on their side, many still blamed relatively well-off or otherwise counterrevolutionary peasants, or kulaks. For example, Josh Sanborn relates that an official looking for reasons for military failure in southern Russia pointed to the presence of "'kulak or half-kulak elements.' These kulaks, because of the 'political ignorance of the mass of soldiers,' were able to act as disintegrating forces and led to the misfortunes of the army."[57] Throughout the war, Red Army officials spoke in internal documents of their fears of "kulak rebellions" within the military.[58] Mistrust of peasants led in turn to their own mistrust: "If the state is a workers' state, and the party a workers' party, then don't put us (peasants) in the army."[59]

Another common categorization is of course ethnicity. Research on ethnic identity in armed forces and civil conflicts is converging on two conclusions that are quite consistent with what this chapter finds in Spain. First, unlike what some 1990s scholarship on ethnic conflicts concluded, ethnicity is far from a guaranteed predictor of loyalties.[60] There is no automatic link between belonging to a particular group, whether the officer corps or an ethnic out-group, and disloyal behavior. Plenty of soldiers in repressed ethnic groups stay loyal, just as plenty of officers did in the Spanish Republic.[61] Second, despite this lack of an automatic connection, the actions of regimes and of rebel groups can make an ethnic cleavage salient.[62] In particular, states often use "ethnic security maps"—images of who is loyal and who is disloyal on the basis of their ascribed ethnicity.[63] This is basically a rule of thumb in a low-information environment.[64] They then keep suspect soldiers under especially tight surveillance and limit their access to positions of authority where their defection would be especially damaging. As we will see in chapter 9, this was a basic strategy in Syria and drove much of the defection pattern in the regime's armed forces; beyond Syria, Iraq under Saddam Hussein and under Nouri al-Maliki pursued the same type of policy, as have regimes in Bahrain, Jordan, Burundi, Togo, Chad, and Sri Lanka, among many others. But this type of policy creates clear incentives for members of out-groups to try to defect, if they can.[65] In sub-Saharan Africa, according to large-scale statistical analyses, ethnic stacking pushes members of ethnic out-groups in the military to launch coups, leave the military to launch rebellions, and defect during uprisings from below, including civil wars.[66]

In other words, dynamics of polarization, where people join up with the side they are "supposed" to, are a common feature of civil wars. This chapter suggests strongly that they are far from inevitable, however, and depend on the decisions that actors in civil wars take to respond to mistrust. It provides evidence—from an extreme case, certainly—of a mechanism of mistrust that helps explain how polarization occurs.

MILITIAS IN THE SPANISH REPUBLIC, SUMMER–FALL 1936

> Mud, cowardice, misery, they all exist as well. But it was none of those things that most struck one. A revolution is a process. It is difficult to be a coward when your companions are being brave. Or at least to be one for long.

—Miguel Nuñez, militiaman

The previous two chapters tested key individual-level hypotheses for my approach to desertion, showing that soldiers are less likely to desert when surrounded by committed compatriots and that efforts to punish ostensible deserters often provoke desertion instead, when there is severe mistrust. This chapter begins an analysis at the macro level, showing how these factors differentiated units and armed groups from each other. It begins in the summer of 1936 in the Republic, where civilian militias experimented in military organization. With state power shattered and confusion reigning, the capacity to effectively deter desertion by accurately detecting and punishing it was weak, for the most part. Militias tended instead to rely on norms of cooperation to keep their soldiers fighting. Those that did so most successfully insisted on a clear display of a commitment to a cause and a willingness to fight. But many of these militias did not.

Though many joined the militias enthusiastically at first, this conviction often did not translate into strong norms of cooperation. Political belief did not mean a willingness to sustain the hardships of fighting. In any case, many militias recruited opportunists as well as the convinced, and competition among different political tendencies undermined trust further. Combatants in many units did not trust each other to fight, did not develop strong norms of cooperation, and suffered pervasive desertion problems.

There were, however, important exceptions. The communist-organized Fifth Regiment units insisted from the beginning on strict discipline and made it clear that this was what recruits were signing up for. Other units, even some militias of the antimilitarist anarcho-syndicalist unions, adapted in similar ways over the course of the first months. The Fifth Regiment and other well-disciplined militias combined voluntary recruitment with other forms of costly signaling, joining a commitment to a cause with the demand to prove a willingness to fight. Developing strong norms of cooperation, Fifth Regiment units gained a reputation for holding the line.

In other words, then, the summer and fall of 1936 were a period of experimenting with different ways of raising and fielding military forces, against a backdrop of questions about loyalties. This period lets the researcher trace why different armed groups experience more or less severe problems of desertion. The ways in which various armed groups on the Republican side assessed loyalties shaped trust among combatants and hence norms of cooperation, and in turn had an important influence on desertion and defection throughout this period.

I summarize the basic comparisons in table 6.1. This table remains admittedly vague. Most militias did not insist on very strong signals of a willingness to fight, but there were variations. Because there were so many separate militias, few really stand out. The key comparison is between the bulk of the militias and the crucial exception, the Fifth Regiment, though I also discuss variation among the former where appropriate. In the remainder of the chapter, I lay out the background to the militia period, analyze the variety of motivations that members of the militias had, and examine the various sources of trust and mistrust that reigned in the militia period and their results for desertion.

TABLE 6.1. Military unit characteristics and hypothesized overall desertion rates—Republic, summer–fall 1936

		THREAT OF VIOLENCE WITHIN ARMED GROUP		
		HIGH; AT MOST OCCASIONALLY STEREOTYPED OR FACTIONALIZED	LOW	HIGH; SYSTEMATICALLY STEREOTYPED OR FACTIONALIZED
Information about motivations	Clear and positive		Fifth Regiment and some other Republican militias	
	Unclear or negative		Most Republican militias	Officers under Republic

Note: Units are placed according to the independent variables.

Setting the Stage: The Coup and Its Aftermath

After months of political polarization in the spring of 1936, workers' militias were prepared to fight once the coup broke out on July 18. These included the fifteen-hundred-strong communist-organized Milicias Antifascistas Obreras y Campesinas (MAOC), concentrated in Madrid; the socialist La Motorizada force; and the anarchist Nosotros group, which planned to call on two thousand militants.[1] These preparations allowed these initially small militias to help defeat the rising in various cities in the Republic. Militia leaders were, of course, subsequently to exaggerate their own role compared with that of loyal officers and Civil Guards, without whom the militia could rarely put down the rising by themselves.[2] But it is clear that the militia made a difference, particularly in conjunction with uniformed security personnel, and that militia units acted quickly and cohesively.[3] In this, they drew on the capacity for collective action they had developed over the previous months of preparation. In other words, they acted essentially as Staniland's combined social-political networks: groups of activists who were veterans of previous political fights and who knew each other both personally and politically.[4] It was, then, not the "masses" that defeated the coup attempt; to the extent that workers' groups played decisive roles on July 18, they tended to be the organized, prepared networks.

In any case, the workers' militias expanded quickly after the initial crisis of July 18–19, 1936. The different groups of union and party militants formed the committed, motivated core of subsequent militias. The MAOC, for example, established a headquarters in Madrid and began to organize militia units there. This process was the origin of the communist-organized Quinto Regimiento, or Fifth Regiment.[5] The preexisting anarchist command in Madrid, which was able to send out a force against General Emilio Mola's forces on the second day of the war, then served as the basis of new Confederación Nacional del Trabajo (CNT) columns starting on July 21, with "a trustworthy militant" at the head of each column.[6] The network of core, active organizers now fanned out across these new units rather than concentrating in single militias as in the very first response to the uprising. The expansion drew on ordinary union and party members—the rank and file, not the highly active militants who had formed the initial militias—and the thousands of new recruits these unions and parties gained once the war began.

To expand their militias, the major labor unions called on the government for arms. Facing the government's initial refusal out of fear of revolution and disorder, many unions seized arms for themselves or obtained them from sympathetic officers.[7] The seizures themselves were scenes of chaos. In both Madrid and Barcelona, even anarchist leaders, generally enthusiastic about arming the workers from government arsenals, watched with deep worry as people took weapons without control and without any sense of who would wind up with them. As one such leader said, "They could be fascists for all we know."[8] After these seizures the new government of José Giral made a virtue of necessity and began authorizing these arms transfers.

Armed with these weapons, and with improvised arms like hunting shotguns, thousands of new militia members joined, from the key cities of Madrid, Barcelona, and Valencia, and from the countryside around. Militias manned the forward defense of Madrid in the Sierra north of the city, and headed out from Barcelona and Valencia to retake the region of Aragón and its capital, Zaragoza, from the Nationalists. They were joined by those regular soldiers, Civil Guards, Assault Guards, and Carabineers who had remained loyal to the regime, and formed makeshift columns that included both soldiers and militiamen in varying proportions. On the Aragón front there were some seventeen thousand men in the first months; in the center, according to Ramon Salas Larrazábal, there were thirty thousand militiamen and a similar number of men from the uniformed security services by September 1936—indicating the militias' rapid growth beyond the initial core.[9]

These militias thus emerged autonomously, from the bottom up, without common standards for recruitment, training, or discipline at first, or a common command structure. The government in Madrid attempted some forms of coordination. Most important was the creation of the Inspección General de Milicias on August 8. This body attempted to regularize the process of requisition, indicated to the parties and unions that raised the militias where they were most needed, and paid a wage of ten pesetas per day as of August 15, disbursing the funds through improvised, often chaotic channels.[10] These steps later formed the basis of attempts to impose common procedures for recruitment and discipline, as the Inspección General started to impose conditions on militias in exchange for payment and materiel. However, the militias retained their essential autonomy for the time being. Each militia column went about recruitment its own way. Military coordination was extremely poor; the parties and unions often did not respond to the government's efforts at coordinating deployment.[11] Further, regions such as Catalonia, the Basque Country, and Santander maintained their own, autonomous regional governments. These did not always comply with the central government's directives.

Indeed at many levels, the coup attempt fractured state authority. The collapse of central, uniformed military and police commands gave local workers' committees and their associated militias considerable power. The militias quickly demonstrated that they were able to act autonomously from the regular security forces.[12] Local governments in Barcelona and Madrid accommodated the parties and unions: the head of government in Catalonia offered on July 20 to resign or stay on as the anarchists wished, while in Madrid, local police forces such as the Cuerpo de Investigación y Vigilancia integrated party and union members who continued to take instructions from their political backers.[13] Further, as central authority crumbled, a social revolution emerged, especially in Catalonia and Aragón. Local workers' committees, especially those led by the CNT, took power in many localities from the established civil authorities. They expropriated property, established worker control over factories, and collectivized agriculture.[14] This was much to the dismay of moderate bourgeois Republican leaders. At the same time, the Communist Party took the position that much more moderation was necessary to keep the middle classes on the side of the Republic and win the international favor of the French and British.[15]

It was thus in a context of severely weakened central authority and considerable autonomy and power for the workers' militias that the Republic now confronted war. The socialist activist Julián Zugazagoitia claimed that "the power of the state lay in the street, pulverized, and a fragment of it lay in the hands and at the disposal of every antifascist citizen, who used it in the manner that best suited his temperament."[16] This is somewhat of an exaggeration: the central government in Madrid continued to exist, as did many of its institutions. But to a large degree they were colonized from below by the parties and unions and their militias.

A brutal wave of violence followed.[17] Laia Balcells's systematic analysis of this violence finds that, above all, it affected politically divided communities, where armed patrols and local actors combined to target rightists to tip the local political balance.[18] Rather than a state enforcing penalties for disloyal behavior in a systematic fashion, then, the practice of violence included arbitrary killings and other abuses against those who were suspected—or could be plausibly portrayed—as being rightists. The victims included landowners and factory managers, nuns, priests, and over a thousand military officers. As we saw in chapter 5, the stereotype of officer disloyalty meant that these efforts to control their defection very often backfired.

At the same time as this kind of violence targeted people for their presumed or pretended disloyalty, actual desertion very often went unpunished. In the coup attempt, thousands had left the forces of public order such as the Civil Guards. Though these forces were actually more intact than many assume, prejudice against members of these services led to a purge, further reducing their effectiveness. To add to this, the coercive apparatus that *did* exist, the local militias and militia-dominated government forces such as in Madrid, focused on targeting social actors and internal enemies over the summer and fall of 1936; tracking down deserters from the militias did not appear to be a high priority. Indeed, as we will see below, many militias did not even penalize leaving. Finally, local government was in an uproar with committee takeovers of many municipalities. This meant that a key bureaucratic tool to track down deserters—communication between armed forces and local government in order to investigate and try to determine a deserter's whereabouts—was often unavailable.

There were therefore few efforts to track down militiamen who had left the front and punish them for doing so. The Republican officer José Martín Blázquez, working in the War Ministry, found that there were noncombatants with rifles all over Madrid. According to him, "The streets of Madrid swarmed with militiamen promenading with rifles, but when we needed them only few presented themselves."[19] Indeed, early on the CNT declared its opposition to any effort to round up arms in the hands of militiamen behind the lines.[20] That many of these men with rifles were deserters becomes clear in the conflicts in some militia units over soldiers returning home with their weapons. Narciso Julián served in the Del Barrio column organized by the Partit Socialista Unificat de Catalunya, the Catalan Socialist-Communist party. He relates that after an air raid, when many men wanted to leave and the column had to reorganize, he was assigned to ensure that the men did not leave with their rifles:

> The heart went out of us all when we saw the numbers coming to hand in their names to leave. . . . Without exception, those who wanted to go refused to surrender their arms, even when told that hundreds upon hundreds of peasants were waiting to use them. Finally, I pointed at the two machine-guns. One of the men threatened to shoot me all the same. "Go ahead, not one of you will be left alive." Trueba, the political commissar, harangued them and at last they handed in their weapons. Then they were put on two trains and sent back to Barcelona.[21]

It could therefore be difficult to persuade militiamen to surrender their arms, even though their returning to the home front—permitting them to stop serving—was in this case a relatively organized process. In a mass flight, it would have been all the more difficult to prevent soldiers deserting from keeping their weapons. Individuals who left militia units, even with rifles, faced few sanctions in the home front from doing so. The Republic thus lacked the key form of coercion that can actually effectively prevent desertion—punishment following an actual attempt to desert.

New militias, then, emerged in a general condition of disorder, without clear, centralized control behind the lines in much of Republican Spain. Central authorities could neither chase after deserters at home nor, for the first few months, enforce central standards on militias. In these circumstances, militias varied widely one from the next, and these differences shaped patterns of desertion.

A Spectrum of Motivations

The militias had a war to fight, and their composition had a strong effect on their ability to do so. For example, in late August 1936, the Oropesa column fought on the main highway controlling the southwestern approach to Madrid, and suffered numerous reverses. Colonel Mariano Salafranca wrote that many of that column's difficulties had to do with the variety of different motivations within the militias:

> The retreats are caused by the general structure and heterogeneous character of the militia. They are a formless mass which contain noble spirits, valiant and passionate for the cause they are defending, together with completely opposite types . . . and . . . an amorphous mass, ready, according to the situation, to follow their leaders, without ideas of their own and, when things become difficult and dangerous, seeking egoistically the easiest way to save their lives.[22]

Salafranca captured the variety of motivations in many militias. Alongside real enthusiasm and ideological commitment were many reasons for opportunism, and for simply following along. Moreover, Salafranca's observation captures the general tendency that the distribution of a willingness to fight and to endure hardship greatly influenced the character of the whole unit—whether it would fight with determination or melt away.

Many of the recruits to the new volunteer militias were sincerely enthusiastic and committed to the defense of the Republic. These enthusiasms are of course the stuff of legend in the Spanish Civil War, but much of this is genuine, as Michael Seidman—whose general argument strongly emphasizes opportunism—readily argues.[23] With the rising defeated, huge marches and rallies led to recruitment to the front. Josep Cercos, an anarchist metalworker, discusses the enthusiasm in Barcelona to head out west to Zaragoza, capital of Aragón, to stop the Nationalist advance: "We were all workers. There was a tremendous fever to reach Saragossa, to take it."[24] A Partido Obrero de Unificación Marxista (POUM) militant, Wildebano Solano, confirms: "The people's revolutionary instinct was amazing. . . . They knew they had to inflict one defeat after another, move ahead every minute. There wasn't a moment to lose. The cry went up—'To Saragossa.'"[25] Members of the militias themselves evoke their motivations poetically. Rosario Sánchez Mora, one of many women who served in the militias, describes the faith that her unit had in eventual victory: "We were young and we thought that the young, alone, would end the war, that we were going to devour the enemy."[26] Julia Manzanal, an instructor in the Fifth Regiment militias, explains that personal, local, and political motivations were mixed together: "Many went out to fight, to defend their own, their parents, to defend Madrid and to defend the country. . . .

On the 16th of February [the date of the Popular Front electoral victory] the people had won and on the 18th of July there was an uprising against that same people, who responded the way they had to respond." On the other hand, according to Manzanal, "I believe that nobody knew where the whole thing could go. I myself did not know what it could bring either. Something similar had never happened."[27] These extracts talk in collective terms—it is easier to find accounts of the commitments of *others* ("they"), or of a collective "we," than of the witness him- or herself. Equally interesting is that the statements of motivation are not expressed in sophisticated ideological rhetoric but in an everyday understanding of the stakes: workers, the fervor of youth, defending a town, defeating the enemy. These fighters were no less committed to a cause for the straightforwardness with which they express it.

But political and ideological motivations are one thing; fighting a war is something else. The real enthusiasm for defending the Republic did not necessarily translate into a willingness to fight and die for it. A French military attaché put the basic problem in a report to Paris about the situation in Madrid: the militiamen "leave, without understanding, for the front, where they discover, too late, that war is serious."[28] The columns that headed out to Aragón from Barcelona, fueled by this popular fervor, soon felt the costs of war. This is what Juan García Oliver found, for example. An anarchist leader from Barcelona, García Oliver raised a column called Los Aguiluchos in late August 1936 to break the deadlock that had emerged in Aragón. García Oliver recounts considerable discontent among his men the first night, setting up camp in the woods with cold rations because the local townsfolk in Grañén, Huesca province, refused to billet them. In his view, his men "were taken at a stroke away from the comforts of home. Against blunt reality, the revolutionary fantasy had ended, and they felt themselves caught in a trap."[29] García Oliver says that his own soldiers got used to the new conditions, but others did not. Captain Manuel Uribarry attributed the mass desertions in his unit in August 1936 to these everyday conditions: "One might say that men fled for a lack of fighting spirit, but I must confess to you that many times, when I saw them flee and I saw their unshod feet covered in sores, saying to me, 'I cannot continue,' I said to myself, 'Perhaps I would have fled sooner than you.'" After all, Uribarry continued, his feet were fine, and he had not had to deal with hunger or cold.[30] The right politics were not enough.

Nor did everyone share the initial political enthusiasm. Far from it: there were clearly many reasons short of a strong commitment to a cause that impelled recruitment to front-line units. According to Julia Manzanal, among those who joined for the "euphoria of defending the cause" were many who were going simply because it was what others did: "¿dónde va la gente?, donde va Clemente"[31] (Where are the people going? Where Clement is going). As time went on there were additionally the formal material rewards. The Republican government announced on August 15, 1936, after one month of war, that militiamen would earn ten pesetas per day—between two and five times the typical wage for a rural day-laborer in much of the Republic, and indeed over five times the prewar military pay.[32] George Orwell, who generally insisted on the "straightforwardness and generosity . . . [the] real largeness of spirit" of the POUM militiamen with whom he served in Aragón, also noted that "boys of fifteen were being brought up for enlistment by their parents, quite openly for the sake of the ten pesetas a day which was the militiaman's wage; also for the sake of the bread which the militia received in plenty and could smuggle home to their parents."[33] In Madrid, in the context of severe wartime hunger, the communist-affiliated aid organization Socorro Rojo Internacional (International Red Aid) apparently only delivered food aid to the families of militia members.[34] Militiamen in Madrid enjoyed some material privileges.[35] They traded on the social value of appearing to be heroic—for example, gaining the ability to eat in cafés without paying.[36]

Still more opportunistic motivations emerged as well. Militias in various locations not only requisitioned goods but also pillaged.[37] The Columna de Hierro, or Iron Column, gained particular infamy for looting and violence, both in Valencia province (where it was from) and in Teruel province in Aragón (where it was often stationed). Begun by anarchist firebrands in Valencia, it counted hundreds of prisoners from San Miguel de los Reyes Penitentiary among its ranks, including both anarchist political prisoners and thieves who, according to Bolloten, "had entered the column for what they could get out of it, adopting the Anarchist label as a camouflage." The Iron Column would steal precious metals from jewelers' shops to pay for war material, and cut a swath of "purifying" violence through Valencia province.[38] Looting is, of course, a common consequence of war of all kinds, and the regular Popular Army conducted its own abuses against the civilian population much later on in the war—for example, with uncompensated "requisitions" of food in Aragón.[39] But those abuses take on a different cast in a volunteer army than in a conscript army: in the latter they probably did not affect recruitment, as individuals had to join anyway. In a volunteer force, looting changes what was in it for someone to join a militia, given that they could stay home if they chose.

Violence against suspected right-wingers in the Republic generated further self-interested reasons to join the militias: in order to pass. Some rightists caught on the Republican side joined militias deliberately in order to cross the lines. This happened with some regularity in the first days, as rightists attempted to flee the Republican zone. In Barcelona, *Solidaridad Obrera* reported eight fascists in a militia who defected to the Nationalists at the beginning of August 1936.[40] José Cirre Jiménez, a rightist artillery officer who found himself on the Republican side at the outset, remembers meeting a man in his unit who had joined the militia because in his home province of Murcia, he felt in danger; the militias offered him a way out and possibly an opportunity to defect.[41] Cirre's story was repeated elsewhere, as officers and soldiers of the regular army whose sympathies lay with the Nationalists waited until their units were sent to the front to rebel and defect.[42] Gerardo Martínez Lacalle, a Falangist organizer hidden in Madrid, joined the combined socialist-communist youth wing, the Juventudes Socialistas Unificadas (JSU), through a connection who knew his politics: "I don't know who told me it would help me to join them. But I found that in that group we were all fascists."[43] Lacalle raised money for the JSU and conducted physical training of militia recruits, in order to enjoy the political protection that the membership offered and to work surreptitiously for the fifth column in Madrid. The militias were far from full of Republican idealists.

Trust in the Militias: Assessing Motivations and Developing Norms

With many different motivations for joining up, militia members and leaders tried to figure out whether they could trust their fellows. The formal procedures for joining up did provide a limited degree of confidence in others and the basis for norms. Beyond this, though, militiamen used a variety of less formal conditions to learn whom they should trust and mistrust. They built on preexisting networks based on neighborhoods, villages and union locals. Experiences of combat taught militia members a lot about each other, and about themselves, enabling one important costly signal. Finally, some militias attempted to make use of self-selection by making clear to their recruits that they would have to submit to military discipline, that fighting would be hard and costly. The latter underpinned the major source of variation among militias, for many did not insist on discipline at all. Those that did, however, thereby required of their recruits a clear and indeed costly signal of a willingness to fight: their volunteers joined conscious that, once fighting, they could not shirk. Accepting this choice willingly provided an important basis for trust.

Answering the Call: Voluntary Recruitment as a Basis for Trust

What did the formal process of voluntary recruitment mean for combatants' motivations? The evidence of multiple motivations that we have seen already suggests fairly strongly that just joining up was far from a perfect guarantee of a belief in a common cause or a commitment to fight. While the formal requirements for new recruits helped to a certain degree, they did not go very far. Recognizing the risks of opportunists and especially of political opponents joining militias, the workers and parties began to require new recruits to present either a union or party membership card, or a voucher from a trusted union or party member. But the parties and unions were growing dramatically at the outset of the war, perhaps tenfold in the case of the unions.[44] Indeed, parties and unions had incentives to maximize membership numbers to strengthen their demands for access to funding, arms, cabinet posts, and other resources of the central government.[45] And membership cards could be had through theft, connections, and cash payment.[46]

Still, voluntarism in Spain *did* mean something, especially compared with what conscription would have meant. Above all, those who had little political interest in the Republic or little desire to fight could still generally stay home, until conscription came in during the fall of 1936. Indeed, it was a manpower shortage that drove the Republic to impose conscription in the first place. At that point, as we shall see in the next chapter, the political commitments of typical recruits declined even further. Similarly, during the militia period opportunists often looked to join home-front patrols and committees rather than front-line units. Revolutionary committees appropriated the assets of wealthy landowners, for example, providing opportunities for theft.[47] This dynamic selected out unreliable recruits from the front-line militias to a certain extent.[48]

Hence, militiamen sometimes saw their fellows' voluntarism itself as worthy of a degree of trust. As we have seen, militia members who spoke years later of the motivations for war tended to speak in terms of *we*, and to underline the motivations that they saw among others who went off to the front willingly. This voluntarism would then serve as a basis for norms of collective action. For example, Cipriano Mera, leader of the CNT Del Rosal column, underlined this voluntarism when trying to induce his charges to improve their self-discipline: "We who are gathered here have come on our own account and we have made a commitment among ourselves. He who would withdraw without first defeating the fascists across that mountain would be a traitor to this commitment."[49] The "Promise of the Popular Militiaman," which new recruits to the Fifth Regiment all made and which enjoined them to fight, to obey, and to make others do so, begins as follows: "I, child of the people, citizen of the Spanish Republic, freely take the status of Militiaman of the People's Army . . ."[50] Commanders such as Victor de Frutos, a CNT militia leader in Madrid, often judged that the fact of voluntarism should stand a militiaman in good stead to begin with, and thought that latecomers showed relatively less commitment.[51] As we shall see in the next chapter, when the Republic shifted to conscription, it lost some element of this trust: those who had stayed home when the call came in the summer of 1936 were now in the army.

There were, however, clear limits to the trust that the fact of voluntarism could generate. There were many for whom joining up was a means to a different end, as we have seen. In consequence, many militiamen did not trust their fellow combatants. This requires us to go beyond the formal requirements and examine the informal conditions that also contributed to trust and mistrust in the militias.

Knowing Your Friends: Prewar Networks

Knowing combatants from before the war was a critical source of information about their motivations, and underlay trust among combatants. The militias varied in their social composition, but on the whole they built on local recruitment and very often had prewar social ties. The initial cores of the militias, as we have seen, came from long-standing activist networks above all. Prewar ties—such as those based on locality or political membership—were a way in which someone else's self-sacrifice would provide an example, serving both as a basis for recruitment and a way of solidifying a unit. Local unions joined the militia en bloc. The Los Comuneros battalion recruited out of the Centro Abulense, a community center for people from Ávila province in Madrid, which put out a call for volunteers for a "Castilian column." It recruited groups of Castilians, including those already in Madrid, who were often members of the center already, and those who had been displaced at the outset of the conflict.[52] Two-thirds of those recruited before January 1937 were from Old Castile, the large majority of these from Ávila, and the unit attempted to make sure that replacement personnel came from the same provinces.[53]

This local recruitment drew on interpersonal ties. All of José María Aroca's friends and colleagues in the anarchist youth league Juventudes Libertarios in Barcelona joined the Durruti column early on, inspiring him to do the same.[54] Timoteo Ruíz, a young peasant from Toledo province, had been attracted to socialism and to the Soviet Union in the years before the Civil War because of the highly unequal distribution of land in his village. He joined the Fifth Regiment in Madrid with friends: "When I came from my village in Toledo province with a few other local youths who like me wanted to fight, we met a lad in Madrid from the village who had joined the communist youth. He told us that the best unit was the 5th Regiment which the communists were forming."[55] Upon joining the Fifth Regiment and completing its training, recruits were typically able to select the unit they wanted to join, and clustered by region or by profession, with names that sometimes reflected these origins: the Voluntarios de Andalucía or the Artes Blancas for bakers.[56]

These ties could help solidify combatants' sense of commitment to each other. Victor de Frutos's CNT forces emerged out of improvised militia based on neighborhood groups.[57] He argues that the fact that his Primero de Mayo battalion was largely recruited from the same neighborhood in Carabanchel Bajo, southwest of Madrid, gave it a strong sense of mutual reliance in the first days of the rebellion. Someone from elsewhere still generally joined only if he had friends in the unit, and "in this way became a man we could rely upon."[58] In particular, the sense of defending one's own home gave Primero de Mayo particular cohesion when the battle got to Carabanchel Bajo itself. The unit requested permission to be stationed there, and now "the militiamen had a stronger sense than at any time in the past four months that they were defending something that was their own."[59]

A dissimilar social background, in contrast, could fuel mistrust. Aroca, the young anarchist student and militiaman from Barcelona, recalls being treated with skepticism as a student. He says he was almost prevented from joining because the man known as "el Murcia," who examined his Juventudes Libertarias credentials, suspected him of being a rightist since he looked like a cleric and not like a worker. El Murcia was, to Aroca, "a typical example of a case that was repeated innumerable times in the Militias: . . . of the illiterate who, with a happenstance position of authority, takes pleasure in humiliating all those who know how to read and write." Once in the ranks, Aroca discovered that class tensions undermined the unit, provoking mistrust and accusations. "On one occasion, I myself was labeled a fascist by a comrade who did not brook my bourgeois custom of cleaning my teeth."[60] Of course, Aroca's own class prejudices come through here as much as those he alleges of el Murcia.

Positive social connections thus gave militia members a sense of whether they could rely on someone and provided a more solid basis for trust. In various accounts of this period, they seem to have facilitated fighting together above all. As we shall see in the next chapter, when the Republic began conscripting en masse, local ties carried on facilitating soldiers' goals—but now the goal was as often to desert as to keep fighting.

Proving Yourself: The Experience of Combat as Signal

We saw earlier that the key motivations for combatants include not just political goals but the willingness to endure military life. This also meant that service itself offered a chance to send a costly signal, proving oneself directly to be up to the challenge. Battle could expose the fragility of initial enthusiasm in maintaining a willingness to serve. Many militia columns fell apart from *desbandadas* (disbandments): instances of panicked flight and, often, large-scale desertion. These occurred especially early on when units had their first taste of battle.[61] Air attacks were particularly intimidating.[62] Narciso Julián, a communist railwayman who had joined the communist-organized Del Barrio column, recalls the extreme panic that set in after an air raid in Huesca province on the Aragón front. "Everyone, including the anarchist machine-gunner, leapt for cover; I never saw him again. The engine driver was the only one to show any control." In the aftermath, "[s]o many men left the column . . . that they had to remain in the township of Gra-ñén to reorganize."[63] Like aircraft, Moroccan units, presented in racist Republi-can propaganda as Moorish hordes, provoked particularly panicked responses.[64]

The hardships of military life and of battle, and the fact that many decided to leave rather than endure them, also meant that those who stayed and fought will-ingly showed a clear signal of commitment. There were the acts of heroism that battle allows. For example, Rosario Sánchez Mora became a public hero in Ma-drid for having her hand blown off while laying dynamite; a poem was written about her, entitled "Rosario, dinamitera."[65] Julián relates how a militiaman who had blown up a tank described it at a rally:

> "Well, look, it's—it's very easy. You lie on the ground with a bomb in your hand and you let the tank get to within three metres and you throw the bomb at the tracks. If it explodes, the tank blows up on the spot. And if it doesn't—if it doesn't explode—" He stopped, not knowing how to continue. "If it doesn't," he added finally, "the tank crushes you."[66]

Heroism had an important impact within military units in promoting trust. Sán-chez Mora relates that in her unit of the communist-organized Fifth Regiment, there was an initial reluctance to serve under an officer. However, she says, "when that man came, wounded with his head bandaged, who had been fighting at the head of his unit, well, we changed our minds."[67] Simply joining early and endur-ing could be a basis for trust that could overcome social barriers. For example, JSU militia member Miguel Nuñez recounts that it was discovered that a unit-mate was in fact a priest in hiding. When this came out, belief in "the ecclesiasti-cal hierarchy's responsibility in siding with the fascist reaction against the people" spurred a suspicion of the priest himself in the unit, but, as Nuñez recounts, his honesty—and his military record—saved him:

> As soon as he knew he was discovered, he displayed a willingness to dis-cuss the matter openly and frankly, and his fearlessness won him a cer-tain sympathy. Moreover, like the rest of us, he had been fighting rifle in hand against the enemy. And he went on to say that he believed history was on the side of the poor, not the rich. He came out of it pretty well, indeed freed of the fear with which he had been living.[68]

As time went on—as we shall see in the next chapter—the cooperation that this helped create among militiamen stood in sharp contrast to the new recruits that the Republic brought in once it imposed conscription.

Bearing up well under the strain of conflict created normative obligations (others are fighting so you should too), whereas *not* enduring such conditions well could undermine mutual effort and mutual confidence. Victor de Frutos, a CNT commander, tells a story that illustrates the importance of mutual influences, norms, and signals.[69] On the highway heading from Madrid to Extremadura, some twenty kilometers from the capital, the advance of the Moroccan cavalry had begun to demoralize his militiamen. In this context, de Frutos tells of one Ramírez who complained about the difficult conditions of fighting, especially the lack of good weapons, food, and even shoes. "Either they give us something to set fire to those bastards [the enemy] or I won't endure any more!" In response, a sergeant nicknamed "El Calabaza" told him to quit complaining and accused Ramírez of wanting to desert and of complaining in order to find someone to go with him, as a way of justifying his departure. "But I assure you, you won't succeed, because nobody is going to move from here!" El Calabaza acknowledged the poor quality of their arms and supplies, but said that that was what they had to fight the fascists with. Ramírez continued to complain about not having shoes, this time saying that El Calabaza got special treatment when he had received his own, the day before. El Calabaza threw Ramírez his own pair and headed to the front trench to fight—barefoot. Shamed, Ramírez changed his attitude, gave de Frutos back the shoes, and followed El Calabaza to the line.

The story illustrates the mutual influence, both positive and negative, that militiamen could have on each other. El Calabaza's primary concern is not Ramírez himself but how he could affect others. El Calabaza's costly gesture, for de Frutos, teaches a lesson in "the dignity of the combatant," pushing Ramírez to grit his teeth and fight. It works as a costly signal and reinforces a norm. While de Frutos claims that each of the two antagonists was "incapable of deserting"—for him, Ramírez was primarily letting off steam in his complaints—it is not difficult to see how Ramírez's "defeatist" talk could have that influence eventually, if it were not met by an even stronger gesture in reverse. El Calabaza, for his part, is quite aware that Ramírez needs another militiaman to go with him to create a normative framework in which it is acceptable to leave. According to el Calabaza, the critical thing is that Ramírez cannot find anyone to do so. The group's willingness to endure and to fight creates mutual obligations.

Submitting to Rules: Discipline, Norms, and What Voluntarism Meant

Voluntary recruitment, local ties, and battlefield displays could all facilitate trust, and there were no obvious systematic differences across most militias in their use. Instead, the militias in the early months of the war varied, above all, by the discipline that their recruits would have to accept. This variation allowed for costly signals, as the uncommitted tended not to join militias that would demand much of them.

It was often not difficult to learn which units to join if one wanted to avoid strenuous service. Notably, light discipline was practically advertised in anarchist publications. At the beginning of the war, anarchist newspapers printed the requirements for militia service, indicating clearly that they were rather lax—for example, explicitly noting that militiamen had the "liberty to enter and leave as free men."[70] The CNT in Valencia published a resolution in its mouthpiece, *Fragua Social*, making clear to new recruits that its units were different from others: "When a comrade enters the CNT barracks, he must understand that the word barracks does not signify subjection to odious military regulations consisting of salutes, parades, and other trivialities of the kind, completely theatrical and negating every revolutionary ideal."[71]

In large part, the rejection of military discipline was out of philosophical opposition. Antimilitarism had been fundamental to prewar Spanish anarchism.[72] It was very difficult to reconcile the opposition between the liberty of the individual and the idea of obeying an order, against one's inclinations, to go out to fight and die for it. Instead, the priority for many was the opportunity to reshape society that the revolution offered. Josep Cercos, a CNT metalworker from Barcelona, expressed this view clearly:

> It was the fever of the revolution which carried us forward. We had preached anti-militarism for so long, we were so fundamentally anti-militaristic, that we wouldn't have gone simply to wage war. That was something we couldn't envisage.[73]

Despite these idealistic roots of antimilitarism, many who profited from it were not especially high-minded. Militiamen who preferred light duty without much discipline sorted themselves into less demanding units, for example leaving during initial training.[74] They would often attempt to leave front-line units for militia units remaining close to home.[75] Such an approach would allow them to gain the benefits of service—ten pesetas per day, social perks, the opportunity to appear to be a hero, or political cover—without having to pay the costs of fighting, since they could frequently avoid doing so. Similarly, right-wingers joined those unions that were least demanding of political credentials.[76]

The result of incorporating relatively opportunistic soldiers, in many units, was the emergence of norms of lax behavior. In some militia units, militiamen frequently argued about or refused orders.[77] Others, according to Martínez Reverte, "held a vote to decide whether to attack or retreat."[78] At the militias' siege of the Alcázar of Toledo in July–September 1936, according to Hugh Thomas, "many were 'tourists' of war, who drove out with their wives or girl friends from Madrid for an afternoon's sniping."[79] Militia members could often return home at night, as in Madrid:

> They set off for the sierra as though they were going on a Sunday outing, to shoot rabbits. . . . How amazing it seemed when in the evening they all came to spend the night at home. The next morning the scene was repeated.[80]

According to Broué and Témime, in some units "you went back home between two turns at guard duty, and you were regarded as a madman if you refused to sleep when you were on guard at night." Hence, militiamen imposed constraints on their units' practices, for to undermine these rights was to risk mass desertion: "a column that strayed from its home base lost most of its militiamen: they liked to sleep home at night."[81] Victor de Frutos, the anarchist commander in the Primero de Mayo battalion, attempted at first to prevent his recruits from going home at night, meeting with incomprehension among his militia members. De Frutos therefore reluctantly granted permissions to return, but had great difficulty in inducing these individuals to leave their rifles in the unit.[82]

That these norms spread from one recruit to another seems clear. Cipriano Mera, an anarchist commander in the Del Rosal column operating near Madrid, relates that in mid-August 1936, some men "of maximum confidence" wanted to go to Andalucía, but, before the transfer, one of them wanted to return to Madrid for a day's rest in more comfortable conditions. Mera says he was wary, for if one went back, others would ask to as well, which is what happened the next day; Mera had to threaten to use force to make them return to sentinel duty. His fellow commander Teodoro Mora had apparently found himself in the same situation. But the coordination secretary of the Center Regional Committee of the CNT told both Mera and Mora to be lenient with their militiamen.[83]

Shirking by some militiamen, as well as its prospect, could have an especially detrimental effect on others in the unit in cases of *desbandada* or mass disbandment. A report from Mera's Del Rosal column on September 15, 1936, lamented that "militiamen abandon their positions with thousands of excuses."[84] De Frutos witnessed *desbandadas* firsthand in his unit; he vividly captures these excuses and the mass process they could kick off: "Sometimes the pretext was a lack of munitions; others, feeling sick and looking for a corner to relieve one's bowels, and, other times, the men yelled openly, 'They're cutting us off!' This spirit would become a contagion, until the retreat became universal."[85] Thus, despite the fact that de Frutos's men were largely from the Carabanchel Bajo neighborhood near Madrid, and that they had had a greater degree of enthusiasm fighting there than at any other time, his unit still suffered a panic at Carabanchel after the influx of a new company of untested, fresh recruits, none of whom, according to de Frutos, really showed that they wanted to fight.[86] A militia commander writing in September 1936 about *desbandadas* near Sigüenza, Guadalajara province, noted the importance of confidence in one's comrades. When such confidence was lacking—for example, in new units where militiamen had not had the chance to learn whether they could rely on their colleagues—a *desbandada* was much more likely. They "began with the spontaneous retreat of a few groups of scared men," provoking the rest to flee as well. To remedy the situation, this commander not only recommended the imposition of harsh penalties for sowing discontent and indiscipline but also instructed militiamen "that those who fled to avoid their own death or injury created situations that magnified the possibilities of casualties. Soldiers should be drilled to instill confidence, strengthen obedience, and induce group trust."[87]

In contrast, when units insisted on discipline, making it clear that they would impose rather strong demands on their members, they tended to induce more committed fighters to self-select into them and developed stronger norms of cooperation. Further, though no unit appears to have been immune to disbandments, insisting on discipline appears to have improved some units' resistance to them.

Some militia leaders recognized the importance of imposing discipline early on. This included voices within the anarchist camp. For example, the CNT journalist Eduardo de Guzmán thought that the war needed to prevail over the revolution:

> This was not a revolutionary riot. This was a war, with all the pains and demands of a war. To win, neither enthusiasm, nor faith, nor heroism was enough. To win, it was necessary to organize. To win, it was necessary to act without vacillation or dismay, with serenity and invincible energy. . . . We are antimilitarists; we continue to be so. But today, against the dramatic realities of a war which we can do nothing but accept, we must adopt warlike methods. If it is necessary, we must bury our ideas to defend them heroically.[88]

However, it was still unclear just what that would mean: "We are not asking for a barracks discipline. But we are demanding a minimum of priceless responsibility, according to the needs of the war."[89]

The most notable instance of a unit insisting on discipline from the early going was the Quinto Regimiento, or Fifth Regiment, which demanded immediate and unquestioning compliance with orders from the very beginning of the war. Organized by the communists from a headquarters in Madrid, the Fifth Regiment served principally as a focus for training and organizing militiamen of many political stripes on the central front.[90] To begin with, the Fifth Regiment incorporated organized militias that had emerged locally and autonomously, but beginning in mid-August 1936, it set up various recruiting stations in order to take charge of recruitment directly.[91]

Members of the Fifth Regiment felt the costs of war the same as anyone else.[92] Where it distinguished itself was in military discipline. While the Fifth Regiment's internal document "Military Instruction" emphasized, much like the anarchists, that what was required was "conscious discipline, self-discipline, not the discipline that comes from repression, from fear, from punishment,"[93] obedience was still very much the order of the day. Another internal document, entitled "Camaraderie and Discipline," noted that there were militiamen who demonstrated insufficient obedience: they "advance and retreat as they like, mock their superiors, sow confusion and indiscipline. With such militiamen, it is necessary to speak seriously, and if they persist, they must be expelled from the militias." While insisting on compliance, however, it also required commanders to exercise restraint in how they treated their subordinates. It noted that some commanders thought that they had "many rights and few duties"; a chief should instead "never forget that his militiamen are his companions, volunteers like him; and if he is chief, it is because of them." Hence, the responsibilities of commander and subordinate were reciprocal. "A chief who treats his militiamen like automata is a bad chief; a militiaman who does not obey his chief is a bad militiaman. Neither has the right to be in the militias."[94]

Leaders of the Fifth Regiment appeared to have been conscious of the importance of mutual trust for combatants, and the role that discipline could play here. Vittorio Vidali, an Italian Stalinist who under the nom de guerre Carlos Contreras helped found the Fifth Regiment, cited the disintegration of the militias in the face of combat as the key problem with the militia system. In particular, writing admittedly after the war, Vidali interestingly references the isolation of committed individuals within what he regards as the undisciplined militia system. For him, other militias had little to fall back on but "acts of individual heroism"; hence, "large columns of militiamen, lacking intermediate officers and commanders capable of leading them, became demoralized at the first sign of difficulty whatever the will (*voluntad*) of individual militiamen." The solution, to Vidali, was capable and trusted leadership that imposed discipline on troops.[95] Here, discipline was not just an individual trait but a collective one. The Fifth Regiment's Promise of the Popular Militiaman included explicit pledges to participate in maintaining others' discipline, maintaining norms of cooperation:

> I commit to keep, and to ensure that others keep [*guardar y hacer guardar*], the most rigid discipline, precisely obeying all the orders of my chiefs and superiors. . . . If I voluntarily fail in these solemn commitments, may the disrespect of my comrades fall upon me, and may I be punished by the implacable hand of the law.[96]

Further observations confirm the interest among key communist leaders in mutual confidence among combatants, with norms upheld both through positive influence and through sanctions. Vidali told a *Moscow Daily News* editor in 1937 that twin slogans underlay the "iron unity" of the Fifth Regiment's units. One was rather positive: "Never leave a comrade wounded or dead, in the hands of the enemy." But another conveyed a much more sinister side: "If my comrade advances or retreats without orders, I have the right to shoot him."[97] It is unclear how widely the latter rule was followed, but the Soviet journalist and agent Mikhail Koltsov recorded it as well in his war diary.[98]

In this context, the Fifth Regiment actively attempted to cultivate a reputation for discipline and to influence recruits' self-selection. In order to be accepted into the Fifth Regiment, a recruit had to declare a willingness to accept military discipline, in addition to good health and proof of antifascism, such as a left-wing union or party affiliation. However, these standards were relaxed at the beginning of the war and during the siege of Madrid in November 1936, when the political guarantee was "the only criterion that was insisted upon strictly."[99] New recruits had only eight days of training, "as much theoretical as practical."[100] Julia Manzanal relates being named an instructor for weapons use and marching, after having joined up herself only a few days earlier, on the day the war began.[101] Still, *Milicia Popular*, the Fifth Regiment publication, discouraged individuals from joining up if they were unwilling to subject themselves to discipline. In an early issue it published the Promise of the Popular Militiaman publicly.[102] In laying out the requirements for joining the Fifth Regiment–organized Acero companies, *Milicia Popular* made an effort to make those requirements appear strenuous, including that militiamen "commit to submit to a rigid discipline." It validated individuals' contributions *outside* the militias in order to give those who sought to prove their revolutionary credentials incentives to select themselves out: "Not everyone can meet these obligations. One can be a good militiaman, a good revolutionary, a good anti-fascist, but still not have the preparation needed to meet these obligations."[103] Again, on September 20, *Milicia Popular* dissuaded those who disagreed with discipline from joining: "If there is anyone who does not agree [that indiscipline must be punished], it is better that they stay home."[104]

With such indications, in sharp contrast to the signals sent in anarchist publications, and with a reputation cultivated by word of mouth, the Fifth Regiment encouraged the self-selection of combatants who were willing to accept the need to fight once at the front. This included, interestingly, many otherwise anticommunist military officers, attracted to the Communist Party because it alone seemed willing to accept that the war had to be fought with discipline.[105] The appeal extended to ordinary civilians. A teacher in Madrid, Leopoldo de Luís, stopped giving classes to the children of militiamen and joined the Fifth Regiment with a group of friends, "because they were the best organized battalions, those best able to face the fascist rebellion."[106] Some particular units formed by the Fifth Regiment, like the Thaelmann or Acero battalions, gained a reputation that led some to seek entry into those battalions specifically.[107] Domingo Malagón relates a similar story, joining the Fifth Regiment with a group of colleagues from the La Paloma art school:

> I cannot say I was a communist at the time . . . but we thought that the best thing to do was to go to the Fifth Regiment, since we saw that that group hadn't disappeared in one or two weeks. In fact, a few days after the rising, my teacher told me: "This will be a Civil War and we will need to face them with an Army of our own." I believe that, at the time, he was one of the few who thought that way.[108]

Ultimately, then, the discipline policies of different militia units had downstream effects on recruitment. They enabled a self-selection process, allowing different militiamen with different degrees of a willingness to fight to sort themselves into units accordingly.

There is general agreement that Fifth Regiment–affiliated units performed comparatively strongly and tended to maintain their cohesion more effectively than many other militia units. Martínez Reverte reflects a general historical consensus in arguing that, in defending the approaches to Madrid, the Fifth Regiment stood out from the other militias in following orders immediately rather than debating them.[109] Further, according to Ramón Salas Larrazábal's account of the central front campaigns, while other militia "disbanded faced with the smallest difficulty," the Fifth Regiment, alongside the Civil Guard and regular army, provided the core of Republican resistance to the rebel General Varela's advance.[110] However, it is important to note that Fifth Regiment units were not immune to panics. An internal report on October 5, 1936, noted that they certainly did occur, often in the face of artillery and aviation bombardments, and typically in newly created units, while the commander of the Lenin battalion (part of the Regiment) complained of similar abandonments the following month.[111]

The Comandancia General de Milicias's statistics on disappearances and other casualties seem to confirm a generally greater capacity for resistance in Fifth Regiment units. (Many, but not all, of these disappearances were most likely desertions.) These statistics were broken down by the militia the combatant belonged to, among other indicators.[112] Though these records do not clearly identify Fifth Regiment units, I compiled a list of the militias mentioned as being affiliated with the Fifth Regiment by Juan Andrés Blanco Rodríguez, Robert Colodny, and Vittorio Vidali.[113] In 1936, Fifth Regiment–affiliated units recorded 523 disappearances and 1,286 deaths, or 2.46 deaths for every disappearance. The remaining units recorded 1,186 disappearances and 1,755 deaths, for a ratio of 1.48. (The Lenin Battalion, which Matthews cites as having indiscipline problems, is exceptional here in having had more disappearances than deaths.) In short, the Fifth Regiment seemed substantially better able than other militias to keep its soldiers fighting, and dying.

Discipline was the most obvious difference between the Fifth Regiment and other units, but were there other reasons for its relative success at limiting desertion? While it stood accused by other political factions of getting better supplies than anyone else, notably because of its Soviet connections, the first Soviet shipments did not arrive until mid-October 1936; and in any case the professional officer José Martín Blázquez at the Ministry of Defense, who was responsible for signing off on requisitions, found the communists' to generally be more limited than others'.[114] This therefore does not appear to be a compelling alternative explanation.

Factional Rivalries, Stereotypes, and Desertion

The wide variety of militias thus had a wide variety of practices, permitting different norms to emerge. But another influence on norms came from the very fragmentation among the different militia factions in Republican Spain. These divisions reduced coordination and trust in militia units, and may have led to increased desertions.[115]

The many different factions on the Republican side had a long history of conflict; up until the war, in fact, the Republic and the CNT had considered themselves enemies. Josep Cercos, the CNT-affiliated metalworker from Barcelona, expressed quite clearly that politically committed activists could fight against Franco without any strong loyalty to the regime: "We didn't give a damn about the republic, we were concerned only about the revolution. I wouldn't have gone to the front if not to make the revolution."[116] This approach sat in uneasy alliance with the more moderate preferences of the Left Republican and Communist parties, preferring to focus on organizing the war effort and limit the re-distribution of property from the middle classes.

The multiple different interests and jockeying for power among these factions generated problems of coordination and cooperation among them. The problems of cooperation were apparently particularly strong among the militias on the Aragón front. In the village of Angüés, a bit behind the lines near Huesca, a CNT-affiliated peasant observed the anarchist Roja y Negra column on one side of the village and the POUM column on the other: "When the former went into action, the latter sat back with their hands in their pockets, laughing. When the POUM was in combat the anarchists, I have to admit, did the same. That's no way to fight a war, let alone win it. They should have got together to fight the common enemy."[117] Major Aberri, a Republican officer sent to Aragón to assist in the organ-ization of the front, reports a striking example of the absurdity of this situation: "I was once in a position where there were several 10.5 guns, but there were no munitions. These were in the possession of a nearby column, which refused to part with them although it had no artillery itself."[118]

The lack of coordination increased the costs of war to the combatants and re-duced their confidence. An illustrative example is the fiasco of the assault on Huesca, a key provincial capital in Aragón, in November 1936. According to Ma-jor Aberri, Huesca was poorly defended and ripe to fall. But the assault was to-tally undermined by a lack of coordination among the militias. At a meeting where the commander of the Aragón front presented the militia leaders with a clear plan to take the city, "those present listened to his plan, which was discussed in detail, but unfortunately they finally decided to consult their respective trade-union organizations before accepting anything. In the end the discussion took a very regrettable turn because the commander's request that some of the columns should hand over to other units the additional material they needed was rejected out of hand."[119]

Ultimately, this lack of coordination doomed the assault on Huesca when an anarchist unit attacked too early. José María Aroca, the anarchist student and mi-litia volunteer, admitted that he decided to leave the militias because the failed Huesca assault ended the last vestiges of his confidence in the unit's organization and leadership: "I decided to abandon the militias when the occasion to do so 'with dignity' presented itself. That is how far I had been discouraged by the mess that reigned in the militias, a mess that could play with criminal callousness with the lives of three hundred men."[120]

The other principal source of mistrust in the militias was the place of the regular security services. While we saw in the previous chapter how intense mistrust of officers drove some of them to desert, it also worked the other way: antimilitarist militiamen would sometimes desert if ordered to serve under military personnel.[121] As with military discipline, the communists in Madrid represented an important exception to these patterns. They had laid the groundwork for cooperation with officers before the Civil War, with a close association with the Unión Militar Republicana y Antifascista, the pro-Republican officers' organization.[122] In organizing the Fifth Regiment, then, the communists made it a standard practice to make the most of loyal officers, according to the Fifth Regiment commander Enrique Líster, in sharp contrast to other political groupings, which seemed to employ those officers as *little* as possible.[123] The receptive attitude of the Communist Party made it attractive to officers, whether or not they ultimately joined the party.[124] However, even the Fifth Regiment's organizers were concerned about mistrust of officers. Having identified the critical problem of disbandments of militias, Vidali argues that dealing with the problem by giving command entirely over to professional officers was no solution: "Given the total lack of confidence in such officers, giving them militia commands would have aggravated the situation."[125]

During the summer and fall of 1936, the militias fighting against the rebellion conducted a grand experiment in military practice. They needed to expand quickly past their initial nuclei of activist networks, and so they recruited people whose commitment to fighting and to the common cause was not immediately known. Some demanded much from their fighters, insisting they prove their commitment through costly signals. In this way they furnished a basis for trust, mutual reliance, and norms of cooperation, all of which improved their ability to resist in combat and limited desertion. In combat itself, fighters learned about themselves and about each other, and if they fought, they reinforced trust and commitment still further. But in others, joining did not demand much of the recruit, combatants could not rely on each other, and the unit was susceptible to disbandments and large-scale desertion. Social ties played an important auxiliary role, facilitating norms of cooperation when they allowed committed combatants to recognize that commitment in each other. And the environment of mistrust, against factional rivals and above all against stereotyped rightists such as military officers, pushed many to desert who might have fought.

This is a complex history, and so a fair question is, What is gained against simpler existing explanations of desertion patterns? Were desertion rates simply a matter of supply, for instance? It certainly appears that militias abused the requisition system, with each party and union overinflating its rosters. Given the tremendous disruption of the coup and local revolutions, it is unsurprising that militias had to improvise in weapons, munitions, and food. It is possible that poorly connected militia leaders would suffer from supply problems and be unable to hold on long to their militia members. However, this would not explain why Fifth Regiment forces suffered from lower rates of desertion than others.

Can a commitment to the cause alone suffice as an explanation? I argue that there are important tendencies in desertion that this approach cannot explain. The individual's political commitment did not often, by itself, keep him or her fighting. In the militias, enthusiasm for the cause and a passionate interest in defending the Republic often gave way to mass panic, disillusionment with one's comrades, and frustration with the militia system. These phenomena all point in the direction of trust and norms of cooperation—of a belief not only in one's own willingness to fight but also in that of the other members of one's unit. Combatants therefore did not make the decision to desert or to fight in isolation from each other. Their choice often did not reflect the side they wanted to support.

Social ties among militia members did make a difference. Many militias built very clearly on ties from unions and community centers, and social ties could help strengthen trust among combatants, while social difference could get in the way. But as we shall see in the next chapter, the generally positive role that social ties played in the militias, limiting desertion by building trust, very often reversed as conscription became ever more widespread. The impact of social ties in the militias cannot necessarily generalize.

There is, finally, the question of coercion. Generally there was very little coercive capacity in the Republic to keep combatants fighting, and this seems to have permitted them to leave easily. When militia members abandoned the front and went back home, there was little effective apparatus to induce them to return. While the severe mistrust of officers, based on a stereotype, made it so that efforts to punish desertion provoked it instead (as in chapter 5), it might have worked better with militiamen, who did not labor under such a stereotype. In the absence of strong trust, coercion can serve as an important alternative, and as we shall see in the next chapters, coercive control helped keep unmotivated combatants fighting later in the war, and proved a decisive advantage in the Nationalist war effort.

But this raises an important question: Was the variation in the militias *only* to do with coercion? If the Fifth Regiment militias showed a relatively consistent ability to resist and to fight, was this simply because they controlled their fighters coercively, through clear rules and punishments for disobedience? The difficulty with this approach is that militia members took on the burden of discipline willingly. If they were unwilling combatants, kept fighting by coercion alone, they could have joined a unit that did not present discipline as a hallmark. Instead, the attractiveness of a disciplined unit lay in the confidence that others would do their job, that they signaled their willingness to do so. In this context, discipline operated not just on the individual but on the group. It resulted in a self-sorting effect, with some recruits seeking out those militias that seemed to take the war seriously and others looking for light service. In other words, the former sent a clear and costly signal of their willingness to fight, while the latter did not. And they ended up in units where they could, more or less, trust that others would do their share.

THE POPULAR ARMY OF THE REPUBLIC, FALL 1936–39

The militia summer of 1936 had been a summer of chaos as well as of valor in the defense of the Republic. The challenge would now be to maintain the valor while reducing the chaos. As we saw in the previous chapter, the militias that arose to fight the rebels varied widely in their insistence that combatants send costly signals of commitment to fight. Some militias, such as the Fifth Regiment, insisted their recruits follow orders obediently, while others did not. Joining the former therefore sent a costly signal of the willingness to fight and served as the basis for trust and norms of cooperation. Joining the latter, however, did not send a strong signal, and norms of shirking were likelier to develop. The former units, therefore, experienced considerably less desertion than the latter. Factional competition and stereotypes of disloyalty often worsened these problems of mistrust, and the Republic had little regular, centralized coercive capacity to make up for them.

From the fall of 1936 through the spring of 1937, the Republic transformed its armed forces entirely in order to regularize them and put power back in the hands of the state. First, it imposed military discipline and a single command structure on its militia forces. Building on the previous chapter's analysis, I argue that new discipline rules imposed costly signals of commitment on volunteers, requiring that they sign on to more demanding forms of warfare than they previously had. As volunteers left rather than accept discipline, those who remained showed their willingness to go on under new rules, deepening the commitment they made to each other.

However, the Republic also ensured the recruitment of less-committed troops by imposing conscription at the same time. The result was a separation in motivations. On the one hand, volunteers were more willing than ever to accept the rigors of war. They developed stronger norms and resisted more effectively. On the other hand, conscription created new groups of combatants with little commitment to fight. Beset by mistrust, groups of conscripts often fell apart. The result was a clear gap in cohesion across units, linked to the share of conscripts in those units. We saw this relationship at a micro level in Santander province in chapter 4; here, I show that it generalized in the armed forces.

In a third major change, the Republic imposed coercive control over the home front and the front line, catching and punishing deserters more reliably. This change was all the more critical with the new influx of conscripts, since to some extent it made up for the lack of trust. Forced to enlist, conscripts would be forced to keep fighting. However, coercive control provoked desertion as well. In particular, the factional rivalries that had made it harder for militia members to cooperate with each other now undermined the very centralization meant to reduce the chaos of the militia period. It was all too easy to see greater control over the militias as a first step to political repression—with reason. Some anarchist and Partido Obrero de Unificación Marxista (POUM) militiamen deserted rather than accept a new centralization of state power that would allow the state, under strong influence from the Communist Party, to persecute them.

Ultimately, these processes combined to produce three patterns in the Republic's units from the fall of 1936 to the end of the war. Conscript units, the bulk of the army, did not send costly signals and so developed weak norms of cooperation, but coercion kept many of them fighting. The key exceptions—the volunteer militias that now accepted military discipline—offered stronger norms of cooperation and stiffer resistance than either the undisciplined militias of the summer of 1936 or the new conscript forces. They were thus like their predecessors in the Fifth Regiment and other disciplined militias: they fought. Finally, political competition provoked members of the factions losing out in internecine competition—anarchist and POUM militias—to desert in greater numbers. Table 7.1 summarizes this comparison.

Volunteer Militias: Accepting Discipline as Costly Signal

There was a widespread recognition by the fall of 1936 that the militia system needed reform. Though the central Republican state was the key agent of change, the militias themselves often adapted on their own account as well. As detailed in the previous chapter, some units such as the communist-organized Fifth Regiment had indeed imposed discipline from the outset, insisting on obeying orders

TABLE 7.1. Military unit characteristics and hypothesized overall desertion rates—Republic, fall 1936–spring 1939

		THREAT OF VIOLENCE WITHIN ARMED GROUP		
		HIGH; AT MOST OCCASIONALLY STEREOTYPED OR FACTIONALIZED	LOW	HIGH; SYSTEMATICALLY STEREOTYPED OR FACTIONALIZED
Information about motivations	Clear and positive	Popular Army volunteer units		
	Unclear or negative	Popular Army conscript units		POUM and CNT units during militarization

Note: Units are placed according to the independent variables.

without discussion and promulgating clear codes of conduct. In fact, the Fifth Regiment's leaders had begun with the idea of creating the backbone of a regular army, and Fifth Regiment units were the first to be incorporated into the new Popular Army of the Republic.

But even anarchist leaders increasingly turned to military discipline, despite their philosophical objections to it. Cipriano Mera's memoirs indicate, explicitly, a change in outlook. As a political leader of the Del Rosal column of the Confederación Nacional del Trabajo (CNT) operating around Madrid, Mera relied on persuasion to convince his militiamen of the need to keep fighting. In a speech to his troops on August 1, 1936, he referred to the mutual commitment of volunteers to each other (as we saw in the previous chapter), insisting on "the necessity of imposing on ourselves a self-discipline stronger than military discipline."[1] However, as time went on, Mera became increasingly convinced of the need to insist on obedience and to penalize indiscipline. After a shelling that killed some of his friends, Mera reflected on the problems of the militias in general, and resolved on the need for command and for planning. He believed his militiamen were not following self-discipline but abusing their privileges, "making use of an improvised liberty."[2] As I noted in the previous chapter, by August 18, 1936, Mera was threatening to use force to keep his troops on sentinel duty, as was his fellow commander Teodoro Mora. Mera further began to tell his men behind the lines that, once at the front, they would not be permitted to leave.[3] Later, one fifteen-year-old member of the Del Rosal column observed a shift: now military orders from up above were "instinctively and without discussion" obeyed.[4]

However, many others within the anarchist movement resisted this new approach. Writers in *Solidaridad Obrera*, a CNT newspaper, asserted a clear preference for a lack of discipline, with one author juxtaposing "absurd and antiquated discipline" to "true camaraderie."[5] Others, especially anarchist hardliners in the

Columna de Hierro, or Iron Column, insisted that military life remained the exploitation of the many by the few: "Barracks and prisons are the same thing. . . . Who can claim that fighters, once they are militarized, are stronger, more willing to fill battlefields with their blood?"[6]

While some militias began their process of reform autonomously, more did so when the central government pushed them to. Its first effort, an attempt to entice militiamen to join centrally led volunteer battalions in August 1936, failed.[7] Then, the new government of the socialist union leader Francisco Largo Caballero, taking office on September 5, 1936, conducted more forceful efforts toward creating a centrally directed, disciplined army, called the Popular Army of the Republic. Largo did so under considerable pressure from the communists now in cabinet and from the several hundred Soviet and Comintern advisers.[8] These advisers were alarmed at the disorganization of the war effort.[9]

Largo began by appointing career officers with a clear preference for command and discipline to key posts, particularly in the General Staff.[10] But his government's efforts gained a new urgency after the fall of Toledo, just southwest of Madrid on September 27.[11] At the end of September the government declared the subjection of the militias to the Code of Military Justice as of October 10 in the central zone and October 20 elsewhere. However, a member of the militias had the option to refuse, and would be struck from the rolls.[12] The imposition of the code implied, for the first time, common standards of discipline across the militias. It required that militiamen submit to the commands of their leaders, that they stay with their units rather than go home at night, and that once they had joined a unit—or decided to stay under the new rules—they could no longer leave before their term of service expired. In short, a central component of militarization was to put an end to the indiscipline that had set some militias apart from others.

Militarization entailed not only discipline but also an integrated command structure. On October 16, Largo Caballero, as minister of war (a post he held in addition to the premiership), took formal command of all the Republic's forces.[13] Two days later, the government ordered the creation of the Mixed Brigades, the units that would be the basis of the Republic's new army, and the incorporation of the militias into these new units. Six were created immediately, and within a month there were twenty Mixed Brigades in operation alongside five International Brigades of forces from outside Spain.[14] The government militarized the militias most quickly around Madrid and on the central front.[15]

To bring about the militarization, the government used both carrots and sticks. Militias received wages and supplies from the Inspección General de Milicias, and though this bureaucracy suffered oversight problems at the beginning, it was able over time to increase the government's bargaining power with militias as its requisitions were increasingly better administered. Now, any militia unit hoping to receive materiel or wages from the Ministry of War had to accept the militarization order.[16] This offer became increasingly appealing as Soviet aid started to arrive in mid-October 1936.[17] Agents of the ministry now paid wages directly to militia members rather than transferring them in lump sums to the militia leadership, a system that had produced much abuse.

If military aid was the carrot, the stick was the threat of police and military action to force militias to accept a military structure. Against certain recalcitrant militias in Catalonia and Aragón, the regime deployed its security forces to compel them into militarization in the spring of 1937. Factionalism and mistrust undermined centralization in the short run: the centralization efforts were often characterized as communist attacks on the anarcho-syndicalist CNT and the anti-Stalin Marxist POUM, which, it must be said, they often were. The militarization order thus provoked running street battles in Barcelona at the beginning of May, which I explore below.[18]

Alongside the communists and socialists, generally enthusiastic for militarization, much of the anarchist leadership accepted it as well, albeit reluctantly. On October 3, 1936, the CNT Defense Committee in Madrid published Reglamento de las Milicias Confederales, a set of rules for its militiamen. They were enjoined to "fulfill the regulations issued by battalion committees and century and group delegates"; a militiaman could not "act on his own account in matters of war and will accept without discussion any post and any place to which he is assigned, both in the front and the rear."[19] It defined certain acts as "grave breaches" of the rules, to be punished by the Battalion Committee; these included "desertion, abandoning of one's post, pillage, and speaking demoralizing words."[20] The shift to military discipline thus took in even the anarchist movement.

This change across the Republic had paradoxical effects. It induced many soldiers to leave but solidified norms of cooperation among those who stayed. Many refused to accept the new structure of commands and regulations, and left. But this also meant that those who stayed signaled their commitment to fight for the armed group.

A clear indicator of this signaling logic comes in the explicit statements of anarchist outfits adopting discipline on their own in the summer and early fall of 1936. The anarchist militia leader Saturnino Carod not only turned to military discipline to improve his unit's effectiveness well before the militarization order, but also used discipline explicitly as a costly signal of loyalties. He decided to impose greater order on his column on the Aragón front, which included eighty Civil Guards, after a bad defeat. He attempted to divide the column into smaller units with a command structure. "The result was a near disaster; the militiamen abandoned the column and he was left with almost the *guardia civil* alone."[21] However, this process of selection meant that those left behind showed more clearly than ever their willingness to fight. Many of those who left Carod's column later returned, but were still reluctant, as his address to them indicated: "'You can rejoin the column, but first you will have to do a fortnight's training. And your instructors will be the *guardia civil*.' Imagine telling a CNT militant that he had to accept orders from a *guardia*! But I wasn't going to back down. 'In accepting, you will be demonstrating your willingness to become good combatants.' They accepted the training."[22]

Anarchist publications eventually followed the communist lead, described in chapter 6, in encouraging self-selection. Just as the communists had, they began actively discouraging less-committed combatants from fighting, and indeed valorizing *not* serving at all rather than joining only to leave again. In late October 1936, the CNT newspaper *Fragua Social*, in Valencia, published an article that, much like the Fifth Regiment's *Milicia Popular* over two months earlier, explicitly asked the uncommitted not to join and validated that decision:

> If someone wants to help bring about the triumph of the Revolution, he must first examine what he would accomplish as a combatant, and if he does not find in himself the degree of self-sacrifice necessary to be a good combatant, he must abstain from seeking entry into the columns, and instead intensify his zeal and labor in the rearguard, where he can also serve the Revolution, with more loyalty than those who march to the Front knowing that they will not resist the first shot they hear fired.[23]

In other words, the effort now was to encourage only the committed to select into military service.

Repeating the trend of exits from the militias as they changed their rules autonomously, the imposition of militia militarization in the fall and winter of 1936–37 came with a new wave of departures. The militarization order gave militiamen the option of leaving rather than accepting militarization; however, once they joined the Popular Army, they were under legal obligations to accept centrally established standards of service and a central command, and to stay for the duration.[24] Many opted out. It is true that many of the departures that occurred at this point were motivated not by any lack of commitment to fighting but by factionalism, specifically the fear that one's political program would be crushed by the Republic, as I describe below. However, it is also clear that many militia departures had less to do with politics. David Granda, for example, describes the basic motivation in his unit in Asturias: "There were a lot of soldiers, especially the older men who were say fifty years old, who said, 'Right, if we are to be militarized I'm going home. I don't want to be a regular. I want to defend the Republic, but as a volunteer, not as a soldier.'"[25] The wave hit not only the anarchist militias and the POUM, with which the Republic and the increasingly powerful

Communist Party had the deepest and most intense factional conflicts, but other columns as well. Consistent with the abandonment of service when militias changed autonomously, staying around after the militarization order seems to have reduced much of the militias to a committed core.

Within this core, accepting discipline not only improved coordination but also seems to have solidified a sense of collective action and mutual confidence. Anarchist sources at this time show that those who were initially quite skeptical of any kind of military discipline, given their philosophical objections, accepted it as a kind of bond of trust among fighters for the sake of victory. In enacting a central code of conduct for the anarchist militias, the Reglamento de las Milicias Confederales made explicit the collective action that the acceptance of discipline would imply: "Every militiaman must know that he has voluntarily joined in the militias, but, having joined, as a soldier of the revolution, must accept and comply . . . Militiaman! These rules of action and conduct are not barracks discipline. This is a force of all, jointly, united and disciplined. Without such cohesion of energy, no triumph is possible."[26]

Military newspapers indicate how different anarchist militia writers reacted to these developments. Some saw it simply as the revolutionary élan of the militia period, now better harnessed: "With this moral force that we have, adapted to the discipline that the moment requires, our function as warriors, we will be able to achieve every attack."[27] However, other articles saw discipline as a way of establishing greater commitment and a spirit of mutual trust. The newspaper of the Iron Column reprinted the slain anarchist leader Buenaventura Durruti's words on discipline: "As for discipline, it is for me no more than respect for individual and collective responsibility. I am against barracks discipline but I equally reject a misunderstood liberty [*libertad mal entendida*] to which cowards have recourse in order to shirk."[28] One article in *Libertad*, published on the Aragón front, expressed ambivalence, suggesting that the impersonal structures of command reduced militiamen's enthusiasm, and that the newly created ranks and hierarchy led to personal ambitions. However, it still claimed that discipline was the way to win the war, and suggested that accepting discipline implied mutual obligations and self-sacrifice:

> And we, the old *indisciplinados*, the sempiternal antimilitarists, convinced of the necessity of war, we were among the first to take up the responsibility and to demand of our companions that they be, not just companions, but soldiers, and it was thus that they would work, obeying, respecting and fulfilling the orders of leaders. . . . Already the word "discipline" has become familiar, interpreted, rather than just in the vision put into this or that regulation or code, as the sense of duty of

personal responsibility [*auto-responsibilidad*]. A post for every man, and every man in his post. All with a right and each one with an obligation taking shape together. [*Todos con un derecho y cada uno con una obligación formando conjunto.*][29]

Here, discipline matters well beyond the letter of the law. It is a spirit, a mind-set on the part of the militiaman accepting it. Further, and critically, it implies a mutual commitment of soldiers to each other. A later article suggested the same kind of mutual dependence: "The soldier as soldier, the corporal as corporal, the sergeant as sergeant, the officer as officer, etc., we must all and each one of us comply with our obligations and intertwine our duties [*compenetrarse con nuestros cometidos*]."[30] Hence, many anarchists came to accept the vision of a voluntary acceptance of rules and obligations as a basis for trust and collective effort.

As for units that were already relatively well disciplined, mutual confidence now started to extend out to the other militias alongside whom they fought. David Granda, for example, noticed a clear and comforting improvement in Asturias: "There had been moments during the early battles when we couldn't tell who was on our side, it was a real mess. But after being reorganized we could recognize each other more easily."[31] For Timoteo Ruiz, in the Fifth Regiment, militarization meant trust in other groups:

> You could never be sure whether the column to your right or left was still there, or whether you were in danger of being encircled. It couldn't continue like this. We had to have a single command. I was filled with joy when I heard that the militias were to be militarized. Not because I knew anything about military problems, but because for too long I had known what it meant not to be able to count on the units on either side.[32]

How did this solidification of trust and norms of mutual obligation translate into desertion? The Los Comuneros battalion offers a particularly informative window into the scale of abandonment of service at the moment of militarization. But it also shows how a unit could fight reliably in militarization's aftermath. The Los Comuneros documents include a registry book with every soldier in the unit from the beginning of the war to the end, including in the transition period in October 1936 when Los Comuneros became part of Battalion 160 of the Fortieth Mixed Brigade.[33] This registry makes it possible to trace the impact of militarization on a volunteer unit and on desertion patterns.[34]

This unit had more a geographic identity than a political one. The political affiliations listed among its initial members are heterogeneous: principally from the socialist Unión General de Trabajadores (UGT), but with a considerable presence from the CNT and the Communist Party, and a few Left Republicans. As we saw in the previous chapter, Los Comuneros had been organized through the Centro Abulense (center for people from Ávila province) in Madrid, and the large majority of its recruits came from Ávila and neighboring provinces. Indeed, the initial registry forms for new recruits to the "Castilian Militias" emphasized to the recruit that retaking these provinces was the central, common objective, though a recruit could be sent "where it is deemed necessary."[35]

The first version of these forms required that the recruit declare himself "disposed to accept the discipline of these militias and the orders of their leaders."[36] However, the registry forms changed once the militia was militarized, in October 1936, to require somewhat more of the recruit:

> [The recruit] commits to obey the orders of the Government of the Republic, of the responsible authorities and of the leaders assigned to the Battalion. Thus [the recruit] promises to accept the discipline imposed by the official organs of the State. [The recruit] commits equally to join the front or fronts that the superior organs determine.[37]

Discipline thus now came from the Republic and the centralized standard it set, and the recruit might fight on any front; Castile was not mentioned. Participation was now on the Republic's terms.

These latter forms were typically signed on about October 11, 1936, one day after the deadline Largo Caballero had imposed to accept military discipline or resign. At the same time, a wave of fighters was deciding not to sign them but to leave instead. Figure 7.1 shows the monthly totals of resignations (*baja voluntaria*— that is, volunteers resigning their affiliation), desertions, and deaths from the Los Comuneros battalion for which a date is given in the registry book (84 of the 135 total resignations and desertions have such a date).[38] The records begin on August 10, 1936 (the date at which the first members of the battalion were registered). Resignations stopped, with just two exceptions, by October 15, 1936. The large spike in resignations occurs in the first and second weeks of October 1936 and includes thirteen voluntary exits listed explicitly as "for not accepting the Decree of Militarization" (there were an additional fourteen of these without a date listed). Evidently, the moment of becoming a regular military column was a moment of truth for many combatants.

The unit was only authorized on August 23 and did not see much action prior to militarization, so it is unfortunately difficult to make an over-time comparison. However, it is clear that what followed militarization was a low rate of desertion for many months, until spring 1938. This low rate cannot be attributed to an easy time of it. Soon after resignations stopped, the siege of Madrid began and the fighting raged on in the central front. Los Comuneros participated actively in the defense of Madrid in November 1936, particularly in the University

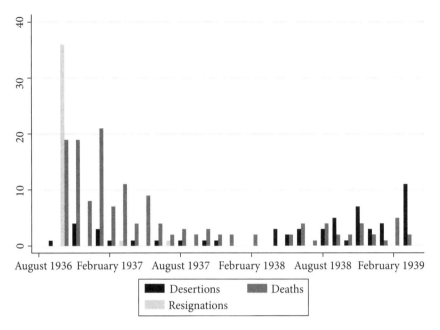

FIGURE 7.1. Monthly desertions, resignations, and deaths from Los Comuneros battalion.

City district where the fighting was especially heavy.[39] The toll of the battle is seen in the monthly death totals in figure 7.1, including eleven deaths in the critical first week of November when the siege began. After the siege, it carried on in essentially the same role in University City, a front that quieted down over time even as Los Comuneros' desertion rate increased.[40] Hence, the overall trend in Los Comuneros is consistent with the unit maintaining—and indeed, given the difficulty of the fighting it experienced, possibly increasing—its resistance to desertion in the wake of militarization before faltering later. For Los Comuneros, the months immediately after militarization stand out as the battalion's finest hour.

Los Comuneros was a unit with a strong reputation and a clear regional identity, making it somewhat of an outlier, but its experience was repeated elsewhere.[41] At battles like the siege of Madrid in November 1936 and again at the Battle of Jarama in February 1937, both on the central front where militarization had proceeded farthest and fastest, Republican forces fought at the peak of their cohesiveness.[42] The First Army Corps, in the Army of the Center, gives a sense of how this generalized in the central front. Its statistics on desertion and defection are available for the periods March–November 1937 and December 1937–March 1938.[43] For the period June 1938 until the end of the war, there are also forty-nine reports, generally appearing every five to seven days, listing a total of

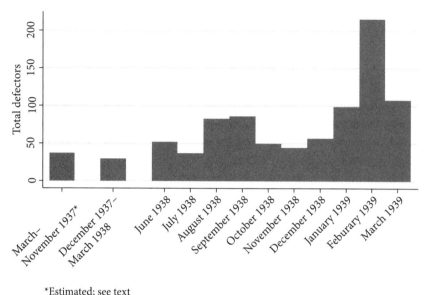

*Estimated; see text

FIGURE 7.2.   Monthly defections, First Army Corps, Army of the Center.

358 incidents of defection or attempted defection involving 832 soldiers.[44] Since defections are counted for the whole period, we can use them for an over-time comparison (figure 7.2). In the year or so after militia militarization, the First Army Corps was composed largely of ex-militia units, including a few from the Fifth Regiment such as Juventud Campesina and the Mangada Column.[45] The over-time trend shows that the First Army Corps fought relatively reliably in the period just after militarization, though unfortunately it is impossible to compare these units with how their component militia performed before militarization; desertion data on militias are rare. More broadly, the Republican forces increased their ratio of deaths to disappearances from 1.48 in 1936 to 2.76 in 1937.[46] Those who had joined left-wing unions and political parties before the outbreak of the war showed an especially high ratio of 4.15 (as against 1.69 in 1936).[47] As the toll of fighting increased, so did the willingness to fight among volunteers.

In the end, combining voluntary recruitment with military discipline had re-sults that neither could achieve on its own. The voluntarism of the militias, with orders endlessly discussed and militia members free to enter and leave, left the militias vulnerable to opportunism. On the other hand, as we shall see, conscripts submitted to rules of obedience were still conscripts, forced to fight. Under nei-ther combination could combatants rely on their compatriots as strongly as when they voluntarily agreed to submit to discipline. This permitted greater trust among combatants, encouraging them to see fighting as a mutual responsibility, and giving them all the more reason to keep at the front rather than desert.

Conscription and Changes in Motivation

Figures 7.1 and 7.2 show a second common theme: the problem of desertion got progressively worse as the war continued into 1938. The Republic steadily lost ground over this period, and this clearly demoralized its forces toward the end of the war in 1939. It also had steadily increasing problems of supply, particularly of food. This was, according to James Matthews, the main reason morale declined over time.[48] I broadly agree about the importance of supply and ongoing defeat. However, it is also critical to underline that the Popular Army suffered with the large-scale incorporation of conscripts. As time went on, conscripts occupied an ever-larger share, as the Republic attempted to confront grave manpower problems. Though it is true that many militias had been prone to opportunism, conscription had an even stronger effect in bringing in combatants who had little preference to fight. Thus, in spite of the improvements in trust with the volunteers who stayed on after the militarization order even though they were free to go, the addition of conscripts weakened the sense of commitment in the bulk of the Popular Army of the Republic. For Matthews, the "paradox" of conscripts, then, was this: "They were needed, but they were not well-regarded nor fully trusted."[49] Conscripts could, indeed, influence their peers to desert.

To enforce conscription, the Republic formally applied the Code of Military Justice to its militias as part of militarization in October 1936. Under the code, draft evaders could be penalized with four additional years of military service on top of the required two. The Republic expanded these penalties successively. On June 18, 1937, it ruled that draft evasion was equivalent to front-line desertion. The penalty for each was hard labor, between six and twenty years, and the guilty party would be assigned to a disciplinary combat battalion for the balance of his military service. The following year the penalties increased again: on April 8, 1938, the government ordered all men who had not joined up when called to present themselves within three days, or face the death penalty as a traitor.[50]

The Republic, of course, faced problems of individuals seeking to shirk their duties by obtaining exemptions. Unions could frequently obtain exemptions for their members, declaring their work vital to the war effort, for example. In late October 1937 this led Indalecio Prieto, the minister of defense, to "cancel all exemptions not ordered by his own department," as Corral puts it.[51]

Many, of course, could not get such exemptions, and many evaded the order to join up. Groups of draft dodgers would sometimes hide in the hills. Civilians could be prosecuted for offering them aid and shelter. This could put civilians in the middle; some groups of Catalan draft dodgers, for example, assassinated mayors for reporting them. To deal with draft evasion, in August 1937, the Republican government set up a new organization, the Servicio de Investigación Militar (SIM), tasked with counterespionage behind the lines, but also with finding draft dodgers and deserters who had gone into hiding. On top of the SIM, the Republic sometimes sent in army and security force units to eliminate pockets of draft dodgers who held out.[52]

With these coercive tactics underlying it, conscription brought in many uncommitted new troops. Santiago Álvarez, the political commissar of the Eleventh Division, worried on the eve of that division's assault on Teruel in late 1937 that the hundreds of new conscripts who had joined were "mostly politically indifferent" and hence unlikely to fight well in battle. Another report, in the summer of 1938, found that the new conscripts were "accustomed to a tranquil and placid prior life, totally out of step with the current moment."[53] Republican censors picked up on the lack of motivation evidenced in new conscripts' letters home. One example, from June 1938: "Even though you suffer hardship, you are at home and suffer hardship for what is ours, but I am suffering hardship for something that has nothing to do with me, so go figure how happy I am; anyway there is nothing to be done but hang on until we see where [the war] is going."[54]

With conscription bringing in men who had no interest in fighting, there was a shrinking basis for reciprocal norms of cooperation in support of the fight. Instead, unmotivated combatants encouraged others to desert. Corresponding to this mutual influence, desertion tended to be concentrated in groups of conscripts, as we saw in chapter 4 in Santander. Lieutenant Colonel Juan Perea, the head of the Fifth Corps of the Republican Army, reported "repeated defections" on the part of soldiers in his 156th Battalion, 138th Mixed Brigade, in June 1937 at the Guadalajara front. That unit, he said, suffered from low morale because its members were "forces that came from the last call-ups almost in their entirety."[55] Moreover, perceptions of deep corruption in draft exemptions meant that those who were conscripted were all the more resentful: they were only serving, they felt, because they did not have the proper political connections to a union or party to secure an exemption, or a friendly doctor who would write a medical exemption.[56] Unmotivated combatants could indeed influence others, including volunteers, to desert, convincing them that the cause was lost or that the unit would not hold together under fire—that is, demoralizing them. Volunteers frequently mistrusted conscripts because they had not proved themselves.[57] Consider the derisive language directed at those who had not joined at the outset of the war in *Libertad*, the newspaper of Division "D" in Aragón: "Recently, there have been signs of life from those who feared to lose it [i.e., their life], and so hid their bodies as well as their intentions in the first months of the war."[58] Conflicts in some units got to the point that political commissars, responsible for soldiers' morale, had to actively battle against stereotypes of uncommitted conscripts: "In the army, and consequently in the 121st Battalion, there are not volunteers and conscripts, but only soldiers; and when one talks in other company about the colleagues in this battalion, we shall refer only to our comrades who fight for the independence of our people." Another commissar gave speeches with titles such as "Fraternization between the Volunteer and the Conscript," "Treatment of the Combatant and Conscript," and "The Conscript as an Integral Part of the Veterans' Combat Plan."[59]

Mistrust meant that combatants influenced each other negatively by their actions as well, eroding positive norms of cooperation. Desertion provoked more desertion, serving as a signal to others of disaffection within the unit. An analysis of desertion written up by the Nineteenth Army Corps in December 1938 serving in eastern Spain noted desertion back to civilian areas as a demoralizing force both in civilian life and in the army itself.[60] Letters from soldiers back home showed their bitterness toward "shirkers (*emboscados*)," the second-most-frequent source of complaints after food, according to Republican censors. In some letters, desertion itself lost its opprobrium: "Some of the disgruntled referred to deserters not as *desertores*, as official terminology labeled them, but rather as *escapados*."[61] When men feared that others would desert, they were themselves much less inclined to serve.

Not just desertion itself but demoralizing talk had a potentially pernicious effect on others, including otherwise loyal men. Officers paid considerable attention to this dynamic, with unit commissars directed to discipline those who, "without negative intent and, by talking too much, spread their complaints, lack of discipline and discontent to others."[62] When men deserted together, their commanders would attempt to determine whether one, through his words, could have influenced the other to leave. For example, in the report of three soldiers defecting together from the Ninety-Ninth Mixed Brigade on February 2, 1939, it was noted that one of them had been a defector from the Nationalist side in the first place. Because he faced the death penalty at the hands of the Nationalists if he were to return, the report supposed it likely that he was an agent provocateur deliberately sent to demoralize Republican troops. Therefore, the defection of the other two men—who had been "of great confidence and of impeccable conduct" up to that point—must have been due to his demoralizing influence, the report concluded.[63] Orders to prevent demoralizing talk came from the highest levels. One day after the fall of Teruel in late February 1938, the minister of defense,

Indalecio Prieto, recognized that men had abandoned their positions without resistance, and ordered severe punishments handed out for "any words that are defeatist or can demoralize commanders and troops."[64]

Faced with these problems of negative mutual influence, one solution the Republican leadership attempted was to reshuffle personnel, breaking up units that were too far gone. In early 1937, the collapsing Córdoba front was plagued with low morale. The Republican leadership faced a dilemma about whether to reinforce the militias fighting there. According to Michael Seidman, the General Staff

> feared that assistance to Republican forces in the south would create a vicious circle: to send resources to demoralized troops might mean throwing good money and men after bad, but to refuse aid would lead to further demoralization and flight. The general staff realized that battle desertions were contagious. To restore discipline, it absolutely insisted upon the disarming of defective units and punishment of the disobedient. Their weapons would be turned over to more reliable forces in the area.[65]

This approach was repeated later and turned into a general policy by Prieto in June 1937: "When the Leaders of the Army consider that a Unit, for its low morale, insufficient instruction, or for repeated acts that reveal inaptitude for combat, does not offer the required guarantees to be employed in combat, they can proceed to disarm [that unit], dispersing its components to the remaining Units of the Army."[66]

Dissolving units was a response to extremes of demoralization, however. In less extreme cases, in contrast, the army believed that the presence of committed troops could reinforce the fighting will of others. Lieutenant Colonel Perea faced, as noted above, "repeated defections" to the enemy among conscripts on the Guadalajara front in June 1937. He therefore asked to swap some officers, noncommissioned officers (NCOs), and privates with a "unit with high morale and spirit, who by their conduct awake the enthusiasm and emulation of the reluctant," requesting a transfer specifically with the Ninetieth Mixed Brigade.[67] In late 1937, the 148th Mixed Brigade on the Teruel front experienced a similar problem, and its officers came to a similar conclusion: that it could be addressed by mixing veteran antifascists with new recruits. Indeed, this was a generally popular method to "promote a combative spirit." As Michael Seidman notes, "Although this method could be effective in boosting morale, it ran the inverse risk of contaminating good soldiers who might begin to imitate the unenergetic and selfish ways of the uncommitted."[68]

Both the positive influence of the committed and the negative influence of the uncommitted are consistent with the importance of trust and norms of cooperation. The dissolution of extremely demoralized units and the influx of more committed soldiers in less extreme cases suggests that the Republican command generally believed that there was some sort of tipping point or critical mass between these two influences: if there were enough committed soldiers, the remainder could be induced to cooperate, while if there were too few committed soldiers, those few who were committed could be induced to desert out of mistrust of their comrades. That this was a dilemma at all can be understood by the argument that the mutual influence of soldiers could be a positive or a negative one for cohesion.

As time wore on in the Popular Army, norms of cooperation appear to have eroded even further, helping to account for the increase in desertion rates over time. In large part, as I argue above, this may be attributed to the ever-increasing presence of conscripts as replacements. However, corruption in this time of straitened supply made matters worse. The Republic's ever-increasing supply problems, with limited funds and food, led not only to demoralization directly but also to suspicion of hoarding and of profiteering by paymasters, quartermasters, and the politically well-connected. It became a common accusation to believe that those in these positions of influence were continuing to eat well, and indeed were diverting food and money, while ordinary soldiers suffered. Many of these accusations appear well founded.[69] It is possible that norms of cooperation in the Popular Army would have eroded to an important degree regardless of conscription. On the other hand, it is possible—though not obviously easy to verify—that the influx of uncommitted soldiers itself affected how the Republican army responded to tightened belts, promoting resentment and mutual mistrust rather than solidarity and sacrifice. Either way, it seems clear that conscription did its share to undermine trust.

Soldiers could influence each other in different ways, and this also reshaped the impact of friendship and social homogeneity among combatants. Earlier, in the militia period, coming from the same background could bolster collective action by allowing militia members to trust in each other's commitment to fight the rebels. Now, increasingly, social homogeneity could allow individuals to recognize others' *lack* of commitment. For example, Juan Brines was well known as a Falangist in his hometown of Simat de la Valdigna in Valencia province, and fled to the city of Valencia soon after the start of the war. Drafted in April 1937, however, he joined the new Republican army. "At the Valdepeñas barracks . . . I had the misfortune to meet the son of the mayor of my village. He told the commander that I was a fascist and that I needed to be killed then and there." Brines only survived because the commander required the mayor's son to repeat the denunciation in front of Brines himself, which he was unwilling to do. Thus the hometown connection only enabled mistrust: it let this mayor's son know that Brines clearly opposed the movement's goals, and could hardly have helped the two of them to fight side by side had they had to do so.[70]

Indeed, such connections might be worse than no help: they might facilitate desertion. Because prospective deserters would be in great danger if their intentions were known, desertions were most frequently done alone.[71] However, desertion could generally be easier in cooperation with another if this was feasible. Because soldiers were rarely on their own, often patrolling or keeping watch with others, they would have to take advantage of rare lapses if they were to get away alone. Coordinating with another could thus make it easier to survive: a hopeful deserter in a two-man post or patrol could much more easily cross the lines by persuading the other to cross too, for example. In turn, because it was so crucial to a prospective deserter not to be found out, such soldiers were typically inclined to rely only on men they knew well. Invitations to desert together could be a sham, a way to roust out prospective deserters. Trust among those seeking to leave was, in general, easier among men who had more long-standing connections.[72] There are thus frequent instances of men from the same hometown deserting together in the accounts of desertion and defection in the First Army Corps.[73] This suggests that the increasing rate of desertion noted above had to do in part with solidarity among relatively uncommitted troops. The connections among soldiers that had enabled militiamen at the outset of the war to recognize the commitment of others and to forge a bond of trust among them now failed to serve such a purpose. In fact, from time to time they *enabled* desertion and defection.

Indeed, friendships with deserters were a common source of interest in monitoring within units. Desertion reports from the First Army Corps asked whether the deserter had any suspect friends within the unit. Deserters' friends within a unit came under immediate suspicion, and some were quickly placed under surveillance. In more than one instance, reports from this Corps indicate that this vigilance over friends of defectors enabled the unit to shoot the friends when they later attempted to defect themselves.[74]

Thus the shift to a conscripted army, in which most men did not have a preference to fight, undermined the basic requirement for trust: a clear commitment to fight for a common aim. Further, social bases of recognizing a shared commitment to fight, such as coming from the same hometown or friendships among soldiers, could now more often serve as a basis of recognizing a shared inclination to desert. These examples illustrate that the problem of mutual influence of uncommitted combatants on each other, particularly among conscripts, appeared throughout the Republic's war effort. These examples are often based on commanders' impressions and are difficult to cross-check, but they are clearly consistent with the micro-level analysis in chapter 4, which showed the influence of conscripts and volunteers on other combatants. Cumulatively, then, they suggest that conscription, producing much less costly signals of commitment across the whole army, undermined trust and norms of cooperation among combatants and thereby encouraged desertion—including among the volunteers who served among these conscripts.

Coercion and Its Dilemmas under Factional Competition

With uncommitted combatants and the difficulty of keeping soldiers fighting through norms of cooperation, the Spanish Republic turned to coercion to prevent and punish desertion. Over the winter of 1936 and the spring of 1937, it imposed clear, uniform penalties on desertion and developed an increasing capacity to impose these penalties. Active mistrust from factionalism initially provoked desertion as coercion expanded, since some militiamen—especially anarchists and POUM members—saw this imposition as persecution. However, in the medium term the imposition of coercion did help deter desertion.

Militarization entailed a clarification and regularization of coercive rules governing combatants. As we saw in chapter 6, the Republic maintained little control over the home front after the coup attempt stripped it of much of its security forces and left the remainder in organizational disarray. There was no central, consistent capability for tracking down deserters. Instead, punishments for disloyalty were in the hands of local committees and patrols, who often focused more on people who were (or could be seen as) right wing than on actual instances of desertion. This changed over time, as the central government steadily asserted its control, disarming the local militias and individual workers.

The central government declared that responsibility for rear-area security, including the tracking down and punishing of deserters, was now the province of the official security forces rather than ad hoc militia committees. The Code of Military Justice mandated that a deserter who did not switch sides could be punished with four years in prison, with an additional eight years given for deserting with arms. Defection constituted treason, subject to the death penalty.[75] Military courts were established to enforce these penalties, with, for example, the Auditoría de Guerra de Gijón set up in mid-December 1936 to apply the code in Asturias. Over half of its cases were, eventually, for desertion.[76] Over time, penalties for desertion increased. As of June 18, 1937, desertion was punished with a sentence of at least twelve years in a work camp, and the death penalty could now be given not just for defection but even for desertion to the home front. Trial and punishment were now to happen within four days, and an execution did not require central government approval if the commander and the political officer agreed that it should take place immediately.[77]

The process of implementing these new control measures, however, was undermined by mistrust. We saw in chapter 5 that the violence enacted against military officers provoked many to defect. A similar dynamic now occurred among the political opponents of the communists. This was especially true in Catalonia and neighboring Aragón. Local CNT and POUM committees were much stronger here than, say, in Madrid, and resisted efforts to control rear areas. Thus, on October 27, 1936, the Republican government ordered that long guns such as rifles and machine guns be handed over to municipal authorities, which had themselves been ordered reconstituted on October 9 to replace local committees. In Catalonia, however, the disarmament order provoked skirmishes between the paramilitary police and resistant local patrols, notably along the French border. The clashes over control of the home front and over militarization of the militias came to a head with running battles in Barcelona on May 2–5, 1937, the Barcelona "May Days." After the defeat of rebellious CNT and POUM forces in Catalonia, control was finally centralized.[78]

At the same time, the central authorities rolled back the social revolution the CNT had put into place in the Aragón countryside, breaking up agricultural collectives, for example. CNT and POUM members saw here the bourgeois Republic's true colors as well as pressure from Stalin to rein in revolution in order to appeal to Britain and France to form an antifascist alliance.[79] And indeed the communists had appealed for caution and restraint, pitching themselves as the best guarantors of middle-class property holders.[80]

The same counterrevolution was thought to be behind the militarization of the militias. This step would put anarchist and POUM militias in the chain of command under a regime for which many had nothing but mistrust, particularly with rising communist influence. The anarchist Diego Abad de Santillán spoke for many when he said that militarization "was not due to considerations of military order, but to the political calculus of counterrevolution."[81] The POUM's official position favored militarization but opposed the way it was conducted, the power it would put into what it considered counterrevolutionary hands.[82] In a statement of its position in its party newspaper in February 1937, it declared: "It is absolutely necessary that control be maintained by revolutionary organizations. . . . In short, resolutely in favor of a regular army, but of a regular army that is the living expression of the Revolution."[83] Therefore, members of the key political forces that believed themselves most targeted by the PCE and by the Soviets—the CNT and especially the POUM—often believed that by fighting in a militarized army, they were fighting against their own cause.

Over the course of the spring of 1937, as the Republic's efforts at centralization and control continued, they provoked immense tension and often desertion. The anarchist Iron Column experienced a wave of over four hundred desertions of men who preferred not to militarize, in March 1937. Many of these may have been among the prisoners that the unit had recruited, who self-selected against military discipline and preferred to steal rather than fight (as we saw in chapter 6), but it is also the case that the Iron Column included many anarchist hardliners who saw service under Republican command as furthering a counterrevolution. Thus it is telling that many of the deserters from the Iron Column later took up arms against the regime in Barcelona two months later.[84] Bolloten recounts a similar wave among anarchist militia at the town of Gelsa in Aragón at the same moment resulting in 1,000 desertions.[85] The Durruti Column was similar even though it was better disciplined than the Iron Column. Though in general it maintained cohesion when it was militarized, it still had men who left because they refused to fight for what they saw as a communist-dominated government. These "Friends of Durruti" advocated armed resistance in Barcelona, playing a critical role in the May Days.[86]

However, many more considered deserting than actually left. The attitude of the CNT leadership was quite important in this regard. The CNT leadership ordered its militants to remain fighting rather than deserting, out of concern for the common cause of defeating Franco and out of fear of the state. The Catalan CNT leader Josep Costa remembers: "The CNT wasn't prepared to order troops to leave the front, for that would have let the enemy through."[87] Helen Graham's analysis concurs, but also cites intimidation by state power, with the Republic willing to call in troops.[88] Hence, the leadership's orders were important in the decisions of some not to desert. During the May uprisings, Ricardo Sanz, commander of the Durruti column after Durruti's death, had five hundred men heading to the Aragón front, where he was ready to link up with other CNT militants and return to Barcelona to fight. But he was ordered to stay at the front by Juan García Oliver, a key national leader in the CNT and the Republic's minister of justice as of late 1936. Sanz's troops obeyed. Sanz recalled later, "My personal feelings didn't matter; I was a disciplined man, a military commander."[89] Sanz was, indeed, disciplined enough to give an interview to the trench newspaper *Libertad* in which he asserted that morale after militarization was "better than ever," in spite of this history.[90]

Beyond the leadership, others who contemplated desertion also ultimately submitted to the state and its coercive capabilities. In the Iron Column, those who did not desert evoked the new power of the state to explain why they acquiesced to militarization when they could have left. They regarded their ultimate conscription as now inevitable and chose to have the unit be militarized so that it could remain together, as a coherent entity.[91] Perhaps suspicious of the influence of other political forces, the CNT leadership, which accepted militarization, still insisted that its units remain majority anarchist, a move that the government accepted lest it provoke further rebellions against militarization.[92] Despite this reluctance, Abad de Santillán argues that the leadership's overall acceptance of militarization was folly: "They approved their own suicide!"[93] Ultimately, however, the increasing control power of the state caused the CNT senior leadership to acquiesce in the supplanting of its local committees and to restrain its troops from deserting. While increasing central control provoked some to desert out of mistrust, over the long run it succeeded in compelling many others to continue fighting.

The POUM came under special attack within the Republic, and these attacks likewise prompted desertion. Though Marxist, the POUM broke with Moscow and with the PCE by supporting the revolution in Catalonia and Aragón. Nor did it help the POUM's relationship with Stalin's Soviet Union that its leader Andreu Nin had been Leon Trotsky's secretary, though the two were now estranged.[94] The POUM's leadership had been more willing to rebel than the CNT's in Barcelona in May 1937, but the CNT's reluctance and the recognition of likely defeat persuaded the POUM's leaders to stand down.[95] One month after the May events, the POUM was outlawed, and police arrested POUM leaders and many of its foreign members.[96] Soviet agents and local allies kidnapped and murdered Nin in June 1937, accusing him of being a fascist spy.[97] The 29th Division—which had formed out of the POUM column—was dissolved, its leaders arrested, and its members dispersed to other units. There, they often had to hide.[98] According to Alba and Schwartz, soldiers who were found to have been POUM members, or even former members of the 29th Division, could be accused of espionage and shot summarily, particularly in communist units.[99]

How did all of this shape desertion among POUM members? Unfortunately, assessment is difficult: mass desertion was in fact one of the charges laid against the POUM in the trial of its leaders in 1938. According to one charge—roundly rejected by the verdict—the 29th Division collaborated to abandon positions to Francoist units. Pro-POUM authors therefore tend to minimize desertion problems, anti-POUM sources to play them up.[100] During the May events, all agree that the leaders of the 29th Division at least considered abandoning the front to fight in Barcelona; some argue that many members of the column attempted to do so but were turned back, while others suggest that there was ultimately little effect at the front.[101]

As for desertion after the outlawing of the POUM in June 1937, pro-POUM sources do not explicitly claim that large-scale desertion occurred and indeed deny it.[102] But in spite of strong reasons to deny much POUM desertion, they offer hints nonetheless. They make the motives to leave, from disgust and fear, quite plain;

Orwell, for example, invokes what a betrayal it was "to send men into battle and not even tell them that behind their backs their party is being suppressed, their leaders accused of treachery, and their friends and relatives thrown into prison."[103] Alba and Schwartz stress that POUM members faced the possibility of death if their previous affiliation were discovered.[104] They also detail POUM members' evasion. Orwell says he and other POUM militiamen returning from the front to Barcelona had immediately to go into hiding, his POUM papers now compromising rather than a credential.[105] Leaving was natural: "the thing we had got to think of now was getting out of Spain. There was no sense in staying here with the certainty of imprisonment sooner or later."[106] More generally, according to Alba and Schwartz, POUM members had to look out for where they would be safe:

> In the villages, where everybody knew them, the situation became even more difficult, and very often a POUM member had to leave for Barcelona or some other place where their politics were not well-known. Many had to leave their families and hide out by changing their residences.[107]

Alba and Schwartz also highlight persecution within military units after the dissolution of the 29th Division, particularly communist-dominated ones.[108] In these circumstances, it is difficult to imagine that POUM members' evasion strategies did not include leaving the army altogether, if possible. Fraser, indeed, claims that the 29th Division's POUM militants left rather than await arrest.[109]

After the initial wave of desertion, the Republic's new measures allowed it a much greater capacity to coerce soldiers into remaining to fight. Under the newly constituted security apparatus, capturing and punishing deserters in rear areas was the task of the public order forces. These included the greatly expanded National Republican Guard (the reconstituted Civil Guard) and Assault Guard. Most notorious, however, was the SIM. Established on August 9, 1937, "to combat espionage, prevent acts of sabotage and carry out duties of investigation and vigilance within the armed forces," the SIM gradually extended its writ to the home front.[110] As we saw, this included finding and punishing deserters and draft dodgers, who would serve their required sentences in SIM-run work camps.[111]

Government attempts at controlling the home front to prevent desertion wrapped soldiers' family members in the climate of coercion. Family members would of course be questioned as the first step in a typical investigation of a deserter. But they were also made to bear the punishment for desertion, and especially for switching sides. The government issued a new order to this effect at the beginning of June 1938. Noting, with sinister overtones, an "excessive generosity of Republican sentiment," it ordered military units and recruitment centers to gather data on soldiers' close relatives, including names, ages, and place of residence. When a soldier defected, that information would be sent on to the SIM.

One male member of the family would then be made to "take the deserter's place in the same unit," and other men would perform auxiliary work like fortification. The place of women in the Republic's conception of military motivation was made clear: female members of a defector's family would be detained "until they could reliably attest, with testimony from members of parties or unions adhering to the regime, that they had done everything they could to dissuade the deserter."[112]

All in all, the Republic now made a much more concerted attempt to find and punish deserters on the home front than had ever been implemented. It finally established the bureaucratic apparatus to do so: security forces, courts, information gathering, and communication between center and local officials. But it was clearly of variable effectiveness. Deserters were often difficult to find. Official provincial bulletins frequently printed orders to particular deserters to present themselves, and according to Pedro Corral, in 1938 these constituted some "90% of announcements in some provinces."[113] Interrogated by Nationalist agents about whether they feared reprisals against family members, many defectors, according to Corral, "averred calmly that there were many who deserted without anything happening to their families."[114] Rough terrain made it particularly easy to hide and resist government capture. Thousands of deserters hid in the hills of La Mancha, requiring public order forces to conduct operations against them in the spring and summer of 1938.[115] Soldiers from hill country possessed the local knowledge to be able to evade government capture for long periods of time and were thus better able than others to desert. Indeed, my past work on deserters in Santander shows that soldiers from mountainous regions were more likely to desert than lowlanders, and that they and their families took specific advantage of the terrain to evade punishment.[116]

The army also sought to punish desertion at the front. Men attempting to cross the lines would typically be warned to stop, and if they did not, they would be shot. Eventually, this applied not just to defectors but to those deserting to rear areas. As of August 21, 1937, the Republican Army of the East had placed machine guns behind the lines. The order did not say in so many words that this was for shooting deserters, but it did say that the machine guns were there "in case our infantry abandon the trenches." In some units, such as the central front's Twenty-Seventh and 138th Mixed Brigades in the period October 1938 through February 1939, the Republican army shot more of its own men for desertion than the Nationalists did in combat.[117]

Vigilance in preventing desertion was the province, initially, of the political commissar. In the militia period, the Fifth Regiment had imported the Soviet Red Army's political commissar system into its units, to maintain the motivation of the men to fight fascism and to monitor the political sympathies of the officers and men. Upon militarization, the army placed commissars in units from the company level up, until, in October 1937, the Ministry of War restricted them to the brigade level and above. Desertion in a commissar's unit would be held against that commissar, as a testimony to the poverty of his political work. At different points, officers and commissars were ordered not to sleep at night but to patrol the trenches in order to prevent desertion.[118] Later, the SIM took over many of these functions.

Under the risk of being shot while trying to defect, typically a defector would try to separate himself from his fellows one way or another. Common pretexts in the First Army Corps were going to gather firewood or to answer a call of nature. One soldier, for example, managed to cross the lines on August 6, 1938, when he was separated by a crag from his partner on guard duty.[119] Defectors needed to be particularly wary of their NCOs such as *cabos* (corporals). Defection reports frequently indicate that soldiers left when an NCO was arranging for sentinel posts to be relieved. Much, in fact, depended on the reliability of those NCOs: soldiers whose NCOs defected gained a prime opportunity to defect as well, and there are occasional reports of a whole guard post—for instance, one *cabo* and two soldiers—crossing the lines together.[120]

Thus, soldiers' chances at desertion depended critically on how tightly they were monitored. If they were under continual surveillance, getting away would be extremely difficult. It was, however, hard to maintain constant vigilance at all times over all soldiers, and so units tried to prioritize. Men who gave particular grounds for suspicion would thus come in for tight surveillance—for example, assigned guard duty always with more reliable soldiers. If a defector managed to escape without being shot, questions would arise: had he been under enhanced vigilance? If so, how was it broken? If not, why not? The Twenty-Sixth Mixed Brigade had standardized forms for investigating desertions, asking about the deserter's previous behavior in the unit and what was known about his political history and sentiments. It also asked whether the man in question had been placed under tight surveillance beforehand. Such a report of two men from the 101st Battalion, Twenty-Sixth Mixed Brigade, indicated that both had been under close surveillance for their demoralizing comments; one had apparently threatened a corporal with death. But they took advantage of the absence of their section's sergeant to escape.[121]

Soldiers under particularly tight vigilance were apparently more likely to be shot trying to escape than others. Reports of shot defectors from the First Army Corps on the central front often indicate that the men were under particularly tight surveillance because of their past behavior or political history. In general, conscripts came under greater suspicion, with a commander saying about one deserter, "Like all recruits, he was monitored."[122] Such suspicions allowed the men tasked with surveillance to be wary of cover stories and keep alert. For example,

Juan Francisco (a pseudonym), who attempted to defect on October 7, 1938, and was shot, had been friends with men who had defected the previous day. The unit command, concerned that Francisco might attempt to defect as well, assigned him to guard duty with one Héctor Martínez, who was held in much greater confidence. When Francisco attempted to defect, leaving his post with the claim of having to answer a call of nature before running to the Nationalist lines, Martínez was prepared; he witnessed Francisco's flight, demanded that he stop, and shot him when he did not.[123] Other soldiers, who were under less suspicion, were consequently not watched, and they seemed to be able to defect more easily. One soldier from First Company, 393rd Battalion, Ninety-Ninth Mixed Brigade, defected on September 24, 1938, to the surprise of his unit: he had served in the assault on Teruel, one of the most brutal battles of the Civil War to that point, and had lost his toes to frostbite, "which," the report stated, "he boasted as a contribution he was willing to have the war against fascism impose upon him."[124]

Generally, predicting who would desert was an important part of coercive control. That it was not always easy to catch deserters is illustrated vividly by the fact that a man who had lost his toes to fascism was willing to desert. Since it is impossible to have complete information about soldiers' intentions, it would have surely been more effective, in preventing desertion, to watch all soldiers at all times. But that would strain resources and inhibit military operations. Some predictions were necessary. The Republic's standard policy was, first, to base predictions on demonstrated behavior, and, second, to use the information to decide whom to watch rather than to decide whom to preemptively punish. Soldiers would often still serve while they were being watched, with punishment often only inflicted once the soldier attempted to desert. In the meantime, the army enjoined its commissars to be discreet about monitoring.[125] The decision to punish a soldier, then, was generally contingent on an actual attempt to desert.

However, suspicions of a soldier sometimes did not spur a decision to watch that soldier more closely but instead active hostility and persecution. Occasionally soldiers were detained before deserting; at other times they were shot. In some instances this may have had to do with political factionalism, which continued apace. Notably, there were conflicts about the political composition of the commissariat, which was regarded as overly communist dominated, and of the SIM.[126] Much of this competition remained at a rarefied level, and in many ways may not have affected life at the front. But the political commissars and the SIM maintained networks of informants among the rank and file. Within these systems of monitoring, men were encouraged to denounce their fellows, creating what Corral calls "structures of betrayal among soldiers."[127] And these accusations, from time to time, could gain a political inflection: when a CNT-affiliated soldier was prosecuted for having deserted, the CNT, in turn, would level accusations of persecution at the communists.[128] All this should have, according to the provocation effect, suggested to soldiers that they could be prosecuted on trumped-up charges and so increased their willingness to desert. There is little evidence one way or another about its effect on desertion. But there is in any case not much evidence of a provocation effect nearly as severe as in May 1937, or as with the officers in the summer of 1936 (discussed in chapter 5). One possibility is that the deterrent effect was much stronger at this point too, trapping soldiers between the possibility of a politically motivated prosecution and an even higher likelihood of punishment if they actually tried to leave.

The changes that the Republic enacted in creating the Popular Army thus reshaped desertion patterns by altering the bases of trust among combatants. Trust solidified among volunteers, since by accepting military discipline they signaled more clearly that they were willing to bear the costs of fighting. However, the influx of conscripts meant that in the bulk of the army, there was little basis for trust and norms of cooperation, and instead reason to believe that many soldiers would rather not fight. Finally, while strengthening coercive control generally pushed combatants to fight until the last few months of the war, it provoked desertion among anarchist and POUM militia members, who could not trust in the impartial application of punishments. Each of these changes, in other words, operated by and through combatants' trust in each other.

The focus on trust thus leads to different conclusions compared with alternative accounts of desertion. It is impossible to deny the supply problems that the Republic faced, especially as the war dragged on, and these account to a large degree for the increase in the desertion rate over time, as does the prospect of defeat. While not denying this influence, it appears that desertions were concentrated among groups of conscripts above all, and that these units had difficulty maintaining norms of cooperation over time. In other words, desertion had a social dimension and was not just a mechanical response to not being able to continue.

Is it enough to focus on commitment to the cause as a direct determinant of decisions to fight or desert? After all, this chapter traces major differences among conscript and volunteer units. Is it just that volunteers fought because they were more committed to fighting? This argument misses important features of desertion patterns that demonstrate the importance of interpersonal trust. Conscripts and volunteers not only differed in their own willingness to fight. They influenced each other too. The influx of conscripts therefore affected volunteers who served among them as well. And a limited influx of conscripts could be absorbed into a volunteer unit, influenced by the norms of cooperation that the latter had developed. We saw a quantitative demonstration of this at a micro level in chapter 4, and this chapter showed further that the problem generalized to other parts of the Popular Army.

Social ties among soldiers can explain desertion patterns in the Popular Army only with reference to the aims of soldiers. Social ties can strengthen cohesion, have no effect on it, or even undermine it. It depends on how committed to the armed group's common aims the combatants in question are. In chapter 6—and here, in the portrait of the Los Comuneros battalion—we saw that militia units based on common hometowns and unions had a strong basis for interpersonal trust and could avoid some desertion problems. In contrast, conscripts often confirmed through social ties that their unit-mates had little interest in fighting and could use these ties to desert together. Trust among combatants, in other words, has to be put in the context of its goals to be understood.

The centralization and strengthening of coercion in the Republic raises the question of whether the Popular Army kept its soldiers fighting (to the extent it did) essentially through top-down incentives alone. Again, however, coercion can have different effects. It can certainly intimidate prospective deserters into staying and fighting. In so doing, it appears that it solidified the Popular Army, allowing it to reduce the problems created by introducing conscription. At the same time, however, increasing centralized coercion provoked crises among anarchist and POUM militia members. The mutual mistrust among the factions on the Republican side made it all too easy to see coercion as likely to be arbitrary. In other words, the impact of coercion can be traced through existing dynamics of trust and mistrust.

Each of these alternative explanations, then, faces large anomalies. Their key variables sometimes work in the ways they expect and sometimes not. Trust brings in the key missing piece: the expectation of what others in the armed group are going to do. This is what makes conscripts and volunteers influence each other rather than deciding separately, what puts social ties at the service of different ends, and what makes coercion seem likely to be an arbitrary tool of political domination. Trust therefore shaped the process of military reform in Spain, and its results for desertion.

The Popular Army case in this chapter therefore highlights perennial dilemmas of military change on the fly in the midst of civil war and in the face of mistrust and desertion. There appear to be no easy answers when an army in a civil conflict needs troops quickly, and when it suffers from deep factional divides. The solutions the Republic adopted were reasonable under the circumstances. That they fell far short of success speaks to how hard it is generally to build trust from a difficult starting point in the midst of civil conflict.

THE NATIONALIST ARMY, 1936–39

The Republic's adversaries did not suffer from desertion on the same scale. As I noted in chapter 1, Ramón Salas Larrazábal estimates a ratio of five Republican deserters for every Nationalist deserter.[1] The source of this estimate is unclear, but is generally corroborated by the frequency of Republican analyses of desertion, requests for information about deserters, and punishments issued for desertion compared with the lack of the same on the Nationalist side. Why this divergence? Above all, this chapter finds that the key differences lay in the effectiveness of coercive control; the lack of factional competition; and the lack of an equivalent, within the Nationalist army if not behind the lines, to the intense mistrust of army officers on the Republican side. At the same time, this chapter underlines and seeks to explain the significant variation among different Nationalist forces. Though the conscript forces and some volunteer forces with low recruiting standards (the Falange militias) experienced problems of desertion similar to those of their Republican enemies, there existed elite forces on the Nationalist side—the Legion, Moroccan Regulares, and Carlist militias—that selected for discipline and a willingness to fight, and that bore the brunt of the fighting as the Nationalists conquered Republican territory. The Legion is of particular interest because, in it, desertion problems got significantly worse as it lowered its recruitment standards. As table 8.1 illustrates, then, the relational approach to desertion generally expects a lower desertion rate among Nationalist forces, with some important variations.

In other words, many of the same factors that explain variation on the Republican side do so on the Nationalist side as well, and help explain the overall gap

TABLE 8.1. Military unit characteristics and hypothesized overall desertion rates—Nationalist side

		THREAT OF VIOLENCE WITHIN ARMED GROUP		
		HIGH; AT MOST OCCA-SIONALLY STEREOTYPED OR FACTIONALIZED	LOW	HIGH; SYSTEMATI-CALLY STEREOTYPED OR FACTIONALIZED
Information about motivations	Clear and positive	Legion (early) Regulares Carlist forces		
	Unclear or negative	Nationalist conscript units Falange militias Legion (later)		

Note: Units are placed according to the independent variables.

between the two. It is certainly true that Nationalist forces enjoyed other significant advantages over their Republican adversaries: a much more reliable food supply, greater support from Nazi Germany and Fascist Italy, and a string of victories. I grant that these factors certainly help explain the overall difference between the Republican and Nationalist desertion rates and have little to do with the relational approach. Moreover, it is plausible that these factors could have overwhelmed concerns for trust and mistrust. For example, a conscript may well be more trustworthy when well fed and on a winning side, reducing the gap between conscripts and volunteers. In light of this, the fact that I find significant variation among Nationalist forces in line with my approach's expectations is important: it provides a first indicator that the Republican experience was not unique, and it suggests that trust and cooperation dynamics are significant whether facing severe challenges and the prospect of defeat, or more favorable circumstances and the likelihood of victory.

The Nationalist War Effort

The Nationalist forces were initially coordinated by a National Defence Junta formed a week after the rising, operating from Burgos and in practice led, at first, by General Emilio Mola. In the beginning, the coordination of the Nationalist side was rather loose: Mola maintained his own command in the north, General Gonzalo Queipo de Llano ran Sevilla and Nationalist Andalucía as a sort of personal fiefdom, and Franco and his subordinates directed the steady advance of the Army of Africa (the military units stationed in Morocco) through southern and western

Spain toward Madrid. While they disagreed on certain military decisions, the rising's leaders were of one mind on the basic principles of the need for control and unity. Over time, Franco gained in power within this group. He was assisted in this by the successes of the Army of Africa and by his important role as the key point of contact with the rebels' crucial patrons, Nazi Germany and Fascist Italy. On September 28, 1936, he took the positions of generalissimo of the armed forces and head of state in the rebel zone, headquartered in Salamanca.[2] This placed him in ultimate command of all the various rebel forces. In contrast to the fragmentation of the Republican side, it was with relative unity in the apparatus of state power that the Nationalists approached war.

Like the Republic they sought to overthrow, the Nationalists had a heterogeneous force. First were those sections of the regular conscript army stationed in mainland Spain that joined the rising, across northern Spain from Galicia to Aragón and in western Andalucía, as well as pockets surrounded by besieging Republican forces in Toledo and Oviedo. The Nationalists did not make the mistake that the Republicans had made of dismissing enlisted men. They did, however, expel and execute those officers and enlisted men who resisted the rising. Hence, these regiments were not entirely intact. Beyond the conscript forces, beginning some three weeks after the start of the war, the Army of Africa began to be transported to the mainland. In addition to conscripts, the Army of Africa included two volunteer forces, the Legion and the Regulares.[3] The Spanish Foreign Legion, founded by Major José Millán Astray and commanded by Franco in 1921–22, initially recruited mainly among non-Spanish First World War veterans like its French namesake. But by the start of the Civil War almost all of its troops were Spanish, typically from marginal social groups.[4] Franco also recruited thousands of Moroccan mercenaries, Regulares, mainly on a voluntary basis, with the promise of payment and land and out of alliances with local leaders in Morocco.[5] The Legion and Regulares totaled a quarter to a third of the regular forces available to the Nationalists. The figures vary, but Gárate Córdoba estimates 2,800 from the Legion and 9,200 Regulares who crossed the Strait at the outset of the war, while Alpert estimates some forty-five thousand regular troops in the regular Spanish army available to the Nationalists.[6]

Civilian militias bolstered the military forces. The radically traditionalist, Catholic, and monarchist Carlists contributed the Requeté militia, while the fascist Falange's militias grew at a very fast pace through the summer of 1936. As with the workers' militias in the Republic, the Falange and the Carlists were already prepared to support the rising when it came. Individual Falange cells had, in the past, been given instructions to support such a rising, and aided the rising in its success in a few cities. In fact, the Falange, according to Payne, had been itching for a rising. The Falange's leader, José Antonio Primo de Rivera, the son of the old dictator, demanded that Mola speed up the timeline.[7] For their part, the Carlists had built up a substantial militia force over time, and over the course of difficult negotiations with Mola, ultimately promised to contribute ten thousand trained militiamen for the assault on Madrid. Similar to workers' militias discussed above, Carlists had laid a kind of surreptitious groundwork: one Carlist organizer in Burgos hid rifles in his father's bakery, which he then retrieved once the coup attempt began. In the Carlist heartland of Pamplona, six thousand men were mobilized almost immediately after the rising began. Carlist units assisted the military rebels in Álava, Burgos, and Zaragoza. Falange and Requeté units played an important role on the front from the beginning, particularly among Mola's forces in the north.[8]

Estimates of the eventual size of each militia vary substantially, from twenty-four thousand to seventy thousand for the Carlists, and thirty-six thousand to eighty thousand for the Falange.[9] Militia members were in any event a substantial force, particularly in the northern campaigns out from Old Castile to Madrid to the south and the Basque Country to the north. While there were certainly factional rivalries among these forces, the fact that they coordinated even before the rising began was a crucial difference with the Republic, whose government actively feared the revolutionary Left.

Signaling and Norms in Franco's Forces

Volunteer Forces under Military Discipline

Rebel success owed a lot to the Legion and Regulares. These were elite, principally volunteer forces under strict military discipline.[10] They figured into rebel plans even before the war. The Nationalist commanders, most of whom had served long years in Morocco, were utterly convinced of the political loyalties of the Legion and Regulares at the outset. As he planned the coup over the spring and summer of 1936, Mola, who strongly doubted the success of the rising within Madrid itself, eventually gave a prominent role to the Army of Africa and prepared to bring it across the Strait of Gibraltar despite both the logistical difficulties and an unreliable navy.[11]

In the first few months of war, the rebels relied on the Legion and Regulares for their principal territorial gains. After the war bogged down into more static fronts after the siege of Madrid in early November 1936, the Army of Africa was used on the most crucial fronts, both to take objectives other units could not and to plug weaknesses in the line. For Franco, the Army of Africa was, according to

Preston, "a priceless asset," the Nationalists' shock troops.[12] They bore the brunt of the fighting and had the highest casualty rates in the Nationalist army: the large majority of both Moroccan and Legion troops were, it seems, wounded at one time or another; one of eight Moroccans was killed.[13]

These forces generally had high morale in the first year of the war. A British military observer described Legionaries as "fit, alert, confident, conscious of being masters of their trade, certain of victory; and knowing that, are cheerful and gay."[14] John T. Whitaker, elsewhere severely critical of violence committed by Moroccan troops and apt to use racialized language to describe it, observed Moroccan house-to-house combat in Madrid, indicating their willingness to fight and die:

> A detail of 50 Moors would surround the building, silence the ground-floor defenders and rush in. They would then clear the second story with sub-machine-guns and hand grenades. These Moors were calm and tight-lipped, expert workmen. They would clear a building floor by floor. There was only one trouble with this work. By the time the Moors had done the job, there wouldn't be any Moors left.[15]

According to Sebastian Balfour, the Nationalist army was "able, by and large, to maintain the quality of its shock-troops throughout the Civil War."[16] (However, one key exception, when the Legion deviated from these recruitment practices in late 1936 and 1937, stands out; I explore it in further detail below.) The Moroccan forces, in particular, suffered from very low desertion rates, despite suffering from phenomenal casualty rates.[17]

The Army of Africa's recruitment and military practices helped encourage this reliability. Because of voluntarism, troops could self-select. To some degree, recruits were attracted by the opportunity for private gains. Legionaries were paid five pesetas per day as against the usual wage of three.[18] But economic motivations were particularly common among Regulares. A drought in the summer of 1936 in Morocco led many to join the Regulares for a bonus of "clothing, four kilos of sugar, a can of oil, bread proportional to the number of their children, and two months' pay in advance," as well as generally more abundant food in the ranks.[19]

The most depraved members of the Legion may have joined entirely for the opportunity to abuse civilians. Such opportunities were plentiful: the Army of Africa committed horrific abuses against Moroccans during the colonial occupation of Morocco. These then carried on in Spain. Nationalist leaders encouraged their troops to rape women identified as left wing, perhaps most notoriously in the lurid radio broadcasts of General Gonzalo Queipo de Llano in Sevilla. Rape by the Legion carried on in an awful tradition of the abuse of Moroccan women in Spain's colonial campaigns.[20] Nationalist forces, notably Moroccan troops, were also permitted to loot property in captured areas. Importantly, though, looting was not as common on the Nationalist side as on the Republican; property owners were a core Nationalist constituency. Moroccan troops could be sentenced to death for looting the property of "respectable" citizens.[21]

Though they could join looking to profit, pillage, and abuse civilians, volunteers to the Army of Africa had to get used to serious demands that they fight. With Spain's abstention from Europe's wars, before 1936 this was the only section of the Spanish military that had to do much serious fighting: notably in the vicious Rif War (1921–26) and in the turbulent "pacification" of Spain's colonial possessions that followed. Moreover, their style of fighting had steadily improved in the course of counterinsurgency, from daily sorties from blockhouses and slow maneuvers to tactics that emphasized rapid movement, indirect and flanking attacks, and small units. Troops spent long stretches of time away from bases and supply lines, carrying their supplies with them and living off the land.[22] It was, in short, a demanding style of warfare that required troops to endure risk and privation.

In this context, practices of the Legion and Regulares signaled to potential recruits that self-sacrifice was a requirement. The Legion was deeply ingrained with a sense of immediate obedience of orders, with failure to comply punished with the whip, and desertion—and even lesser offenses—punished with death.[23] In Morocco, the discipline was focused on the battlefield rather than on base, where rape and looting were widespread and tolerated with equanimity among Legion officers.[24] Beatings and whippings were also a standard practice within the Regulares; they were administered by Moroccans rather than by Spanish officers so as to avoid one form of interethnic resentment.[25]

Further, propaganda in both forces signaled a strong preoccupation with death. The Legion's slogan, repeated as a chant, was "Long live death!"[26] Millán Astray called the Legionaries *los novios de la muerte* (bridegrooms of death); on a base at Dar Riffien in Morocco was an arch with the inscription "Legionaries onward to fight; Legionaries onward to die."[27] Its subsequent leaders, such as Franco himself and, during the Civil War, Lieutenant Colonel Juan Yagüe Blanco, attempted to continue in this tradition.[28] For their part, the Regulares had, in Spain's colonial wars, "developed a tradition of exaggerated *machismo* scorning protection when under enemy fire" in Paul Preston's words.[29] Those who went over to Spain at the start of the Civil War knew that they were going to risk much. A song they frequently sang went as follows:

> Guard your belt and put another one over it,
> For we are going to Spain to die.[30]

It was clear, in short, that joining was costly.

It is true that the Army of Africa had recruited for a different military purpose, the suppression of anticolonial insurgency rather than fighting enemies on the mainland. However, well before the war, it began to take on its new role. Officers who were veterans of the Army of Africa were at the heart of the conspiracy against the Spanish Republic, while the rhetoric of its military publications and speeches increasingly denounced what was regarded as the antimilitarist decadence of the Republic. Most importantly, in October 1934 it was deployed by a right-wing government to suppress a workers' uprising in the mainland province of Asturias. At this stage the identity of the enemy shifted very clearly from Moroccan insurgents to left-wing activists and workers.[31] This was a precursor to the role that it played in the war beginning two years later.

On the basis of the clear signals of a commitment to fight that they demanded, both the Legion and the Regulares actively cultivated an esprit de corps. In the Regulares, while joining the Nationalist cause frequently had the economic motivations discussed above, Moroccan members of Spain's colonial force had also developed comradeship in combat with the Spanish elements of the Army of Africa. As Balfour points out, the first Regulares units were largely made up of "veterans of the Spanish colonial army, many of whom had fought in the Moroccan war on the Spanish side," with age little barrier to enlistment.[32] It helped that the first units were commanded by so-called enlightened officers whose racism toward Moroccans tended to the paternalistic end of colonialism rather than to explicit subordination.[33] As Balfour illustrates, bonds between officers and Regulares forged in colonial Morocco helped facilitate recruitment and mutually supportive cooperation for the Spanish Civil War:

> During the colonial war and in the post-colonial "pacification" campaigns they had formed a community of soldiers in which fraternity and solidarity were more powerful than ideology or politics. An anecdote reveals the strength of these bonds. A Moroccan sergeant of the Regulares, veteran of the Spanish colonial army, joined up and was sent on the first boatload of troops to Cadiz. During the voyage he was astute enough to suspect that the sailors were preparing to mutiny against their officers. As soon as he landed he went straight to Varela, his old commander in the colonial war, to warn him.[34]

As for the Spanish Legion, it had a long-standing institutional history of intense cooperation among its troops stretching back to its founding in 1920. Legionaries were supposed to be able to call for help under any circumstance with the cry "¡A mí la legión!" Its founder José Millán Astray worked assiduously to convince his men of his personal commitment to them, and in this regard his own wounds helped give him an almost mythic image.[35] As they accumulated battle experience, trust between Legionaries and their officers solidified.[36]

However, the Legion did not maintain the commitment of its forces during the Civil War. Partly this was a consequence of its heavy losses and their replacement with less committed call-ups. The decline in commitment was visible on the Aragón front, quiet during late 1936 and much of 1937. For example, Frank Thomas, a British volunteer in the Legion, deserted in the spring of 1937 out of his dismay at the willingness of Spanish Legionaries to live and let live with Republican forces.[37] Further, as of June 1937 service in the Legion became a punishment for draft dodging, because of the Legion's reputation for toughness. Yagüe complained that this policy was "prejudicial" to the Legion, and the measure was rescinded in January 1938, with the draft dodgers in question dispersed throughout the military.[38] Owing in large measure to these problems of recruitment, the Legion suffered from a fairly high rate of defection to the Republican side.[39]

In general, though, the Legion and Regulares had the capacity to secure reliability on the part of their troops, with clear selection for those who had a high tolerance for fighting and strong norms of cooperation. In addition to their military experience, well beyond anything the rest of the Spanish army could offer, this helped make the Army of Africa the keystone of Nationalist advances, particularly in the first few months of the war.

It should be noted that beyond internal trust, Regulares had particular reasons not to switch sides. Possibly to motivate soldiers and civilians through fear, Republican propaganda deployed racist stereotypes of Moroccans as raping and pillaging Moors threatening European civilization, with the communist orator Dolores Ibárruri denouncing "*morisma salvaje*" (savage Moorishness).[40] One cartoon in the anarchist newspaper *Fragua Social*, entitled "Civilización Cristiana," appeals to racist tropes about Moors—swarthy, with a fez with a white crescent and star, and a wine bottle sticking out of his belt—about to run through a white mother and child with a bloody bayonet.[41] Such propaganda may have persuaded Moroccan troops not to try to switch sides; a Spanish defector from a Moroccan company told a commissar in the Popular Army that Moroccan troops would not switch sides because they feared shooting or torture.[42] This is not a factor that my approach anticipates; it may have pushed Moroccans who would otherwise have defected to stay behind, and may explain especially low desertion rates despite high casualties, economic motivations for joining up, and some conscription.

Similarly to the Legion and Regulares, the Carlist Requeté militia combined voluntarism with obedience (though it did not enforce punishments nearly as harshly). It added to these elements a strong sense of social cohesion. In Navarre, the center of Carlism, the rising was greeted with "scenes of religious enthusiasm, combined with warlike zeal," according to Hugh Thomas; men poured into the provincial capital of Pamplona from outlying villages singing Carlist songs, hailed by the crowds.[43] These songs were one of several collective activities in which a Carlist, Christian identity was reinforced and linked to the military effort, such as public ceremonies, collective confessions, and wearing religious symbols and garments.[44] Drawing on this religious spirit, a document called *The Requeté's Prayer Book* used religious ideas to justify self-sacrifice in the name of redemption and crusading.[45] The Carlist movement also depended strongly on local communities.[46] Some 15–30 percent of men of military age volunteered for rebel militias in Navarre and the neighboring regions of La Rioja and Aragón.[47] According to Martin Blinkhorn, one village, Artajona, "sent 775 out of 800 eligible males into battle."[48] The capacity to recruit whole villages, and a resulting mutual commitment and willingness to fight, played a large part in Carlist propaganda, as Blinkhorn relates:

> A leaflet released in 1937 contained a conversation between a Falangist and a Red Beret; asked who is to be informed should he die in battle, the Red Beret replies: "Tell José María Hernandorena, of the *tercio* [unit] of Montejurra, aged 65. He's my father." And if he should prove to be . . . unavailable? "Then tell José María Hernandorena, of the *tercio* of Montejurra, aged 15. He's my son."[49]

Thus the Carlists played on the sense of a whole community collectively defending its supposed political traditions.

Carlist texts maintained the idea that the militias selected recruits rigorously, based on "cast-iron guarantees."[50] However, the expansion of the Carlist militias brought in many who were not fully committed to the cause. Blinkhorn considers it likely that only a minority of new Requeté recruits had been active Carlists before the war. Carlists set up new branches where they had previously been inactive. Many of the new recruits were thus "unavoidably deficient in their grasp of the essentials of Traditionalism," to use another word for Carlism.[51] However, Carlist units were under military command from the beginning, with military discipline, under the same guidelines for obedience and punishments for desertion as ordinary soldiers.[52] Ultimately, Carlist units proved to be relatively reliable. Indeed, Mola used the Requeté widely in northern Spain to supplement unreliable local militia forces.[53]

The Falange militia seemed to have comparatively greater discipline problems and tended to be less often employed. These problems corresponded to different recruitment and discipline practices, less insistent on costly signals of commitment. Whereas Carlist militias tended to be under military command, a prewar agreement between Mola and the Falange had established that a maximum of one-third of the Falange's militias would be under direct military control.[54] This meant that their units were less subject to strict military discipline. Therefore, according to Payne, Falange militias tended to attract those who wanted to avoid harsh service.[55] Draft-age men would attempt to join militias to get an exemption from the regular army.[56] Indeed, Faustino Sánchez, a Falangist youth from Asturias who fled to Galicia when the rising failed back home, reported that, just like on the Republican side, Falange militiamen could go home at night: "For us volunteers there wasn't much discipline. After we took my home town, I used to leave the column and go home for the night when I felt like it."[57] In addition, the regular army co-opted and integrated the most effective Falange units, leaving the less effective ones to operate autonomously.[58]

The Falange militia often did not acquit itself particularly well in fighting. However, over time, the arm's-length relationship with the military ended, and discipline came down harder. By September 1936, the Falange leadership was more readily accepting military control of Falange units.[59] That December, Franco subjected the militias to military discipline.

In sum, the volunteer forces ranged against the Republic resembled the latter to some degree, in that they varied in their conditions of service. Sometimes they allowed some recruits to enjoy the fruits of military service without paying its costs. But the major difference with the Republic is that Nationalist volunteers would—with the important exception of some Falange units—have to fight. Under military discipline, they accepted that they would be forced to obey orders and endure battle. The sense of mutual sacrifice was especially pronounced in the Legion, Regulares, and the Requeté, where requirements of a willingness to fight and sociopolitical solidarity were greatest. It was much less developed in many Falange units, which often specifically recruited among the politically uncommitted and adopted looser discipline.

Conscription and Weak Norms

Like the Republic, though, Franco relied on conscription as well as on voluntarism; indeed, the rebellious units of the regular conscript army provided the bulk of Nationalist numbers, and Franco later called up successive draft classes. He also cracked down on draft exemptions, ordering on November 1, 1936, that any such request received from a draftee's family or friends be destroyed unread. Later he cut off the option of joining the Falange militias to avoid tougher service in the army. As part of the process of integrating these militias into the army, on April 24, 1937, Franco ordered that every militia member serving in rear areas be incorporated into the army on pain of being considered a deserter.[60] And as on the Republican side, Franco confronted a significant problem of draft dodging: bands of draft dodgers hid in the hills, especially in Andalucía and in Asturias. The Nationalist authorities would send units of Falange and police after these bands. In December 1937 in Asturias, a deadline was set for any draft dodgers to present themselves, after which public order forces would, according to the ultimatum, "open fire on everyone found hidden in the hills."[61]

Unsurprisingly, then, the conscripts who did join up tended to have relatively weak commitment to the Nationalist side. César Lozas, a Republican sympathizer in Valladolid, had a chance at an exemption because he was of dual French-Spanish nationality. However, he joined anyway in the winter of 1936–37, out of fear of reprisals against his Republican father. "The new regime might not consider [his dual nationality] sufficient. There was no way out but to serve. And that, he believed, was what the majority of peasant recruits in his infantry company—he was the only student—felt. They were not politically motivated to fight." Lozas also notes that they were not left-wingers who would try to leave for political reasons: they "lacked the ideological awareness that would have motivated a serious attempt to desert." Another student serving in the Nationalist army on the Andalucía front found, similarly, that the peasantry "joined up with resignation—the sort of attitude that the great mass of people always shows in these situations."[62]

Corresponding to this limited enthusiasm, norms of cooperation were more difficult to maintain among conscript forces—perhaps as difficult as those among Republican conscripts. The internal communications about desertion on the Nationalist side are strikingly similar to those of their Republican counterparts. In January 1938, a note from the head of the Twenty-Second Division to General Gonzalo Queipo de Llano noted, "Each recently organized unit that arrives at the front for the first time is sifted, producing desertions that are difficult to avoid." Fidel Dávila, head of the Army of the North, confronted the same reality in August 1938 with new conscripts from the Balearic Islands, including ten deserters in one week. They lacked training and "do not demonstrate sympathy for the Glorious National Movement, in contrast with the other troops of this division."[63]

However, the Nationalist commanders were caught in a dilemma. As we have seen, the increasing incorporation of conscripts and particularly draft dodgers into the Legion came with weaker norms and a higher desertion rate, and its commander, Yagüe, fought the policy. At some points, other commanders mirrored this reluctance, attempting to keep elite units and conscripts separate and, in Seidman's terms, "regroup the most committed volunteers in new formations."[64] But this also implied that the remaining units would be full of conscripts, and thus more likely to have poor morale and to fall apart. Thus some commanders preferred to mix volunteers and conscripts so that the former could bring up the morale of the latter. This was the policy at the battles of Jarama in February 1937 and of the Ebro in 1938.[65] The inconsistency of these two approaches bore a striking resemblance to the inconsistency in Republican practice. Mixing and separating conscripts and volunteers were opposite reactions to a common phenomenon: men tended to respond to those around them.

As on the Republican side, trust among conscripts often helped them desert. Men were assigned to monitor comrades, so a man's chances at desertion often depended on others. A corporal in the 105th Division, deployed southeast of Zaragoza in Aragón, allowed eleven soldiers serving under him to defect to the Republicans. It seemed that every night he was on sentinel duty, one of his men would cross the lines. Eventually his superiors uncovered this pattern and the corporal himself was driven to defect in November 1937. Friends could therefore help friends desert. For example, two corporals in the First Army Corps were very close and talked about deserting together. On the night of August 7, 1937, the sergeant who was supposed to go on duty with one of them suffered an extremely painful insect bite in the foot, and the two friends were, for the first time, assigned sentinel duty together; they left as soon as they could.[66] Because of the need for trust in such situations, men engaged in a delicate process of steadily discovering whether a compatriot was a leftist. Eugenio Calvo, a Basque communist, joined the Legion after the fall of northern Spain to the rebels, intending to get to the front and defect. In his unit he met four others who were also of the Left: "During the training, he and the four others had, little by little, sounded each other out, small things revealing their thoughts." They planned together to desert, locating a gap in the barbed wire they would all cross. One was wounded in the attempt and another carried him.[67] Personal connections aided this cooperation; in one case, two brothers and another individual from the same hometown deserted on the same night, June 7, 1937, in the Zuera sector in Zaragoza.[68] Here, trust through social solidarity had the opposite effect in conscript units as compared to the Carlist Requeté. Far from forging a commitment to fight, trust often served as the basis for desertion itself—just as we saw in the shift from volunteer to conscript units in Republican Spain.

Coercive Control and Political Unity

The rebel forces thus had an advantage in combining voluntarism and discipline to a greater degree than the Republic. But there was still considerable variation among Nationalist forces on these criteria, with heavy use of conscripts and some plainly undisciplined volunteer forces.

Where the rebels had an unqualified advantage, however, was in their political unity and the high degree of centralized, coercive control that the Nationalist state apparatus imposed on the rebel zone. Control of desertion was part and parcel of the general control that the authorities exercised over society. Unlike the

"uncontrolled" violence characteristic of the Republican zone, the much more severe violence on the Nationalist home front generally occurred as the consequence of central direction and as part of installing the power of the new Nationalist state.[69] There is some disagreement about this point: Julius Ruiz argues that
Republican central government figures were more complicit in violent repression
of fascists than is usually appreciated, while Stanley Payne argues that "in the early
months the Nationalist repression was not at all centrally organized," for regional
and local military authorities were in control of the exercise of violence in the
first several months.[70] There was an understanding that an element of disorder
was inevitable: the instructions preparing the rising argued that "certain disor-
ders under the supervision of armed civilians must be permitted in order that a
number of specified persons can be eliminated and revolutionary centres and or-
ganisms destroyed."[71] Thus, executions were conducted at night and after procedures of denunciation, drawing a certain resemblance to the violence of the "un-
controllables" of the Republic.[72]

These elements of decentralization and private violence do not seriously undermine the general point that Nationalist authorities had much more extensive
control over society than their Republican counterparts, a control that would enable them to punish desertion more effectively. On the Republican side, as we
saw, the phenomenon of violence, decentralized to local authorities and in private hands, created the conditions in which deserters could escape punishment.
In contrast, the Nationalist side kept tighter control over the use of violence. Far
from the chaotic distribution of arms in the first days and the resistance to disarmament by the anarchists and Partido Obrero de Unificación Marxista (POUM)
in Barcelona, the Nationalist authorities vigorously disarmed civilians from an
early date. Ten days after the start of the rising, General Gonzalo Queipo de Llano,
administering Sevilla with a significant degree of autonomy from the other Nationalist leaders, ordered "intensive searches" for arms, which had to be handed
over to the Civil Guard on pain of execution.[73] Thus decentralization to local military authorities, such as Queipo, did not in any sense mean a less thorough or
credible top-down control of society by the state. Every garrison that rose immediately declared martial law in its respective region and replaced the existing
civil authorities.[74] In addition to the order to turn in guns, martial law also gave
a legal justification, however thin in principle, to persecute those who objected to
Nationalist rule as having committed the "crime of rebellion," expansively defined.[75] In any event, by March 1937 Franco was signing off personally on all
executions in the Nationalist zone.[76]

Thus the Nationalist authorities had an extensive ability to round up and kill
the opponents of the new regime—which they did by the tens of thousands. In
conducting this violence, the leaders of the rebellion spoke of a "cleansing" of

enemies of Spain that needed to take place: the purpose was not merely to win a war but "the permanent suppression of the enemy."[77] Hence, as Javier Rodrigo argues, violence during the Civil War "went beyond the necessary control of the rearguard. Apart from its immediate function for the present, terror was intended to have an effect on the future."[78] Thus, killing was not just "connected to the concrete action of the defendant. . . . The 'other' was killed for impersonal reasons: for belonging to the enemy."[79] This was clear from the outset, and implemented from the top down. Mola's orders for Morocco included the directive to "eliminate leftist elements: communists, anarchists, trade unionists, masons, etc."[80] The Nationalist press officer Captain Gonzalo de Aguilera y Munro, a nobleman and wealthy landowner in Salamanca, articulated his extreme contempt to American journalists: "The masses in this country are not like your Americans, nor even like the British. They are slave stock. They are good for nothing but slaves and only when they are used as slaves are they happy."[81] Hence it is important to see Nationalist violence not only as a war strategy but also as a broader political strategy to eliminate an enemy.

This strategy leaves its traces in the overall patterns of violence, and in the differences between Republican and Nationalist patterns. Balcells does find key similarities between the two sides' patterns of violence, studying executions in Catalonia, Málaga and Nationalist-held Aragón. In both Nationalist and Republican Spain, violence peaked in municipalities where Left and Right were equally strong (as measured by electoral results). This is because, according to Balcells, in these municipalities eliminating the supporters of the opposing side could tip the local political balance, and such a violent policy would have significant support locally. However, there are two key differences between the two zones: in Balcells' words, "violence by the Nationalists was more intense but also more territorially concentrated."[82] In other words, fewer municipalities had at least one killing in the Nationalist zone, but those that did had many more. Balcells attributes the difference in severity to Nationalists' top-down orders to kill their enemies.[83]

Very clearly, this brutal repression often gave its victims very little chance to comply. It was often based on past actions, before the rising; on social class and occupation; on ethnic identity, notably with the targeting of Catalans; and on family ties to suspect individuals. If and to the extent that this repression affected soldiers, then, my approach to desertion suggests it should have provoked many of them to desert or defect.

However, James Matthews argues that in the midst of all the mistrust and persecution, Nationalist authorities still often gave soldiers a chance for "redemption" through military service. It was official policy to grant such an opportunity. General Carlos Asensio Cabanillas wrote to the Twelfth Division in December 1937 that "it is necessary for unit commanders to make known to the troops—although not in an official communiqué—that all those who have unfavourable records are, while they serve the cause of Nationalist Spain in the trenches, attenuating or erasing their guilty pasts."[84] Matthews cites a speech to soldiers in December 1938 that explicitly invoked a logic that linked punishment to current rather than past behavior: "Cast yourselves free of the fear that one or other of you had been Red in ideas or action. At the front, your past social or political activities have been erased (*se han borrado*). On your return, you will all be the same; the only ones who will be treated differently are the shirkers (*los emboscados*)."[85] Military service could therefore—theoretically—offer a privileged avenue for avoiding persecution, even if civilian life did not. This service could theoretically also help soldiers' families. In Asensio's policy, "as their rendered services increase, either by the extended length of time in arms or by the military actions in which they have taken part, their good conduct not only benefits themselves, but also their relatives." Asensio was also aware, though, that the credibility of this policy depended on how families were *actually* being treated: "The soldiers must also be made aware that, as soon as they receive news that their social and political conduct before the National Movement is being investigated in their villages, they must inform the commander of their unit. He will inform me so that I can defend the individual concerned and his relatives from possible reprisals, on the condition that his conduct within his unit makes him worthy of this."[86] An additional option for leftists was to join Falange militias, which, according to one Falangist organizer, became known as the FAIlange (referring to the Federación Anarquista Ibérica) because, among other reasons, "we accepted everyone."[87] According to the editor of the Falangist newspaper in Oviedo, fully 20 percent of the Falange in Asturias were ex-leftists, equal to the proportion of Falangist true believers. Falangist documents stated that, in the words of Stanley Payne, "voluntary enlistment for active duty was a clearer sign of loyalty than was ideological purity."[88]

As Matthews makes clear, though, this incentive structure was often poorly maintained: many soldiers and their families were persecuted in spite of their military records, and they often deserted accordingly. A notable case is the Legion unit Bandera Sanjurjo, created in August 1936 in Zaragoza. It made a specific appeal to leftists in the area and encouraged them to "do meritorious actions that can redeem their pasts." Men joined the unit in order to protect their families from reprisals. But the unit was racked with desertion in late 1936 and early 1937. General Miguel Ponte, the head of the Fifth Army Corps under which the unit served, noted that the recruits' families had been persecuted, the bonus due to them for the Legionaries' service unpaid. Ponte clarified the effect this would have had: the men had been "assured that by [joining the Legion], if their conduct was honorable and loyal, they would wipe out the stains and errors of their former lives, which contrasts vividly with reality, as this [the repression of their families] shows that it is no longer just individuals but the Authorities of their home villages who work against their desire for liberation and their material interests."[89]

The Bandera Sanjurjo's experience was repeated elsewhere; for example, leftists in the Twelfth Division were induced to desert when they heard from family members of investigations into their political views.[90] In one episode, Twelfth Division soldiers had to inform their superiors of their last place of employment and provide its contact information. This was supposedly in order to connect them with their jobs when they finished their service, but the form provoked considerable anxiety, with officers suspecting that their men feared that this was a way of checking on their union pasts. At least one soldier defected at the next opportunity after receiving the form. In other cases, soldiers could come under suspicion simply for being Catalan, for example.[91] To be sure, many leftist soldiers just defected in order to join the side they preferred.[92] But the timing of these cases suggests that the fear of persecution for one's past or characteristics—which one could now do nothing about—created incentives to try to leave. In effect it created the fear that one would be punished despite *not* deserting, that is, the fear that can drive the provocation effect. The new Nationalist state had undermined its own assurance strategy: serve with loyalty, and you will be safe.

Though punishments did provoke desertion, the capacity of the Nationalist state for top-down monitoring and surveillance created a powerful deterrent effect that counteracted it. Even when provoked, individuals frequently had little recourse. Deserters would be tried and punished under courts martial organized within their division or corps, administering the Code of Military Justice with its penalties of imprisonment for desertion and death for defection. Local Civil Guard and Falange officials from the soldier's hometown would also investigate his political and social history. Tight central control over safe-conducts and permission to travel made it easier for the authorities to prevent a deserter from getting very far.[93] Even if the deserter himself could not be caught—for example, if he switched sides and thus escaped Nationalist punishment—his family could pay the price. In one instance, Nationalist authorities in La Coruña ordered the arrest of all the adult male family members of two men who had fled to the Republican camp with their arms.[94] Above I noted that César Lozas, a Republican sympathizer in Valladolid, accepted the conscription order rather than dodging the draft out of fears of reprisals against his father. Once in the army, Lozas found that the other conscripts in his unit were intimidated from deserting by the policy of control in place. Though he found them unlikely to try to desert because of their political neutrality, he also noted that "any such attempt could cost you your life—and even if you succeeded, reprisals could be taken on your family. There was considerable terror in the rearguard."[95] The repression of those family members was a bureaucratic endeavor, requiring efforts on the part of the military unit, with its records of soldiers' home-towns and family members, and the local military authorities who were tasked with detaining soldiers' families.[96] This apparatus of punishing family members was akin to its counterpart on the Republican side, but, given the greater power of the Nationalist state over society, more effectively maintained.

There were, however, ways in which deserters could slip through the cracks of this system. In places where it was more difficult to maintain top-down control over society, deserters could hide more easily. Not only draft dodgers but desert-ers as well hid out in bands in the hills of Huelva and Sevilla, facing death from the Civil Guard and other rear-area authorities if they were caught.[97] It appears anecdotally as though desertion was more common among soldiers from moun-tainous areas than among soldiers from flat land, as I have found on the Repub-lican side, because hill country soldiers could take advantage of the difficulty of moving around and their knowledge of the rough terrain to evade the Nationalist authorities.[98]

Home could prove an important resource for a deserter who was hiding out. Among his family or friends, he could receive support and shelter. While many denounced deserters out of fear of further reprisal, others refused to do so.[99] Rec-ognizing the appeal of home, the Nationalist authorities sought to make it as difficult as possible for soldiers to get back to their villages and towns. One tactic was physical distance. On September 23, 1936, Nationalist authorities issued an order that militiamen must serve outside their home regions in order to receive their pay.[100] Within the regular army, various orders over the course of the war transferred soldiers away from their home regions. With Catalan soldiers cross-ing the lines on the Aragón front to head to Catalonia on the other side, and with Galician soldiers on the northern front deserting back to their relatively near home region, in April 1937 Franco's headquarters authorized a swap of Catalans for Galicians between the two fronts.[101] With transportation networks watched vigi-lantly, it would have been difficult to cross such distances undetected.

Very often, soldiers could not take advantage of home because they could not make it out of their units in the first place. Those trying to defect could be shot in the attempt, and in December 1936, Trench Councils permitted summary execu-tions at the front rather than having to wait for headquarters, though documenta-tion on these proceedings is scarce.[102] As in the Republican army, the Nationalists employed particularly tight vigilance against those who were dubious, relying on proven veterans to administer front-line monitoring. For example, the army as-signed one corporal and two veteran soldiers to watch over sixty conscripts at the Battle of the Ebro in 1938, paying particular attention to the newest draftees.[103]

Variation in coercion therefore had an impact. In some circumstances defec-tion was more difficult. For example, crossing no-man's-land was a dangerous proposition when an elite unit with good snipers, such as the Legion, was serving at the front.[104] In contrast, defection was facilitated when such monitoring could not be established. Officers in northern Spain, for example, were frustrated that "the extensive and sparsely covered front prevented competent surveillance," enabling defections to the Republicans.[105]

Deterrence played a particularly essential role in preventing desertion among soldiers who plainly had no reason to stay otherwise. Notably, not everyone with a left-wing past could have it expunged at the front line.[106] Instead, the Nationalists forced some of the most politically suspect troops, as well as prisoners of war and many defectors from the Republican side, into labor battalions doing work to support the war effort (such as building roads). Here, the conditions were extremely difficult, with limited rations, poor clothes, and hard labor; this was punishment. Though forced laborers in these battalions could theoretically begin to "redeem" their pasts, there were clearly strong incentives to leave if one could. However, punishments for further disloyalty were often swift and severe, such as summary execution of soldiers upon having uncovered a plot to defect. Additionally, having placed many of the most suspected soldiers in work battalions, the military then kept these units far from the front in order to limit their chances of defection.[107] It appears that leaving was simply not an option.

There are thus two explanations for why Nationalist violence did not provoke more desertion and defection. For some, the Nationalists created the option of "redemption" through military service, limiting the provocation effect. But they did not maintain this policy consistently. Instead, the coercive apparatus appears to have been too effective for many to defect, even those whom it provoked to. The deterrent effect seems to have frequently outweighed the provocation effect.

Nationalist Factionalism

The centralized, coercive capacity of the new Nationalist state was also able to overcome limited differences in political agendas. Factionalism on the Nationalist side was not as pervasive as on the Republican side, lacking deep substantive differences or a history of violent conflict. However, there were still programmatic differences among some rivals. To the extent that these differences existed, centralized coercive control kept them from producing large-scale desertion.

Over the course of the autumn of 1936 and the spring of 1937, Franco institutionalized unity in the new regime, in two steps: unified military command and a unified political entity. First, the coequal collective decision-making body of the generals, the Junta de Burgos, gave way on September 29, 1936, to a unified command with Franco himself as head of the military and head of the new state.

Franco had two key advantages in this process: after the deaths of key rivals in the first days of the war, he was the most senior general who would be acceptable to all. Vitally, in addition, he had the support of the Army of Africa, as a former commander of the Legion. At the key meeting in which the generals decided on Franco's command, Colonel Juan Yagüe "pointed out forcefully that his legionaries and Moroccan troops wanted Franco as supreme commander."[108] The strong preference for unity among the military hierarchy was probably enough to ensure Franco's ascendance, but Yagüe's intervention suggests that elite forces weighed heavily in the decision.

The Legion and Regulares also lingered in the background in the more difficult process of uniting the Carlists and Falange under Franco's control. On April 18, 1937, from his headquarters in Salamanca, Franco announced a decision to unify the Carlist Traditionalist Party and the Falange in a single entity with the unwieldy name Falange Española Tradicionalista y de las Juntas de Ofensiva Nacional Sindicalista, and to ban all other political parties. There had been mixed feelings among both Carlists and Falangists about the prospects of unification. Before the war, the Falange's founder, José Antonio Primo de Rivera, had had discussions with Manuel Fal Conde, the leader of the Carlist militias, on cooperation in a rising. During the war, Carlist and Falange leaders had broached the idea of political unification and published an exploration of points of agreement and disagreement between the two tendencies. Certainly members of both parties saw the need to unify for the sake of victory in war. Further, both would now come closer to real political power than they ever had.[109] Franco's lack of clearly defined political ideology (other than vicious opposition to the Left and to regional autonomy movements) helped bridge the gap among different forces. His political program evolved over time, combining an appeal to hierarchy and military strength (to keep the various military chiefs together), restoration of official Catholicism (to appeal to the Carlists), a corporate state (to appeal to the Falange), and a cordial but arm's-length relationship between the military and an exiled monarchy (to bridge the gap between antimonarchist officers and those favoring restoration).[110]

But elements of the Falange and Carlists opposed cooperation with the other, disagreeing essentially between Carlist decentralized rural traditionalism and Catholicism and the Falange's preference for centralizing, modernizing, corporatist revolution.[111] In addition, Primo de Rivera had feared domination by the military, believing that it would co-opt the Falange with few guarantees for the implementation of its program. Similarly, Fal Conde, in the preparation for the rising, had been concerned that Carlist support would help ensure military dominance without a clear guarantee that the Carlist monarchy would be restored. Both, though, recognized that in a confrontation with the armed forces, they stood little chance.[112] To some degree, members of each faction appear to have been wary of political unification but to have accepted it because there was little alternative.[113]

If efforts at centralization prompted much less desertion on the Nationalist side, then, it was ultimately testimony to two basic logics. First, there was apparently a greater potential for cooperation on the Nationalist side. The different factions accepted more readily that winning the war required submission to central authority. The Nationalist program was also able to offer both the Falange and the Carlist programs substantive gains. Unlike among many anarchists, there does not appear to have been a widespread sense on the part of either that it would have to give up its whole program in order to win the war. The balance of common versus competing interests favored the former to a greater degree than it did on the Republican side. Second, lingering in the background was the sense that there was very little alternative: that the coercive apparatus of the military would ultimately force unification if necessary.

Why did the Nationalist side experience a considerably lower rate of desertion than the Republican side did? And what explains the still considerable variation in desertion among different rebel forces? The rebellion enjoyed a few critical advantages over the Republic stemming from its profoundly military and authoritarian character. When joined to voluntary recruitment, the insistence on military discipline and submission to authority became, almost paradoxically, sources of trust: the key forces were able to use them to have combatants signal their voluntary willingness to suffer, to fight, to kill, and to die. In this way, the Legion and Regulares built trust through a combination of voluntary recruitment and frightening disciplinary standards, so that in joining up, a soldier was committing to fight, and to fight hard (though in the case of the Moroccan troops, this appears to have been reinforced by Republican propaganda). That this was an obviously brutal and violent path to cohesion should not obscure that it was a path nonetheless. The Requeté likewise used voluntarism and military obedience (albeit of a much more limited character), but community mobilization supplemented these signals to an important degree. Authoritarianism also meant that, though there were certainly different and competitive factions on the rebel side, there was also a greater willingness than in the Republic to accept the necessity of a single hierarchy and leader, ultimately reducing factional competition and largely removing a source of mistrust that plagued the Republic. The centralized, coercive apparatus made perhaps the biggest difference: where the active trust of the Legion, Regulares, and Requeté was unavailable, as among the conscripts who constituted the majority of troops, coercion *did* keep soldiers fighting.

It was therefore clearly *not* that the rebel side had a surplus of enthusiasm or political motivation that was lacking in the Republic. The passion of many Republican militia volunteers, which we saw in previous chapters, gives the lie to this idea. Where there was an important difference was, first, in discipline and, second, in coercion. The former made it so that in the elite rebel forces it was relatively easy for soldiers to show each other a willingness to obey orders and to sacrifice. More relaxed forces such as the Falange militias recruited a larger share of opportunists; and even an elite force like the Legion was undermined when the army introduced uncommitted soldiers into the fold.

Moreover, it was not that the rebels built more successfully than the Republican side on social ties. These ties were certainly crucial to the Requeté, and probably more intense than in Republican militias because Carlist ideology seemed to dominate in some communities, but Republican militias built on ties of place and occupation too. The Legion, for its part, built its trust among recruits who had little prior connection to each other through costly signals of martial intent. And just as in the Republic, local ties could subvert the cause, as among groups of conscripts; social ties were given their direction by combatants' objectives.

The more difficult question that the Nationalist experience raises is whether the coercion approach to studying desertion is sufficient to explain rebel military success. Does the analyst need to bother understanding trust and mistrust at all, or was military power in Franco's Spain built essentially on fear? There is no doubt that the coercive apparatus made a big difference: it was extensive, penetrated down to the village level, and made it so that even if a fighter feared persecution and maltreatment there was not much that he could necessarily do; threats to family members and friends meant that there was very often the threat of worse to come. Exceptions, like the looser penalties maintained in many Falange militias and their higher desertion rates, reinforce the importance of coercion. The deterrent effect was very powerful.

However, this is also not a sufficient explanation. There remains the gap among the more reliable Legion (at least for the first few months, until its recruitment patterns changed), Regulares, and Requeté, in contrast to the regular conscripts, even though they were subject to the same coercive apparatus.

Moreover, coercion itself worked in a manner that at least did not backfire as severely as it did in the Republic. This is perhaps surprising given the utter brutality the Franco regime meted out behind the lines. It is possible that, given the persecution on the basis of stereotypes within Franco's Spain generally, one may have expected a higher desertion rate on the basis of my approach; certainly Catalan soldiers and those with a leftist past appear to have often suffered from severe mistrust. One answer is that Franco's surveillance apparatus ensured that the deterrent effect often outweighed the provocation effect. Beyond this, however, it is critical to underline the distinction between civilian and military life in Nationalist Spain. At the same time that this political project terrorized civilians, it also valorized the army; in doing so, it set aside the army as a place where a leftist could sometimes redeem a dubious political past.

It is difficult to ignore the ideological origins of all this. Valorizing the violence and martyrdom of military power was at the heart of the Nationalist project, alongside conservative Catholicism, tightly restricted gender roles, the persecution of regional minorities, and the demonization of its adversaries. It appears that these ideological priors gave the Nationalists access to a certain kind of answer to the problems of military organization: squaring the circle of the voluntary acceptance of obedience and punishment, diminishing factional competition for the sake of common authoritarian leadership, and setting up a military path to political redemption. Some of the very features that made Francoism so appalling may also have made it militarily effective—and not just through fear but also through the creation of a kind of trust and cooperation, perverse though it might seem.

THE CRUMBLING OF ARMIES IN CONTEMPORARY SYRIA

The previous chapters demonstrated the crucial role of trust and mistrust in desertion in Spain. The purpose of this chapter is to find out how this portrait of desertion applies in the Syrian Civil War (2011–present). I examine five factions in this immensely complicated conflict, with my analysis running up to around the end of 2017. The Syrian war has been marked by very wide variation in desertion. On the regime side, a huge wave of desertion and defection drained the army of manpower and indeed provided the core of the armed opposition that made civil war possible. But at the same time, a core of the army remained loyal, helping prevent a repeat of the cascade that toppled dictatorial regimes in Tunisia and Egypt in 2011. Opposing the regime, a highly variable set of rebel militias and armies has ranged from informal and ever-shifting groupings of fighters that have struggled to keep together, to tightly organized and disciplined armies that have put up stiff resistance. Episodes of this determined fighting in the face of grim odds, like the Kurdish resistance to the Islamic State in Iraq and al-Sham (ISIS, later Islamic State) at Kobane, gained deserved renown.

This variation in desertion patterns, as well as the variation in the military practices of these different forces, makes Syria a good place to test my approach to desertion. As in Spain, the focus is on how different forces in the same war, with the same social, technological, media, and international environments, organized for violence differently and maintained their fighting forces in very different ways. Beyond this, studying a contemporary war helps overcome some of the biases implicit in focusing on Spain in the rest of the book. Does the relational approach to desertion offer lessons for analysts of contemporary armed conflicts? If so, it should give us a good idea of which armed groups will experience higher and lower desertion rates as well as the mechanisms by which these will occur. It should also add insights beyond existing approaches. The task of the chapter is to find out whether Spain has lessons for Syria.

Syria is a preeminent "new new civil war," according to Barbara Walter: it is typical of current conflicts in being fought in a Muslim-majority country, in involving Islamist armed groups that have transnational goals, and in using Web 2.0 technologies to gain support abroad.[1] These characteristics evoke various explanations of military cohesion and desertion. In terms of ideology and personal commitment to the cause, it may be that Syria demonstrates the "extremist's advantage" that Walter sees: a comparatively strong ability to recruit dedicated martyrs.[2] At the same time, local neighborhood groups of activists and networks of Islamists and Kurdish nationalists have underpinned rebel units, evoking the logic of interpersonal political and social ties. The transnational character of the war is felt in the influence of deep-pocketed backers, from states to private individuals and ranging in origin from the Gulf to Turkey to Russia and the United States. Their role reflects the transnational war economies many see as a new and fundamental feature of war.[3] So perhaps preventing desertion has depended on using outside support to keep one's soldiers supplied and paid. Finally, the horrors of the war, perpetrated above all by the regime and by ISIS, put Syria in the lead of the grim upsurge in violence in civil wars.[4] This requires an examination of raw coercion in keeping combatants fighting, for the violence did not spare combatants from their own armed groups.

These explanations are important, and they play into my overall account, which focuses on the origins of trust and mistrust. The groups best able to limit desertion and keep their fighting strength—Jabhat al-Nusra (JN), the volunteer bulk of the Kurdish People's Protection Units and Women's Protection Units (respectively, Yekîneyên Parastina Gel, YPG, and Yekîneyên Parastina Jin, YPJ), the elite elements of the regime's Syrian Arab Army (SAA), and ISIS early on—have done so by building norms of cooperation within their armies, based on voluntary recruitment with demanding standards to insist on well-motivated combatants who signaled their trustworthiness to others. The units that have fallen apart— much of the regime's regular army, most of the Free Syrian Army (FSA) units, and ISIS later—either have not insisted on these standards or have suffered from factional conflicts and stereotypes that undermined trust among combatants at the front. Table 9.1 summarizes my approach's expectations about different desertion rates across these forces.

So the key trends in contemporary conflicts are important, but they have not fundamentally altered how armed groups hold together. Instead, these factors' im-

TABLE 9.1.   Military unit characteristics and hypothesized overall desertion rates—Syria

		THREAT OF VIOLENCE WITHIN ARMED GROUP		
		HIGH; AT MOST OCCASIONALLY STEREOTYPED OR FACTIONALIZED	LOW	HIGH; SYSTEMATICALLY STEREOTYPED OR FACTIONALIZED
Information about motivations	Clear	JN ISIS (early) Regime elite units YPG/YPJ		
	Unclear	ISIS (later)	FSA	Regime regular army

Note: Units are placed according to the independent variables.

pacts on whether soldiers stay and fight or flee have to do with how they shape norms, trust, and mistrust. War may have changed, but these factors are still at the heart of desertion.

This account has much in common with Vera Mironova's analysis of why opposition combatants have defected to different groups over time in Syria, and in fact draws on some of the survey research that Mironova and colleagues conducted.[5] Mironova argues that the vast array of armed opposition groups have competed like firms over a pool of recruits, each trying to demonstrate that it could offer fighters a competent organization that could allow them to make an impact, as well as adequate supplies and pay. However, successful and well-paying armed groups can attract opportunists, with problematic consequences such as undermining cohesion. So armed groups have tried to screen out opportunists through devices like recommendations, the test of combat itself, and compliance with nonmilitary rules such as religiously justified codes of conduct as a test of a combatant's ideological dedication.[6] For Mironova, these mechanisms, and especially the latter, help explain the greater cohesion of Islamist groups as compared with the FSA.

While I agree with Mironova on the importance of self-selection and of screening through costly signals and on some of the devices for doing so, my account differs from hers in a few important and related respects. I include regime forces and the YPG/YPJ alongside the FSA, JN, and ISIS. Excluding the former two, Mironova assumes the latter three groups share a single recruitment pool. Potential recruits, in her view, all have the overarching aim of defeating the Asad regime, and are searching for the best method of doing so given acceptable fighting conditions (or are simply opportunists). This leads Mironova, like Walter, to seek to understand what it is about Islamist groups that seems to give them an advantage over more secular groups, and to examine the functions of ideological signaling within the former. In contrast, in taking on regime forces and the YPG/YPJ, I focus more on costly signals that a variety of armed groups, Islamist or not, can require in order for combatants to signal their commitment. Doing so points to important differences among extremist groups (between JN and ISIS in particular) and to common points with more cohesive groups that do not fall under the Islamist banner, such as the regime's elite forces and the YPG/YPJ.

This book's approach to desertion does not tell analysts everything they need to know about loyalties in a war like Syria's. Notably, it does not build an account of where factional conflicts emerge from, and it does not focus on the splits and broken alliances that have been so common in Syria. For that, other analyses will provide better answers.[7] My focus is instead on groups of ordinary combatants. Thus I examine how factional conflicts bear on the cohesion of fighting groups, but I do not seek to explain either where those conflicts come from or how they result in elite-level splits that tear whole armed groups apart. But this chapter's ground-level focus captures a great deal about the problems of desertion and defection in this civil conflict, while existing analyses of loyalty and cohesion in Syria typically focus on macro divides.[8] In contrast, this chapter allows more attention to the characteristics internal to each group that permitted it to hold together more or less effectively.

Armies and Militias in Syria

The Syrian regime is and has long been brutally authoritarian, dominated from 1970 to 2000 by Hafiz al-Asad and, since then, by his son Bashar.[9] Long before the war, the regime had a deeply feared surveillance apparatus that reached pervasively into people's lives. It comprehensively punished political opposition, constraining the small opening to civil society organizations that occurred during the 2000s.[10] Power in this regime has been held above all by the extended Asad family. Indeed, before the war the regime's base progressively narrowed under Bashar al-Asad, who abandoned many of the socialist policies of the Ba'ath Party in favor of a crony-capitalist economy dominated by business networks centered on the regime itself, deepening economic inequality.[11] Finally, the regime was and is seen popularly as tightly linked with the Alawite community, some 12 percent of the population.[12] Much of the Asad family and its close associates are Alawites, while a large majority of the population, just over 60 percent by most estimates, are Sunni Arabs. There are certainly Sunni members of the regime elite and its business networks, and many Alawites are excluded from access to the regime's largesse and circles of power, especially as Bashar al-Asad narrowed the regime. However, there is certainly a disproportionate share of power in Alawi-tes' hands, and Alawites have long held the key posts in the security services.[13]

Syria in 2011 therefore had many bases for grievances against the regime, but little room for their political expression. The popular demonstrations that ended in the downfall of dictators in Tunisia and Egypt in January of that year changed all that. Beginning in February 2011 in Daraa and Damascus, protests gathered momentum in mid-March and spread around the country, progressively build-ing a sense of an unprecedented opportunity for Syrian activists to have their voices heard.[14] The regime met this challenge with a brutal crackdown, provok-ing a new phase of violent rebellion in the summer. Notably, this armed rebel-lion gathered much of its strength from defectors from the SAA who left with their weapons. Though some demonstrators since 2011 have tried to keep to nonvio-lent activism in the face of a brutal armed conflict, many groups of activists also started to take up arms in order to defend their neighborhoods against the re-gime's security forces. The regime only escalated. Throughout 2011, the conflict in the streets spiraled downward to a civil war.[15] Hundreds of thousands of sol-diers and civilians have died from the regime's poison gas and barrel bombs, rebel groups' improvised explosive devices and car bombs, and shelling and small-arms fire on all sides; millions have fled.[16]

Though at first it was common to talk about a war of two sides, the regime versus the FSA, from an early stage the FSA was more of an umbrella term for an ever-shifting array of highly autonomous armed groups without much central co-ordination. And throughout 2012 the conflict added ever more sides. In late 2011 and early 2012, JN emerged as al-Qaeda's arm in Syria. But in 2013, ISIS appeared and challenged for the leadership of the Salafi-jihadist movement in Syria. ISIS expanded dramatically over the next year in both Syria and Iraq, cap-turing a large swath of territory across the two countries before being steadily driven back over the course of late 2014 through 2018. Meanwhile, in the sum-mer of 2012 the regime's forces suddenly withdrew from much of the largely Kurd-ish north, and the YPG/YPJ stepped in to take its place. It quickly established it-self as the most significant mainly Kurdish armed group, though there have been many others.

Ultimately, then, this is a war of bewildering complexity, with hundreds of more-or-less autonomous armed groups at different times. Information about any one of these groups is very often fragmentary and unclear. In what follows, I ex-amine key characteristics of armed groups under five major headings reflecting the most important broad sides: the regime, an overall portrait of FSA-affiliated forces, JN, ISIS, and the YPG/YPJ. At the end of the chapter, I summarize and compare the different armed groups.

Regime Forces

Desertion in the SAA has posed an immense challenge to the Asad regime. Beginning with individual cases throughout 2011, in early 2012 desertion took off, though in ones and twos at a time rather than whole units.[17] By July 2014, about one hundred thousand soldiers had deserted from the Syrian military—that is, 40 percent of its prewar numbers.[18] Indeed, the regime so lacked for manpower that Asad admitted it publicly in July 2015 and amnestied deserters who had not joined the rebellion.[19] According to Bou Nassif, some three thousand of the fifty thousand to sixty thousand members of the officer corps defected.[20]

But while the regime's desertion and defection problem was by any estimate extremely severe, Asad still retained a determined and loyal core. This was critical to the regime's ability to fight on (though its support from Iran, Russia, and Hizbullah has probably been at least as important).[21] Notably, this loyal core staffed the SAA's elite units. These were at the center of the regime's military strategy, tasked with the defense and recapture of the crucial cities in western Syria while the regime abandoned much of the rest of the country.[22]

What, then, made elite units and most of the officer corps reliable while much of the army fell apart? The answer has a lot to do with very weak norms of cooperation in the latter. These weak norms proceeded from unmotivated recruits, but soldiers' lack of initial desire to fight for the regime does not seem to be a sufficient explanation. Instead, a deep mistrust of those same recruits, coercive tactics that created a warranted fear of arbitrary violence, and widespread, institutional corruption all reinforced the desire among ordinary soldiers to desert.

The bulk of the SAA relied on conscripts among its enlisted ranks. Even the regular conscription system had a difficult time meeting the regime's manpower needs, with many avoiding service through bribes, and with a growing fear of simply being sent to the front to die.[23] A portent of the regime's manpower problems was an amnesty for draft dodgers if they reported for duty, enacted in November 2011.[24] Over time, the regime resorted increasingly to open press-ganging raids (for example, rounding up young men who had gone to cafés to watch an FC Barcelona match in Latakia in December 2014).[25] In contrast, though some supposedly elite units like the Republican Guard evidently had significant numbers of conscripts among their ranks, others, like the Fourth Armored Division, were in the overwhelming majority career volunteers.[26] As for the officer corps, the regime selected recruits based on political reliability, increasingly so as the war has gone on; however, personal connections to the "right" figures were the critical criterion for admission and advancement.[27]

Reflecting the makeup of the population, most conscripts were Sunnis, while volunteers in the officer corps and in the elite units appear to have been mostly—and in some units, almost exclusively—Alawites. This was certainly the case in the Fourth Armored Division, which the regime relied on especially for its critical operations.[28] Alawites had long had a disproportionately large presence in the officer corps, notably in key positions. As the war dragged on, the officer corps became even more exclusively Alawite. Perhaps half of the Sunni officers left, while new officers were much more often Alawite than before the war.[29]

Conscription brought in unmotivated soldiers. In 2011 they became even more inclined to desert when they heard in surreptitious communication with their family and friends about demonstrations and the regime crackdown.[30] (Notably, in contrast, the army set up a closed world to members of the officer corps and their families, who often live in military neighborhoods.[31])

All this suggests that soldiers often had plenty of motivation as individuals to desert, reinforced by networks outside the army. However, this motivation appears to have been compounded by the interpersonal dynamics of trust, mistrust, and cooperation *within* the army as well. Many conscripts had little desire to fight and often attempted to get out of it, demonstrating very weak norms of cooperation. Soldiers often tried to avoid battles, bribing officers to get out of patrol duty.[32] Albrecht and Koehler, statistically analyzing the pattern of desertion among their interviewees, find that desertions were especially likely to occur in provinces and at times when the regime suffered a lot of casualties.[33]

Mistrust was even worse between conscripts as a group and the armed forces in general; conscripts had reason to doubt that the military as a whole would back them up if they chose to fight. Reflecting the reliance on elite, volunteer units and a mistrust of conscripts, conscript units got the oldest tanks and other equipment.[34] Corruption compounded these disparities. Corrupt practices were pervasive in the officer corps especially; its members earned a poor salary, and personal connections within the officer corps served as channels for regime patronage.[35] In other words, corruption was baked into how the officer corps went about recruiting and supporting its members. The result was even worse equipment and conditions of service for soldiers. For example, Major Iyad Jabra of Air Defense claimed that commanders bribed military inspectors to write reports papering over badly maintained equipment.[36] These factors undermined the willingness to fight among conscripts, according to officers interviewed by Hicham Bou Nassif. In the words of one such officer:

> I have always been convinced that if there would ever be war with Israel, soldiers on the front would run away, rather than actually fight.

Soldiers know that their tanks can barely move, that their armament is inadequate, and that generals steal sums allocated for food.

Some senior officers can be bought with a packet of cigarettes. Do you think soldiers would fight and die for such generals, if they are sent into battle?[37]

In other words, soldiers and especially conscripts had little reason to put in much effort given that their contributions would not be matched by those of their officers—far from norms of mutual obligation and effort.

Even worse, conscripts were often suspected of sympathy with the opposition, putting them in grave danger. According to Ra'ed, a conscript in the Republican Guard, "Some conscripts that are not trusted are issued rifles, with no ammunition. . . . I was one of them. I was given a Kalashnikov rifle, but no bullets. Some conscripts who are considered troublemakers are just issued sticks."[38] Activists feared that their political opinions would be held against them if they obeyed the draft call, and that they would be sent to the front as cannon fodder.[39]

During the war, as well, sectarianism increasingly motivated mistrust between Sunni and Alawite recruits. At the beginning of the war, many of the Sunni conscripts interviewed by Ohl and colleagues emphasized their friendships with other members of their units, including across sectarian lines. However, they began to identify more closely with coreligionists as time went on.[40] Sunni officers, as well, long resented preferential treatment for their Alawite colleagues. According to Bou Nassif's interviewees, friendships among Sunni and Alawite officers were exceptional, though they did occur.[41] This should not be taken too far; according to Khaddour, there were social divisions among Alawites more profound than those separating Sunni and Alawite officers. But the sense of social solidarity among officers did not, for Khaddour, suffice to remove religion from the picture.[42]

With many suspect soldiers and officers, the regime relied to an important degree on coercion to prevent desertion and defection. During the war the regime added to the surveillance networks parallel to the chain of command, and officers deeply feared informants in their units. It also invested in its ability to detect desertions after the fact, establishing a system to communicate names of deserters to checkpoints across the country.[43] These measures did help prevent attempts to desert; deserters had to plan their moments of escape very carefully, often did not coordinate with others for fear of letting something slip to a regime agent, and relied on outside networks to get past surveillance.[44]

However, the regime's efforts at coercive control appear also to have often backfired. Coercion often seemed arbitrary: soldiers and officers suffered penalties, including arrest and imprisonment in the regime's feared jails, on a suspicion of disloyalty falling far short of actual attempts to desert. Soldiers felt that every move was under surveillance and any step out of line—such as failing to show indignation toward the rebels when watching TV reports—could lead to arrest.[45] Sunnis in the officer corps had to very publicly display their adherence to the regime to avoid consequences.[46] They even had to hide their religious practices to avoid arousing suspicions. As one officer reported, "I always avoided parking my car in the vicinity of mosques, just to be on the safe side."[47] The regime's coercive efforts, indeed, took on a clear sectarian cast: in both the rank and file and officer corps, Alawites were often feared as especially likely to be regime agents.[48] Ultimately, the portrait that emerges is of soldiers caught between the deterrent and provocation effects: fearing punishment even if they did not try to desert, but fearing the even greater probability of punishment if they did.

Though many soldiers had a strong inclination to desert, they rarely coordinated to do so. However, this was often not by choice; they assessed their ability to desert with others but concluded they could not. The fear of regime agents persuaded prospective deserters to keep their heads down, falsifying their preferences.[49] But some prospective deserters came to trust that fellow soldiers were of a similar mind. Again, as time wore on in the war, such trust could take a sectarian cast: "Most of the people in my unit were Sunnis. You know what that means. You can trust them somehow; they were all with the revolution."[50] In other cases, prospective deserters could tell others their plans and, even if this did not induce others to join, the deserter could at least anticipate that the others would not turn them in.[51]

Although it was hard for deserters to work together, they still followed the example of others. An artillery soldier from Idlib explains how these cascades of opposition could overcome the regime's ability to coerce compliance:

> At first, to abandon my station seemed a crazy idea. Our officers were watching us very closely and wouldn't hesitate to hit us. We had no contact with the outside world. We were given the coordinates of positions to shell and that was it. But gradually, there were more and more refusals to obey orders. I sabotaged our shells so they didn't explode when they forced us to shell a village. In September [2012], I realized that out of 1,500 men in my brigade, only a thousand were left, the others had deserted. I decided to do the same.[52]

Alongside regime losses, these relational processes may help explain why the desertion problem steadily got worse from the outset of the conflict and crested in 2012, as norms further broke down, soldiers pushed each other to desert, and the regime's mistrust of its soldiers only mounted.[53] In other words, the regime could perhaps have had a less severe desertion problem had it invested in the regular force, fought corruption in recruitment and promotion of officers, and exercised greater restraint in surveillance and control so that mere suspicion was not enough to punish a soldier. But many of the soldiers may have deserted anyway, while military corruption and the surveillance state were how the regime built support and clamped down on dissent. It is therefore difficult to think it could have been much different.

At the same time, however, the SAA reflected patterns that go beyond this book's hypotheses. The regime's military experience also suggests that the dynamics of trust extend to relationships outside the armed group. This is notably the case in the key role that soldiers' families played in facilitating their desertion, as Koehler, Albrecht, and Ohl's interviews showed. Mistrust extends outside the armed group as well. Notably, it seems clear that many Alawite soldiers have remained fighting for the regime not out of a strong attachment to it but out of fear that other factions would target them even if they deserted, defected, or surrendered.[54] In other words, the stereotypes that helped push some Sunnis to desert also helped keep some Alawites fighting.

The Free Syrian Army Umbrella

It is hard to say the FSA was ever a coherent fighting force; rather, it was a disparate gathering of many different groups. Samer Abboud describes two types of outfit under the FSA banner. First were small, highly localized groups getting some resources from the FSA command and nominally coordinated by fourteen provincial Military Councils united under a General Command, though these local units operated highly autonomously. Second, larger brigades typically had their own external sponsors and were much more mobile, operating across regions.[55] Many of these brigades broke away from the FSA over time or started independently of it, and groups added or dropped the FSA label according to local circumstances.[56] It is difficult to estimate the number of groups claiming an affiliation with the FSA, let alone the number of fighters. It was, in short, a thoroughly decentralized and loose militant network. In important ways, then, the FSA has resembled the disorganized militias of Spain in 1936, though with worse coordination and even more extensive infighting.[57] In this context, I discuss above all the desertion of individuals and small groups rather than the bewildering array of changes in alignment of whole groups, which are better treated in terms of alliances rather than desertion.

FSA-affiliated units dominated in the armed Syrian opposition in 2011 and the first part of 2012, and thus deserve their share of credit for the effective resistance kept up against an intense repression campaign. Beginning in 2013, however, and ramping up over the next two years, units under the FSA umbrella started to experience a growing wave of defection to other forces such as JN and ISIS,

and of fighters leaving combat entirely. This included not only whole units changing camp but also individuals and small groups leaving. Indeed, some FSA units
dissolved altogether.[58] In Aleppo, different FSA fighters estimated a desertion rate
of 50 percent in 2014 and 2015.[59]

FSA units built on preexisting network ties to an important degree. Civilians
joined on the basis of political networks like groups of activists, and more personal networks of family and friends; frequently, these groups had demonstrated
in the spring of 2011 and then, as the crackdown continued and worsened, took
up arms to defend a neighborhood.[60] As noted, regime defectors themselves depended on their own network ties to get out and join the FSA; these ties provided
an immediate link to opposition activists or to people within the FSA.[61]

What did these ties mean for the signals that FSA fighters sent each other? Joining demonstrations and defecting from the regime armed forces certainly implied grave risks, so joining indicated a willingness to sacrifice for the sake of opposing the Asad regime. On the other hand, the often arbitrary character of
coercion within the government armed forces that I noted above, and the highly
indiscriminate nature of the regime's bombardments of neighborhoods and villages with strong pro-opposition sentiment, increased the risks of *not* joining the
opposition and the armed rebellion.[62] While the regime's crimes provided a strong
motivation to many to oppose the regime, it may also have meant that FSA fighters were looking above all to survive. Further, the demonstrations themselves had
clear cascade dynamics, as people who had never participated in opposition actions joined these demonstrations because others were as well. Many hoped that
mass action could provoke a regime breakdown as in Tunisia or Egypt, or robust
external military intervention as in Libya, and hence help bring down Asad. So
demonstrating did not mean that an individual was prepared to take the special
risks and costs that attend on fighting for a long period of time, in addition to
the moral and strategic objections that many activists raised against the turn to
armed uprising. Many demonstrators therefore hesitated strongly about fighting,
taking up arms only because they felt that they had no choice, rather than because
they were really prepared for soldiering.

FSA units recruited voluntarily, on the whole, but the requirements were not
high compared with those of other groups. Recruitment was quite open, and for
some time rebel groups were vulnerable to infiltrators from the regime.[63] Training was highly variable, with some larger groups setting up training camps in the
countryside while others had very little instruction; and there is little evidence,
one way or another, as to how often training has been used as a screening or signaling device.[64] In local FSA units, fighters were often essentially part time, staying
at home and joining for operations, without uniforms, rather than submitting to
tight discipline.[65]

Finally, it is critical to underline the importance of money across much of the armed opposition. In a stagnant economy further devastated by war, the wage that armed groups could often (though not always) pay became increasingly attractive, including for army deserters who would have particular trouble working.[66] Moreover, as the war wore on, armed groups began to control the oil and grain trades in much of Syria, and to gain financing from transnational networks. This gave them cash to recruit and arm fighters, and meant that economic incentives came to be more important for recruitment to various armed groups in late 2012 and 2013.[67] As noted, some of the brigades that emerged with outside financing did so under the FSA umbrella, even if many did not. Hence, according to Abu Suleiman, an FSA commander in Manbij, "When we first raised arms, we had only five Kalashnikovs between us and we got around on motorbikes, but at least the people had respect for us. . . . Now, 70 percent of those who say they are in the Free Syrian Army haven't even been to the front line," occupied instead with profiteering.[68]

At the same time, the central organization of the FSA lost out on the competition for financing, pursuing American and other Western backing that did not materialize to the extent hoped for, even after various largely unsuccessful attempts to unite and provide greater structure and hierarchy in order to respond to American demands. Saudi Arabia and Qatar began funding units outside this structure, in competition with each other. Private financiers also bypassed the FSA.[69] Over time, then, the official FSA umbrella could not provide its troops with wages or military supplies to nearly the same degree as other groups.

In this context, the principal motivation for desertion in interviews by Mironova, Mrie, and Whitt conducted in 2014 was the belief that it was impossible to win. A clear majority of deserters mentioned this, and almost half said it was their main reason.[70] The sense of futility had several sources, some of which correspond to my relational account, others less so. Having joined up on the basis of popular demonstrations in the hope that this was a revolutionary moment that could, in a cascade, bring down the Asad regime, many were left frustrated by the long-haul war that emerged, and that they thought they would likely lose.[71] Hence if they had signaled their willingness to take to the streets against Asad, they had not necessarily shown a willingness to fight a war. Deserters frequently cited a lack of discipline in their armed groups as a principal reason to leave.[72] One key reason for changing brigades was a sense that others in the old group lacked motivation.[73] Financing issues also emerged here, diminishing the sense of collective action. Well-motivated, committed fighters whose priority was overthrowing Asad rather than earning a wage became deeply embittered at the corruption of others. A strong sense built up over time among many FSA fighters that the senior FSA leadership especially was corrupt, interested only in its own material gain, and that competition over profit centers like checkpoints and oilfields had come to be more important than fighting Asad.[74] Moreover, fighters who changed groups often did so with their friends, suggesting that as the motivation to keep fighting for one group diminished, fighters would still draw on their more purely social trust to desert together.[75]

At the same time, other dynamics appear to have influenced the sense of futility. The first was simply a lack of funds. Fighters passed from the weakening FSA to groups that could pay a wage, whether in run-of-the-mill brigades or larger outfits like JN and ISIS.[76] A lack of wages pushed others to abandon the fighting altogether.[77] Further, the decline in financing for many FSA groups simply left them without arms and ammunition.[78] Similarly, fighters often changed groups out of a sense that their own was poorly organized—it did not take care of its fighters, for example, or it lost battles too frequently.[79] Finally, external agendas in the civil war, and the lack of commitment from the United States especially, left FSA fighters with the sense that what had started as *their* revolution was now a bloody battlefield for regional and global powers.[80]

Importantly, then, desertion from the FSA often had to do with a failure of collective action, and often did not. For many, it was futile to continue to fight because their contributions were being let down by indiscipline or by the cynicism of commanders and other fighters on the take. These explanations for desertion reflect the relational approach's concern for trust and cooperation among combatants. But on the other hand, for many it was above all a lack of bullets, not a lack of solidarity, that ended their participation in the FSA.

A deeper look at the FSA deserters reflects these different explanations. While around 70 percent of both current FSA fighters and deserters said that defeating Asad was an important initial motivation for themselves, only 44 percent of deserters thought it was important for most other FSA fighters—suggesting a suspicion of others' motives. But these deserters were far from fully cynical: they still thought that others had joined for collective aims like community defense (67%) or the armed group's goals (70%), or at least for expressive motivations like revenge against Asad (81%); these are comparable numbers to the self-reported motivations of both current fighters and deserters. Moreover, deserters were highly likely to cite social motivations like inspiration from others and joining because all their friends had joined (93% each)—much more so, in fact, than current fighters (54% and 51%, respectively).[81] The portrait that emerges, then, is one of fighters who joined the cascade of the revolution and then either did not want to carry on as the war dragged through its bloody course or would have continued but for a lack of trust in others or a lack of weapons. Norms of cooperation, and their lack, thus played an important role in why the FSA fell apart, but norms may also not have sufficed to keep it going without supplies. The desertion rate in the

FSA was therefore considerably higher than my approach would have expected based on the factors I focus on.

Jabhat al-Nusra

In contrast to the FSA, Jabhat al-Nusra, al-Qaeda's longtime affiliate in Syria, enjoyed possibly the most consistent military effectiveness of any rebel group in the conflict. It proved especially cohesive, and as my approach expects, this cohesion derived from JN's norms of cooperation. On the other hand, JN lost perhaps half its fighters in 2013 when the Islamic State in Iraq (ISI), out of which JN had emerged, changed its name to ISIS and tried to take over operations from JN. This major factional divide has had far-reaching consequences. The rupture itself, treated as a breakdown of an alliance from the top down, does not enter this book's remit of the day-to-day of desertion and loyalty directly, except insofar as it shaped trust and mistrust among ordinary fighters.

JN's leader, Abu Mohammed al-Jolani, crossed the border from Iraq in August 2011 on orders from the ISI and its leader, Abu Bakr al-Baghdadi. Jolani founded JN in October of that year, and the group conducted its first attack, a suicide bombing in Damascus, in December. Throughout the spring of 2012, JN grew patiently, conducting terrorist attacks at a slow pace. However, over time it shifted to guerrilla and conventional warfare at a larger scale, often in conjunction with other groups. It eventually numbered five thousand by about 2013, and ten thousand by 2016.[82] In July 2016 it changed its name to Jabhat Fatah al-Sham and formally dissolved its link to al-Qaeda, and in early 2017 it merged with other jihadist groups into Hay'at Tahrir al-Sham.

There is consensus about JN's battlefield effectiveness.[83] For example, from the autumn of 2012 to the spring of 2013, its participation was vital to a series of rebel victories against the regime, even though it was considerably smaller than the FSA.[84] While effectiveness is not the same thing as a lack of desertion, and I have encountered no comparative estimates of desertion specifically, JN's effectiveness does seem based, among other factors, on a willingness to fight rather than run away. JN fighters gained a reputation for courage in combat. They made a notable contribution to the battle to control Aleppo in late 2012 alongside other factions, with FSA officers praising JN fighters for their bravery, though this sentiment is far from universal in the FSA.[85] In combat they have served as an elite force in alliance with other factions, drawing on their combatants' motivation as well as on their tactical expertise, according to Charles Lister.[86] Notably, JN units show evidence of strong interpersonal norms of self-sacrifice, alongside relatively good supply. According to an FSA commander near Aleppo, "Al-Nusra fighters rarely withdraw for shortage of ammunition or fighters and they leave their target only after liberating it. . . . They compete to carry out martyrdom [suicide] operations."[87] Mironova, Mrie, and Whitt's interviews with Islamist fighters and deserters—including members of Ahrar al-Sham alongside JN, meaning that these numbers should be taken with a grain of salt—reveal interesting differences among fighters and deserters about their perceptions of the motivations of the other members of their groups.[88] While deserters and active fighters alike agreed that their compatriots often had political motivations like defeating Asad and defending their communities, deserters were on the whole more cynical about their compatriots. Many more deserters than active fighters thought other members of their group had joined for money (29.8% vs. zero) and family pressure (19.2% vs. 8%) while far fewer deserters than active fighters (14.4% to 85%) thought their comrades supported the goals of the group specifically.[89] Deserters, therefore, seem to have had less trust in their compatriots than did soldiers who kept on fighting.

The overall norm of sacrifice in JN corresponds with, and may be related to, military practices emphasizing strong signals of commitment. JN's recruitment patterns favored motivated combatants over sheer numbers. They did so in two ways, each of which would have provided clear information to serve as the basis for trust: building on network ties and insisting on costly signals of commitment from new recruits. Before the war there had been jihadist networks in Syria; indeed, for a time they were supported by the regime to fight in Iraq against the American occupation. Beginning in March 2011, the regime released numerous jihadist prisoners, supposedly as a conciliatory gesture but widely seen as a way to paint the opposition as extremist and thereby broadcast the regime's narrative of the conflict internationally. The jihadist networks and freed prisoners started to form cells in Syria, which JN then set about coordinating.[90] From the beginning, then, JN drew on interpersonal ties forged in political conflict. As it expanded, soon after its first attacks, JN maintained a network approach.[91] It insisted on a personal recommendation or *tazqiyya* from at least one current JN member, with two exceptions: members of smaller allied groups could request a transfer to JN, which was done with mutual agreement of commanders; and JN absorbed and kept intact other groups that had formed independently.[92]

New recruits also had to signal their commitment. Fighters went through a training program including military and religious instruction. Estimates vary about the length of training, ranging from one month to six to eight weeks to several months.[93] Newly trained fighters had to then demonstrate their commitment in combat in an explicit process of evaluation.[94] JN also maintained a strict code of conduct.[95] It was relatively well financed—from oil and gas fields, from ISI initially, and, after the split in April 2013 caused the withdrawal of its support and an ISIS takeover of much of its oil and gas resources, from Turkey, the Gulf, and the spoils of its military success.[96] It built on these resources to attract recruits by outbidding other groups for wages.[97] However, JN had a reputation for being less corrupt than other groups and for centrally directing the resources it obtains.[98] So, while fighters could certainly earn a better wage in JN than in other units, it would have been comparatively difficult to profit greatly from one's JN affiliation. On the whole, then, recruits often self-selected for a demanding military experience, and those who were not ready for it could find other groups to join. Just as in the Fifth Regiment militias in Republican Spain, some fighters joined JN accepting that it would entail strict limits on their behavior, while others left and joined other groups to be able to come and go more easily.[99]

Despite this general picture of commitment in JN reinforcing norms of cooperation, there is a damaging factional rift between foreign fighters and Syrians. With its origins in the ISI, next door in Iraq, and its links to al-Qaeda, JN's leaders feared incurring a reputation as an outside actor seeking to impose its will in Syria. To embed itself more successfully and gain local support, JN worked closely with many other local armed groups in its military operations, delivered civilian services like bread, utilities, and health care, governed locally in cooperation with other groups, and did not openly state the ISI linkage until the ISIS split forced it to in 2013.[100] JN focused its recruitment on Syrians, who have made up the majority; estimates range from 60 to 80 percent.[101] Sensitive to its interactions with civilians and other armed groups, JN has actively discouraged its foreign fighters from joining the religious police and combat commands.[102] The leadership has thus long been conscious of an important distinction between Syrians and others.

Tensions between the Syrian and transnational bloc, which Gerges calls "the basic fault line within al-Nusra," underlay the rift with ISIS in 2013. On a few occasions in late 2012 and early 2013, Jolani refused Baghdadi's demand to openly declare JN's links to ISI, which would make it more difficult for JN to operate with its embedded networks in Syria and force it to rely more heavily on its Iraqi patrons. On April 8, 2013, after JN had foiled a project by ISI to attack the FSA, al-Baghdadi made the link public and announced that JN would now be folded into a new, expanded ISI, to be called ISIS. Jolani refused this rearrangement and instead declared his loyalty to al-Qaeda leader Ayman al-Zawahiri. JN split in two over the issue, from the top down. ISI having worked within JN ranks to build up loyalists, Lister estimates that over half of JN's personnel defected to ISIS.[103] Many of these defectors appear, indeed, to have been the foreigners in JN, while its Syrian forces were more likely to remain in JN.[104] But non-Syrians have continued to have an important presence in JN, and the tension has endured; according to Gerges, Jolani has continued to be preoccupied with defection of foreign fighters, one reason he resisted breaking JN's formal affiliation with al-Qaeda Central until July 2016.[105] The bulk of the disloyalty problem in JN, then, has been due above all to an elite split (which my approach does not attempt to explain) involving many fighters, but the lingering divide between Syrians and others has represented a check on the general sense of norms of cooperation and trust within JN. My approach would expect this source of mistrust to increase the likelihood of desertion on an everyday basis by impeding the cooperation between Syrian soldiers and others, but I have not found any confirmation of this.

Islamic State in Iraq and al-Sham

Perhaps unsurprisingly for an armed group with tight links initially to JN, ISIS's military approach was in many ways similar. But it differed in some key respects. ISIS drew on similar means of communicating a willingness to fight, in which it built on network ties and costly signals, and it experienced similar mistrust among Syrian and foreign fighters. At the same time, ISIS did not maintain selective recruitment over time. Instead it attracted fighters through its success and through economic pressure, and eventually resorted to conscription. Its extreme brutality deterred many potential deserters but provoked others, both implicating them in horrific crimes and leading them to fear arbitrary violence within the group. Hence, its spectacular expansion was to an important degree short-run. While it was able to put up tenacious resistance as it began to lose ground, its morale collapsed over time, hastening its battlefield demise.

ISIS was, at its peak, considerably larger than JN, commanding tens of thousands of troops.[106] After its emergence from the ISI and its split from al-Qaeda in 2013, ISIS rapidly gained control over a huge swath of territory from northwestern Syria to central Iraq, establishing a capital in Raqqa in Syria and proclaiming a "caliphate" in June 2014 after it took Mosul, Iraq. ISIS quickly became the focus of regional and international intervention in the Middle East, with its destabilizing conquests, revolutionary message, franchising to incorporate Salafi-jihadist movements from Nigeria to Southeast Asia, recruitment and inspiration of terrorists around the world, and with the sheer brutality of the physical and sexual violence it committed. From 2015 to 2018, a wide array of adversaries with their own conflicts among each other steadily pushed ISIS out of its territorial possessions in Iraq and Syria.

Among ISIS's key advantages over many of its opponents in 2013 and 2014 was a clear edge in cohesion, most glaringly when Iraqi army units broke and ran from Mosul in the face of a much smaller ISIS force in June 2014. In the face of its defeats, it maintained effective resistance and fought doggedly in late 2014 and 2015.[107] Correspondingly, there are reports of relatively strong mutual commitments at this time: according to Gerges, both combatants and commanders "fight side by side and die side by side, which explains a high rate of casualties among regional commanders who lead the charge in battles."[108] Even an ISIS defector reported that "ISIS members support each other to the death. The others are not like that."[109] However, even at this point it was losing some fighters to defection and desertion, beginning in early 2014 and gathering pace in 2015.[110] By the spring of 2016, U.S. military sources were reporting increasing rates of both desertion and malingering; by the autumn of 2017, as ISIS lost Raqqa, desertion appeared to be further on the increase.[111] Ultimately, if ISIS does not appear to have witnessed the mass desertion of the Syrian army or FSA groups, it did seem to have a much higher desertion rate than JN as time went on.

ISIS's recruitment methods resembled those of JN. ISIS drew on prewar jihadist networks, notably among prisoners in U.S.-occupied Iraq and in Syria. New fighters in 2013 and 2014 required vouching from an existing member.[112] They also sent clear costly signals, submitting to several weeks each of military training and of religious instruction that emphasized obedience to religious authorities. According to different reports, new fighters had to personally execute a prisoner, serve on guard duty, or serve at the front at the end of their training period.[113] ISIS also implemented two levels of commitment, permitting another signal: fighting with the group without joining it, and pledging lifetime allegiance on pain of death if the fighter leaves (a decision that brings more money and status to the fighter).[114]

At the same time, ISIS was more vulnerable than JN to opportunists. While many joined ISIS out of ideological attachment and a sense of belonging or valorized identity, many self-interested motives drove recruitment too.[115] As ISIS expanded rapidly, the prospect of joining a winning side helped attract new recruits and defectors.[116] So did ISIS's ability to pay high salaries and, flush with cash from oil, to do so consistently; it could outbid JN, to say nothing of FSA groups. After two and three years of war, with ever-increasing hardships, these factors weighed heavily.[117] And, especially horribly, ISIS appealed to some new recruits through the chance to commit rape.[118]

But on the other hand, ISIS imposed costly signals and norms of obedience. To an important degree, this meant that, as in JN, even self-interested recruits had to signal a commitment to fight. However, many appeared to join in order to escape from ISIS repression, and others were forced to fight, cutting against this interpretation. Not only did increasing poverty drive some men into ISIS in search of the stable salaries it offered, but ISIS itself accentuated this dynamic by levying high rates of taxes and limiting access to resources among families without a member who was fighting.[119] A similar process occurred among the defectors it recruited from other groups. ISIS theoretically insisted on costly signals to some degree by accepting only those defectors who "repented" outside of the context of a battle, but defectors from other groups who eventually left ISIS still reported defecting out of fear that they would be killed because of their earlier affiliations.[120] This points to a major difference between ISIS and JN. While JN continually worked with other opposition groups as a conscious strategy, ISIS rarely did so, instead always attempting to assert its own primacy over other groups.[121] It was therefore not possible to benefit from an association with ISIS while still retaining membership in another group, as it was with JN. ISIS insisted that people choose. This would have weakened the motivations of its resulting membership, since many seem to have chosen ISIS out of intimidation and to join a winner. Once ISIS started losing and stopped being able to pay, then, these self-selection dynamics may well have worked against it. Finally, as it ran into increasing problems in recruitment over 2015 and 2016, ISIS began to resort to conscription in areas it controlled.[122]

In general, then, the signals ISIS fighters sent each other were therefore less evident than in the case of JN. Perhaps corresponding to a diminished sense of loyalty among fighters, severe mistrust emerged around combat: fighters felt that going to the front was a way for leaders to get rid of combatants they did not like. Having to fight while others held back was a principal motif, indeed, in ISIS defectors' narratives.[123]

Overlaid on this were tensions among national contingents. Groups of fighters from outside Syria and Iraq often acted together within ISIS, maintaining distinct subgroups based on language.[124] This should, by the lights of my approach, have reinforced norms of cooperation *within* these units, but tensions among national contingents cut against this trust. Syrian and Iraqi troops resented foreign fighters. The latter were given greater incentives to join, seemingly had lower training standards, and, according to Syrians and Iraqis, were sent to the front less often. Additionally, Syrians and Iraqis often thought that they should be the ones to govern ISIS's territory in their countries.[125] Deserters therefore often cited this resentment of and lack of cooperation with other national groups. Interestingly, both locals and foreign fighters who deserted reported that they were the ones to be used as cannon fodder.[126]

With fighters having several motivations to defect, ISIS used its brutal coercive methods to keep members fighting. It created blocking detachments to prevent desertion, for example.[127] ISIS considered desertion to be apostasy and punished it with death and reprisals against the deserter's family, enforced by its internal security police. These measures have effectively intimidated fighters from attempting to desert.[128] Here, however, ISIS's shocking violence also backfired. Defectors have said they had left for fear that the leadership's spies would denounce them maliciously and arbitrarily, and that they would be killed in short order.[129]

ISIS's policies therefore pointed in different directions when it comes to trust and norms. While ISIS insisted on costly signals of obedience and willingness to fight in some regards, the intense pressure it put on individuals to join, its insistence on its own supremacy, and its vicious violence left it with plenty of uncommitted and mistrustful fighters, reinforced by mistrust among national contingents. Correspondingly, it experienced more frequent desertions than other jihadist groups, particularly as time went on.

The People's Protection Units (YPG) and Women's Protection Units (YPJ)

The YPG and YPJ together constitute the largest Kurdish force in the Syrian Civil War, with thirty-five thousand fighters claimed in 2013 and sixty thousand by the end of 2016.[130] Though claiming to be independent, the YPG/YPJ retains a close association with the Partiya Yekîtiya Demokrat (PYD) or Democratic Unity Party, an affiliate of the Kurdistan Workers' Party (Partiya Karkerên Kurdistanê, PKK), the primary Kurdish militant group in Turkey.[131] In July 2012, the YPG/YPJ established its control over Rojava or western Kurdistan when the regime suddenly pulled most of its forces out of northern Syria to focus on the core of the country.[132] Since then, the YPG/YPJ has fought regime forces remarkably little but has had major clashes with ISIS, JN, FSA affiliates, and other Kurdish groups.[133] It has formed the lion's share of the Syrian Democratic Forces (SDF), the principal American on-the-ground ally against ISIS.[134]

These battles established the YPG/YPJ as a relatively effective force. There is some disagreement about its tactical prowess, but general consensus on the YPG/YPJ's cohesion.[135] This was on display most clearly in its effective defense against an ISIS siege in Kobane in late 2014 and early 2015. The fact that its fighters carried on resisting rather than fleeing to the nearby Turkish border with the civilian population testifies to an impressive ability to prevent desertion. Digging in and fighting ISIS house to house, the YPG/YPJ bought crucial time for U.S.-led coalition airstrikes to begin.[136] It then played an important role in offensives taking cities from ISIS with the SDF.[137] However, at the same time, there are reports of defection and desertion among Arab members of the SDF, notably among conscripts, including in 2017 as the SDF was scoring considerable victories against ISIS.[138] Still, the bulk of the YPG/YPJ was able to fight hard with limited desertion.

This ability seems based, to an important degree, on interpersonal norms: outside observers commented on the commitment that fighters displayed to each other and their willingness for self-sacrifice.[139] In turn, these norms of cooperation correspond—just as in JN and ISIS—to preexisting networks and to costly signaling in recruitment. The PKK had operated out of Syria and had recruited thousands of Syrian Kurds for its insurgency in Turkey in the 1980s and 1990s, though Syria shut down the PKK's camps and expelled its leader Abdullah Öcalan in 1998. The PYD itself was founded in 2003 alongside other PKK-organized civil society organizations and retained close ties to the PKK.[140] The PYD founded the YPG militia in 2007, keeping its fighters outside the country in Qandil in northern Iraq.[141] While the PYD had perhaps a greater potential to mobilize the civilian population than the old political parties that had existed in one form or another since 1957, the regime's repression limited its presence.[142] In the spring of 2011, however, around a thousand fighters affiliated with the PKK and YPG came from northern Iraq at about the same time as Salih Muslim, the key PYD leader, and began establishing the YPG more strongly in Syria.[143] Its women's militia, the YPJ, was founded in 2012.

As it expanded, the YPG/YPJ established relatively strong standards for new recruits. The YPG/YPJ fighters themselves were recruited on a voluntary basis.[144] Training lasted only fifteen days at the end of 2013, but this eventually increased to three months at the beginning of 2014 and included military and political components.[145] Recruits had to sign on to strict discipline and an austere, demanding military life.[146] However, these standards were not applied consistently. With a very large front line, the YPG/YPJ often delegated recruitment to local commanders, leading to the recruitment of child soldiers in some places, and to a relaxation of training when under pressure.[147]

In July 2014 a conscription law was passed in Rojava (though there are reports of forced recruitment earlier). This law was enforced by the PYD's internal security service, the Asayish, on pain of prison.[148] Conscripts received forty-five days of training and then served for nine months in the so-called Self-Defense Forces. They were tasked officially with guard, checkpoint, and logistical duty, with the idea of freeing the YPG/YPJ and its volunteers for actual combat.[149] Conscripts also fought, in early 2017, though reportedly selection for combat duty among conscripts was voluntary.[150]

In general, conscription provoked resentment of the PYD, reinforcing divides with other factions in northern Syria. Indeed the PYD did not enjoy unanimous support in Rojava, far from it; other Kurdish factions rallied together under the banner of the Kurdish National Council, supported by the Kurdistan Regional Government in Iraq, and the two groups have fought. The PYD claimed Rojava to be a common project across parties, but the PYD dominated local government, Rojava checkpoints flew the PYD flag, and the Asayish was often seen as acting for the PYD.[151] This generated resentment and fear and a willingness to hide one's true motives. An activist from the Future movement claimed, "If one of their fighters dies, we go to the funeral. Everybody does. If you don't go, you show that you are against them. We are afraid to show that we are against the PYD."[152]

Another axis of discord was mistrust across Kurdish/Arab lines. The YPG/YPJ was not wholly Kurdish, having recruited non-Kurdish fighters in separate brigades.[153] Moreover, the YPG/YPJ worked with other, predominantly Arab groups, and increasingly so as time went on. With the Syrian National Council having refused to recognize a Kurdish right to self-government, relations between the YPG/YPJ and the FSA were often fraught, including armed clashes. However, from time to time the YPG/YPJ and FSA fighters worked together against ISIS. For example, after failed FSA offensives in Raqqa and Aleppo, some FSA fighters retreated to Kobane and then fought alongside YPG/YPJ personnel in some joint operations. They left decidedly mixed impressions of their ability to trust each other.[154] SDF offensives into ISIS-held territory, such as Manbij, put Arab fighters in a leading role.[155] However, ethnic tensions still ran high. The YPG/YPJ is accused of human rights abuses in Arab towns under its control. Many Arab residents of SDF-occupied territory were concerned about arbitrary detention by the Asayish in particular. The recruitment of Arabs to the Asayish was often regarded as too little; the impression was that "the Arab recruits have no authority."[156] The apparently high rate of desertion and defection of Arab members of the SDF may well be linked to this general mistrust along identity lines.

Thus, there is mixed evidence about the sources of trust and mistrust in the YPG/YPJ: on the one hand, a core built on network ties and costly signals; but on the other, the use of conscripts and considerable pressure to join despite factional and identity differences. Notably, the PYD's internal security apparatus, considered by many observers to have a very high degree of surveillance and enforcement capacity, sometimes reinforced these divides.

In broad strokes, then, the differences in armed groups' rates of desertion corresponded to how they recruited, managed, and controlled their fighters, and thus to conditions of mutual trust and mistrust within them. The most effective groups—JN, the YPG/YPJ, elite regime forces, and ISIS in its early years—used voluntary, typically networked recruitment and relatively demanding terms of service, while groups most prone to desertion either conscripted (as with the bulk of the regime forces and ISIS eventually) or did not demand strong signals of a willingness to fight over the long haul through rigorous vetting and training (as in FSA-affiliated units). Corrupt practices, profiting at the expense of military success, further reinforced the sense of the futility of fighting in the regime and FSA. Finally, the widespread, brutal violence enacted by the regime and by ISIS on their own troops both kept some troops fighting and provoked others to desert in order to get away from the threat. Interviews and surveys give a portrait, from within the armed groups, of the critical relational character of trust, in which trust is self-reinforcing and mistrust is too: combatants looked to each other and to their commanders to figure out whether fighting was worth it, and armed group leaders who mistrusted their combatants could, as in the regime forces, threaten them with arbitrary violence that only made mistrust worse.

On the whole, these are the same mechanisms of desertion that I found in Spain in the previous chapters, with resentment at corruption and war profiteering playing perhaps a more prominent role in Syria. These findings suggest that the trust/mistrust approach can help analysts understand conflicts well outside of the Spanish Civil War. Understanding desertion and cohesion in armed groups in contemporary conflicts requires a sense of the factors that can underlie interpersonal trust: the activist networks and recruitment and training practices that help soldiers signal their commitment to each other, the stereotypes and factionalism that can generate mistrust, and the coercion practices that can overcome some problems of mistrust but not all.

But this does not exhaust the necessary analytical tools. First, the relational approach does not examine key, basic issues in desertion like whether the army can keep its wages paid and its soldiers supplied with food and ammunition. Just as with hunger in Republican Spain, this was a critical factor in desertion in the FSA. Desertion appears to have been at least as high in the FSA as in the regime regular army, with whole units dissolving in some instances, and this is *not* as my approach would predict; on the basis of the factors that I identify, it should have been lower since I do not have much evidence of provocative violence taking place within FSA units. Second, my approach does not much consider the problems of mistrust between an armed group and prospective deserters or defectors in a *different* armed group, such as the fear of being singled out for their identity that seems to have kept a number of Alawite SAA soldiers loyal despite exhaustion and frustration with the Asad regime.[157]

With these caveats in mind, this chapter shows that the trust and mistrust approach to desertion can shed new light on armed groups in Syria's civil war. First, much work on armed groups in Syria focuses on high-level alliances and splits. But armed groups also crumbled from the inside. A focus on trust shows us how. Second, analyses of Syria's armed groups and their effectiveness have tended to focus on macro-level factors such as financing, foreign patrons, and ideology. In contrast, this chapter shows that the micro level of interpersonal relationships of trust and mistrust, which in turn are shaped by the armed group's organizational practices, had a major impact on cohesion and effectiveness.

One important way in which these organizations differed, particularly on the rebel side, was in their attention to the short and the long term of fighting a war.

It is no accident that the most cohesive armed organizations were those that had roots in armed groups *before* the war: JN and the early ISIS in their roots in jihadist networks from both Iraq and Syria, and the YPG/YPJ with its PKK connection. In each case, long-running militant groups provided doctrinal models about how to run an insurgency, whether Salafi-jihadist theorists or the PKK and its Marxist-Leninist tradition. These groups had prepared for a *war*, and could recruit militants who had shown that they were similarly prepared and whom they knew well. Their background also gave them a set of experienced commanders and a relatively clear, established leadership.

JN and ISIS offer a particularly instructive comparison given their similarities. While JN seems to have consistently favored careful recruitment into its own ranks, often preferring to work with other organizations rather than insisting on absorbing their members, ISIS's spectacular rise and its brutality along the way saw it favor short-run success over long-term, sustainable trust. It attracted many who looked to join a winning (and wealthy) side, or were cowed by fear and a binary choice, to be part of ISIS or against it. To an important degree, its successes in 2014 set it up to lose many supporters in the years of battlefield defeat. Thus, while ISIS grew to have tremendous territory and resources and to have a broader transnational impact than any other armed group, this success was to an important extent unsustainable. JN, meanwhile, stayed smaller but endured. These organizational points suggest a basic difference in strategy, whether to favor the short term or the long term. This offers a tool to characterize conflict environments, because it suggests not only which groups are strong now but which groups are likely to continue to be strong into the future, shaping the incentives that other armed actors have for forming alliances and for facing particularly severe short-run threats. From this point of view, JN may have been an especially attractive alliance partner not only because of its effectiveness but because of its resilience—it could more easily survive to repay favors. ISIS' rapid success, in contrast, proved deceptive.

The more fundamental contrast is between the FSA and these other opposition groups. Growing out of networks of activists gave many FSA units the interpersonal solidarity of political opponents who had taken grave risks to demonstrate against the regime, but also meant that for many of them, fighting was more a matter of a felt necessity and a tragic evolution of the uprising than something for which they had prepared and committed. Moreover, the FSA inherited a decentralized, chaotic character from the acephalous mass protests of 2011. It was the fruit of local, ad hoc reactions to protest and brutal repression, with survival a critical motive. It was extremely difficult in these circumstances to develop clear standards of recruitment and training or to insist on effective vetting. Thus, at a basic, important level, there was a disconnect between a mass movement that had emerged in a matter of weeks and an army developed over months or years. Some groups are better suited to war, others to nonviolent protest, and the passage from the street to the front is not an easy one.

A final issue emerges from what Barbara Walter calls the "extremist's advantage" in civil wars.[158] For Walter, extremist groups, and particularly Salafi-jihadists in contemporary wars in the Muslim world, have a few assets that other groups do not. Their ideology, according to Walter, means that they can offer low-cost rewards in the afterlife; that they recruit particularly committed followers at first, because joining a group with an extreme ideology tends to be isolating at the beginning, when it is weak; and that they can more credibly signal that their political order would fight corruption, compared with other groups. Mironova similarly argues that Islamist groups used conformity with religious practices within the group as a costly signal of adherence to an ideology and therefore of a long-run commitment.[159] This view is consistent with mine in some important respects. Notably, I agree with Walter and Mironova that JN and ISIS had important advantages in imposing costly signals on recruits.

But it is also worth pointing out that JN and ISIS (at first) insisted not only on a demonstrated adherence to Salafi-jihadist doctrine but also on a willingness to fight, which ideological adherence itself need not necessarily provide. This is because of the specifically military context of civil war and the critical role of interpersonal trust here. Ideologically minded recruits might still be unwilling to fight and risk death, but their comrades need them to do so. Both groups thus insisted on undergoing demanding training regimes and proving a willingness to fight at the front line. It is not clear that, in the absence of this kind of specifically military signal, the extremism of the ideology would have been enough to build a military force. Walter argues that extreme ideology outperforms the purely secular institutions of training: "Boot camps demand money and personnel and are an inefficient way to determine commitment because only a certain percentage of recruits are able to complete the program."[160] However, it is precisely the fact that not everyone passes that makes training a source of costly signaling. And these are, of course, organizational practices that do not depend on the content of the ideology; after all, the YPG/YPJ and regime elite forces also adopted them, to good effect. Walter also does not distinguish between JN and ISIS in terms of key organizational practices, practices that led to more uncommitted combatants in ISIS despite similar ideologies. ISIS insisted on swearing loyalty only to it, and appealed to fighters looking for better pay, luxuries, or opportunities to commit violence.[161] Ultimately, we have to analyze these groups' military, organizational practices to really understand how ideologies translate into interpersonal commitments and norms of cooperation.

This is not to deny that adhering to an extreme ideology entails costs that could certainly add to this military signal. Members of the core jihadist networks out of which grew JN and ISIS signaled their willingness to fight in the political and social wilderness for a cause. The YPG/YPJ likewise built on the networks and signals formed in a period of similar isolation, growing out of the PKK's long struggle against Turkey. There is clearly a connection here to the content of the groups' aims, whether jihadist or nationalist: states marginalize some groups rather than others. However, this is more because of the exclusion of the ideologies than their extremism, a label it is hard to apply to the YPG/YPJ.

But beyond their exclusion, all three of these groups were linked directly to civil wars in Syria's neighbors, Turkey and Iraq, that had raged for years before Syria fell into conflict. These armed groups therefore cashed in a legacy of war. They had a committed and trusting core, military doctrines and the expertise to train new fighters, an understanding of what a war would take, and a coherent leadership that could (if it chose) put in place these critical organizational practices to build trust. This connection, then, is not especially hopeful for the future. Signaling a commitment to fight over the long haul creates a sense of trust that can be a resource for future wars, including across borders.

CONCLUSION
Desertion, Armed Groups, and Civil Wars

As the Spanish Civil War progressed, the Republic's grave disadvantage in desertion took its toll, helping Franco's forces win. When a defecting officer took with him the defensive plans for Bilbao, it was of immense value in the rebel conquest of the city; on a larger scale, mass desertions undermined both Republican offensives and their efforts to hold territory.[1] Along the way, as each side tried to deal with desertion, it set up practices that affected life at the front (like militarization and punishment battalions) and at home (like patrols and propaganda). I have set out in this book to explain desertion in civil wars in terms of the complicated, often counterintuitive, dynamics of trust and mistrust at the heart of military units in times that tear countries apart. In this conclusion, I want to draw out the implications of this book's approach for civil wars more generally, in theoretical and practical terms.

The approach I have used in this book helps bridge a long-running theoretical debate about how to understand people's motivations in civil wars. Do big, common causes really matter for many people, given how far removed they can seem from the everyday fears of surviving and getting by in wartime? My answer is that the grand causes of civil wars matter through the interaction of combatants. This synthesis accepts that civil wars are both political and personal. It focuses our attention on relations among combatants as key mechanisms driving armies forward. In this chapter I spell out this synthesis and its importance. Then I suggest a new theoretical extension that goes beyond this book by looking at interactions among armed groups. I next move one step back from the book's focus on signals, trust, and desertion, proposing arguments about when armed groups are likely to adopt the practices that I think are important for fostering trust and limiting desertion. I conclude by then looking one step ahead, discussing the consequences of military cohesion and desertion for civil wars and their legacies.

Grand Causes and Armed Groups: A New Synthesis

Because studying desertion and defection is a way in to studying how armed groups stay together or fall apart, the analysis in this book allows for some lessons about how armed groups work generally. One critical question here is about the role of the grand ideological causes that supposedly animate civil conflicts: Do these causes really shape people's behavior in civil wars? This question has provoked ferocious debate. Relational theory offers a truce, and a way forward, in which causes matter through relationships among actors, and particularly relationships of trust and mistrust.

The disagreements have focused on how acceptable it is to interpret armed groups in terms of the appeal of their demands. It often seems natural to do so—to talk in terms of communists versus capitalists, Muslims versus Croats versus Serbs. Ethnic conflict analyses in the early 1990s used this view. Asking what ethnic groups will do when the state breaks down, for example, presumes that members of an ethnic group tend to act together.[2]

There are several powerful objections to this line of thinking. They should give pause to anyone hoping to apply "the cause" in a straightforward, direct manner. First, there is the classic collective action problem: even if you believe in a cause or identify with a social group in conflict, it may not make sense to go through the ordeal of fighting when it will not change whether the cause will succeed or fail.[3] This problem underwrote the turn toward economic analyses of conflict in the late 1990s and early 2000s, suggesting that the key thing armed groups needed was cash to pay fighters selective incentives.[4]

But the collective action problem has many different solutions. Among them, notably, are norms of cooperation in which combatants rely on each other.[5] Combatants are in a position, through their own efforts, to substantially increase or decrease the costs of fighting that their fellows pay, and to create obligations that they have to fulfill. It is true that soldiers do not think too much about the final goal. But trust in fellow combatants and obligations toward them—what they *do* think about in the moments of quiet after action when they sometimes consider whether to slip away—require at least a basic commitment to a banal sense of common aim, lingering in the background. I also find an important role for community ties, but I underline that more fundamental than these ties is the purpose they are put toward, and whether combatants tend to agree on some common aims.[6]

A second line of scholarship turned instead to survival, power, and war winning. Civil wars, in this view, are vicious contests among armed groups and can entail tremendous violence against civilians. So ordinary people in civil conflicts are generally only weakly drawn to one side or another and are motivated above all by survival in the midst of violence.[7] This "in no way implies that coercion is the only factor or that popular grievances are irrelevant," according to Kalyvas, but these causes depend on power to put them into practice.[8]

The survival motive is of course essential in civil conflicts, and the exercise of coercive power can certainly keep combatants fighting rather than switching sides. But a soldier's prospects for survival depend greatly on other soldiers and the bonds of trust that they can establish among themselves. And we have seen in this book that while coercion works to a point, it is often deeply affected by judgments of who is likely to defect—judgments that draw lines around different groups of combatants, constructing some as likely to be disloyal. And it is the way "the cause" is defined that will often tend to suggest who is in and who is out.[9] In brief, a cause can help soldiers survive. It does so when a group of combatants comes together and can trust in each other's cooperation. A cause can also kill, including when combatants find themselves trapped on the wrong side and under immense suspicion. Causes, and the way they are manifested in the relationships in an armed group, matter for the survival motive.

Increased attention to socialization processes in civil wars has raised a third objection to devotion to the cause as a motivator.[10] Combatants might be socialized to adopt the values the group wants them to adopt. In this way, prior commitments to a particular ideology would not be the reason that combatants fight; instead, they fight first, and obtain commitments to a cause later. Scott Gates argues that abductees in some rebel groups in Sierra Leone, Uganda, and the Congo have proved just as willing to stay and fight as volunteers, if not more so.[11]

Socialization is indeed a critical civil war process, and it plays an important role in how groups of combatants influence each other to fight or to flee. But it should not be understood as coming only from the top down. Recruits can also resist socialization, and one of the ways they do so is collectively. A critical mass of recruits can fight back against the behaviors and values the organization charges them to adopt.[12] This finding coheres very well with what we see in desertion in the rest of this book: each individual soldier is more likely to desert when others around him are uncommitted. In other words, socialization is a powerful force but works through, and is limited by, groups of combatants and what they bring into an armed group in the first place.

My analysis here accepts crucial aspects of all three critiques of grand-cause thinking. What relational theory offers, then, is a compromise. It looks at how characteristics of armed organizations connect large-scale political projects to the more direct motivations of individual combatants, who worry about the costs of fighting and look to ensure their survival, and who can be influenced and persuaded by their fellows. Militia members answering the call in 1936 in Spain and in 2011 in Syria wanted to know whether others in the unit would do their part too. Lukewarm fighters could be deeply affected by the strong motivations of the bulk of their unit-mates. Rightists in the Republican forces, leftists on Franco's side, opposition sympathizers in the Syrian regime forces, all trying to pass long enough to cross the lines, would try to assess whether they had a possible ally in the unit who could help them out. Officers in Spain looking only to uphold the Republic and follow their commanders' orders, or Sunnis in the officer corps in Syria, may find that they were presumed to be for the other side, and feel they had to flee to be safe.

So, despite the importance of common aims, we cannot simply expect to see ideologues fighting and opportunists deserting, treating each individual in isolation from the whole. Military units are more than the sum of their parts. Putting people together in a military unit in a civil conflict raises all of the usual questions about combat motivation along with deeper questions about whether a fighter may actually want the other side to win. A combatant who worries that unit-mates will not pull their weight or fears falling under suspicion of disloyalty is a combatant who is much more likely to desert. These judgments depend on the delicate interplay of combatants, who arrive in an armed group with their preferences and intentions but find that these must respond to the preferences and intentions of everyone around them and by how they are perceived. Tracing these second-order, contingent, endogenous intentions is one of this book's key contributions.

Indeed, these second-order effects help provide new insight into the key empirical puzzle for simplistic understandings of "the cause." This is the fact that people act in ways they are not supposed to in civil wars—that Tamils sometimes fought alongside the Sri Lankan government, that Sunnis still make up a very large part of the Syrian army, that "geographically loyal" leftists in Spain fought for Franco, that one can be opportunistic and apolitical and join up anyway, and that ideologues collaborate.[13] This certainly is strong evidence against any straightforward link from grand projects to individual behavior. But the relational approach helps us understand when and why people actually do fight for the side that they are "supposed" to, and when they do not.

First, people's personal motivations and their behavior may not line up. For example, Serbian nationalists may desert from nominally Serbian nationalist militias while ordinary, fairly apolitical people may keep on fighting. The relational approach expects such "exceptions" to depend on military units and their composition. As we saw in chapter 4, a personally committed individual may desert when surrounded by the uncommitted; an unmotivated soldier may stay and fight when pressured by unit-mates who are committed.

Second, people may fight despite what their personal characteristics suggest about their loyalties—for example, someone who is identified as an Alawite may fight and keep fighting for the Syrian opposition, and someone identified as a Sunni may fight and keep fighting for the regime. Many people's political motivations differ from their social categories—there are, after all, Alawites who believe deeply in the importance of opposing the Asad regime and Sunnis who are fiercely committed to keeping it in power. What the relational approach to desertion helps explain here is when people are forced to line up with their social categories. When an army uses stereotypes to infer loyalties, fighters may be more likely to join the side that everyone expects them to even though they would have been willing to fight for the "wrong" side, like defecting officers in Spain. (In turn, these defectors reinforce the stereotype itself.) When an army does not rely on stereotypes, and allows soldiers to prove their willingness to fight, they can transcend what an identity narrative says about who they should fight for.

A Theoretical Extension: Bilateral Interactions

One could extend a similar logic to interactions across armed groups, not just within them. The approach that I have developed in this book focuses only on one side at a time, which was already a large undertaking. But since civil conflicts are interactive, and in particular since they are fights over polities with common reference points and social cleavages, it is natural to suppose that the dynamics of trust and mistrust in desertion and defection stretch well outside a single armed group. Above all, can a combatant trust in good treatment on the other side? Or will they fear being treated as untrustworthy by their former adversaries if they lay down their arms or defect?

If a soldier fears mistrust and persecution from the other side, defection may be a losing option—the flipside of my argument that mistrust within an armed group often provokes defection. Those that an armed group characterizes as implacable foes are unlikely to defect to join it. These problems are exacerbated if opponents cannot make credible commitments *not* to repress defectors. Soldiers may fear that they will be mistrusted as possible spies or as individuals prone to switch sides again. They may also fear that opposing leaders will have incentives to present themselves as good nationalists by targeting out-group members. And they may fear that their support is ultimately disposable: useful for the other side to win the conflict, but not likely to induce its leaders to make substantive concessions to one's group. Thus, for example, Alawite soldiers in Syria have feared, both in the Muslim Brotherhood uprising of the late 1970s and early 1980s and again in the civil war since 2011, that they would be targeted for persecution because of their close identification with the regime, and their defection rate has consequently been quite low.[14] A similar dynamic happened in Spain. As we saw in chapter 8, Moroccan troops may have remained loyal to the Nationalist side out of fear of ill treatment on the Republican side, given the heavy use of anti-Moroccan propaganda by the latter. Both sides interrogated defectors and examined their background to determine whether they were spies.[15] One Communist Party member who defected from the Nationalists recalled finding these interrogations justified, but still very difficult to go through.[16] On the other side, the Nationalists attempted to determine the political alignment of soldiers who defected.[17] Nationalist propaganda promised good treatment only to defectors "without bloodstained hands," and instead vowed "inexorable justice" toward "assassins" trying to switch sides.[18]

The discussion suggests several important questions: What practices by side A, especially labeling groups of people as loyalists for side B, deter a potential defector? What incentives exist for side A to implement such practices? That is, is it ever rational for an armed group to limit its potential to receive incoming defectors, and if so, why? Is there a trade-off between mobilizing one's own constituency and deterring defection from the other side? Examining these questions would, I think, help get a better handle on when civil wars just carry on, with one side's fighters continuing to slog on in the face of continued defeats, because defecting and surrendering would simply be worse.

Tools for Policy Analysis

How can the relational approach to desertion aid in understanding contemporary armed conflicts? Drawing on the Spanish and Syrian cases, I offer some guidelines for assessing which armed group practices and characteristics help reduce desertion rates; the constraints in the conflict environment that can prevent armed groups from adopting these practices; and the long-run consequences of military cohesion in conflict and post-conflict environments.

If the relational approach in this book offers ways to link common causes and the ordinary concerns of combatants, these links depend on organizational factors: on how armed groups arrange themselves to have combatants send costly signals and to draw on local networks; and how they investigate loyalties and pursue military justice. So examining how an armed group uses these practices is critical to analyzing the degree and nature of the desertion problems they will face. In turn, the relational approach stresses that combatants can create strong bonds of trust or mistrust with each other, which then shapes their behavior toward each other; these links can have major implications over the long term.

Which Armed Groups Hold Together?

I find above all that the most cohesive armed groups, the ones best able to limit desertion, were those that imposed the costliest signals. These came in two critical varieties: drawing on highly committed cores of preexisting networks of activists and militants, and, given that these networks are rarely large enough to effectively fight a civil war, recruiting new troops voluntarily but with an insistence on training and military discipline. We saw this across different settings in Spain and Syria.

These signals work by giving combatants the chance to show that they are highly motivated to fight. So should we expect armed groups that motivate people especially strongly, that successfully make mass appeals, to hold together more effectively? For example, can armed groups that successfully engage grievances, emotional indignation, or well-crafted, ideologically resonant claims hope to enjoy lower desertion rates?[19] They can, but this depends on their ability to connect these motivations with an organizational structure allowing combatants to display their willingness to fight, creating confidence in each other's motivations, whether through initial networks or subsequent recruitment practices. Throwing together well-motivated recruits who do not know each other and have little basis for trusting in each other's commitment may not really work. Allowing soldiers to experience that commitment, by knowing that recruiting standards are high, by passing through training and combat together, and by drawing on local ties among committed members, works much better, but takes patience and investment.

A related nuance is the importance not just of a commitment to a cause but of a willingness to actually fight in a war for it. Political motivations and a military commitment are not the same thing. As we saw in Spain with the deep antimilitarism of many left-wing activists, and in Syria among opposition members who had strong moral and strategic reasons to favor nonviolent activism against the state, there can be an important disconnect between the intensity of political belief and the willingness to take up arms. And the decentralized structure that helped unions respond quickly to the coup plot in Spain and helped activists mobilize across Syria's cities also made it difficult to achieve the central standards and disciplinary practices that help create military cohesion. This disconnect suggests an important point: violent and nonviolent resistance is not always just a matter of strategic choice, with groups selecting one or the other based on the demands of the moment. The choice also has to run up against the nature of the organization and of its membership, and confront the question of what strategy the group is most apt to carry out.

A second key aspect of armed groups is their coercive capacity. Should analysts expect that armed groups monitoring their combatants and punishing desertion will have lower desertion rates?[20] This book has shown that while armed groups rely on coercion when fighters cannot be trusted to fight, coercion is also weakened considerably when mistrust is too great, when combatants have good reason to fear arbitrary violence. As we saw in the Spanish Republic, in the Syrian regime, and in the Islamic State in Iraq and al-Sham (ISIS), violence very often provoked combatants to defect. Understanding stereotypes and the often personal interests of those doing the punishing is critical to understanding what effects coercion is likely to have.

Because fighters influence each other's choices, this book's findings suggest caution in reading macro-level factors down to individual combatants. After all, it is often those one would not expect to desert who do. For instance, a lack of strong motivations may well produce large-scale desertion—but not just among the unmotivated. For example, after the crumbling of the Iraqi army at Ramadi in May 2015, U.S. secretary of defense Ashton Carter declared: "What apparently happened was that the Iraqi forces just showed no will to fight. They were not outnumbered, but in fact, they vastly outnumbered the opposing force. And yet they failed to fight."[21] Carter's statement takes a serious problem with cohesion and attributes it to the Iraqi forces broadly—with the risk of suggesting that anybody who ran from ISIS did so because of a lack of underlying motivation. Critically, however, my approach stresses that we cannot read such lack of motivation directly into any given soldier's decision to desert. In Iraq, for example, many combatants may have genuinely wanted to fight against ISIS. But when they served in an army with many "ghost soldiers" (who were allowed to just show up long enough to collect a paycheck, as long as they gave a kickback to their commander), they may simply have wondered what the point was.[22] Their will to fight was not an individual property, dependent only on their own commitments and wishes. Instead, it had much to do with their relationships.

A similar lesson applies to severe mistrust on the basis of stereotypes within an army, as with officers in the Spanish Civil War. It is certainly possible that the soldiers who are stereotyped as disloyal really are. But, based on the findings in this book, members of persecuted groups are likely to come under particularly intense suspicion of disloyalty, like Sunni soldiers in Syria or Tamil soldiers in

Sri Lanka. This suspicion, in turn, could very well reinforce their interest in deserting, out of fear of additional arbitrary persecution within the military itself. The result would be to worsen still further a problem of mistrust. In other words, many deserters may have wanted to stay and fight, in principle, just as many who fight may prefer to leave if they can. The stories we tell that say, "Well, of course Sunnis are deserting the army in Syria; it's an Alawite regime and a Sunni rebellion" obscure the complex, interactive processes that may push someone to leave.

This has important ramifications. First, analysts seeking to learn from desertion what the underlying problems in an armed group are need to understand that the profile of deserters is not necessarily a good indicator of who wants to fight and who does not; it is as important to investigate the conditions they faced in their units, such as unit composition, practices of recruitment, and punishment and coercion. Second, programs such as amnesties for combatants and Disarmament, Demobilization and Reintegration, which seek to help former combatants reintegrate into society, need to recognize that troops may leave an armed group and still take its cause to heart; under better circumstances, with more trustworthy compatriots or better-managed systems of control and punishment, they might have stayed. Even deserters may look for other ways to keep supporting the armed group's objectives, and may react badly to denigrating the group's aims. Third, it is important to recognize how critical social connections can be for deserters—that their mistrust of unit-mates can be a strong reason for them to want to leave, and that their ties with other deserters may have helped them depart. As soldiers try to reintegrate into civilian life, these social ties can be of critical importance.

Barriers to Adopting Successful Practices

If there are practices that can help prevent desertion, why do some armies not adopt them? This is not the central question of the book, but the relational approach to desertion provides a theoretical basis for answering this question, and the cases themselves add some more insights. Three key factors emerge: the strategic environment, with both external and internal threats to the armed group; the ideological environment, both motivating soldiers and generating stereotypes; and structural constraints on armed groups in the form of preexisting network ties and factional alignments.

The key strategic problem that the relational approach identifies is about patience. It takes time to carefully observe a soldier in order to assess loyalties based on behavior and costly signals. So, in the first place, an army has to limit its growth and invest precious resources in a long period of training and evaluation of new recruits in order to use stringent costly signals and recruit only those who pass the test. Further, it requires careful, discreet monitoring, as well as surveillance of the home front, to limit punishments only to those who actually try to desert. It is cheaper to rush to judgment on the basis of stereotypes.

Hence, armed groups under pressure for numbers—for example, the Spanish Republic in late 1936—should be likely to loosen standards, with serious long-term consequences for desertion. This is already fairly well understood; the cases in this book reinforce this lesson, and add the important finding that loosening standards does not just let in prospective deserters but undermines the willingness of even old veterans to fight.[23] The cases in this book also suggest that patience can be a strategic choice, not just a response to pressure. In Syria, for example, the long-run strategy of Jabhat al-Nusra (JN) to stay small and work with other forces on the ground contrasts clearly with ISIS's strategy to try to grow quickly, wipe out other forces, and strike a knockout blow. These two groups had quite similar aims but divergent political strategies for achieving them, and very different time horizons.

But if external threats can make an armed group impatient to recruit, internal threats can make them impatient to coerce desertion away. In 1936, the Spanish Republic faced defeat not only in combat but also from defectors leaving in droves in the coup attempt and its aftermath. This was the key context for the executions of officers that drove still others to defect. Internal crises of disloyalty may be critical to explaining these kinds of purges. The onset of a rebellion can call certain regime soldiers' loyalties into question, as with Sunni soldiers in Syria in 2011. Shifts in alignment can have similar effects, like the emergence of ISIS and its effects on JN. To take another example, the emergence of a new pro-Hutu militia in eastern Congo in 2007, the Coalition of Congolese Resistance Patriots–Armed Forces of the People, provoked Hutus to leave other militias such as the National Congress for the Defense of the People.[24] In these kinds of cases, fearing disloyalty, the armed group may react preemptively and provoke more disloyalty. Thus, if external pressures for numbers cause an armed group to, in effect, be overly trusting of new recruits, internal threats may cause them to be overly mistrustful.

If armies respond to these strategic considerations, they must also account for the environment of ideology. The relational approach to desertion suggests two critical roles for ideologies in armed groups: they motivate and designate. Ideologies help mobilize followers (in conjunction with signals and personal relationships, as we have seen), but they also appeal to some groups and designate others as enemies—social classes, ethnic groups, and so on. So if armed groups often have trouble adopting the model that keeps desertion rates low, it may be because there are very difficult trade-offs in doing so: strong ideological appeals can help create trusting, cohesive units, but they can also undermine trust by designating some members of the armed group as natural adversaries. Finding a best-of-both-worlds solution that both motivates followers and keeps the armed group open to committed recruits from unexpected social groups would help limit desertion but may often be very difficult.

Finally, armed groups can face structural barriers to establishing effective trust among combatants. An important part of the story of trust is how armed groups build on preexisting network ties, so they are constrained to an important degree by the pattern of these ties as it exists when they get going.[25] In my view, recruitment, training, and discipline practices are a critical second avenue to signaling a willingness to fight and creating trust among combatants, allowing armed groups other options than just relying on what already exists, but it is clear that preexisting ties are an important source of trust. Relatedly, some armed groups simply confront more severe problems of factionalism, generating additional reasons for mistrust and desertion. This book has emphasized a particular problem here: factionalism does not just generate the risk of a split, with one faction breaking away from its alliance with others, as scholars have emphasized, but can undermine relationships between individual fighters too.[26] Even if armed groups hold together at the level of high politics, they are likelier to lose a steady trickle of deserters in the everyday course of the war. Integrating multiple factions into a single organizational structure may help reduce the risk of fragmentation, but it comes at increased risk of mistrust among combatants at a ground level. In other words, it is very difficult for factionalized armed groups to escape their origins.

Long-Run Consequences of Trust, Mistrust, and Desertion

The norms of cooperation that military units can create, or not, may have important long-term effects. The ability to sustain a fighting force may be transferable to other settings. Having fought together in one conflict and having proved themselves to each other once, a group of combatants is well placed to act together again. Desertion, in other words, may well shape what Elisabeth Wood calls "the wartime transformation of social networks."[27]

Most obviously, this can be in renewed conflict. It is possible that desertion and defection in civil conflicts play an important role in how a civil conflict might restart, having once ended. Combatants who have fought together and who trust each other are clearly a risk factor. The Legion and Regulares, having served actively in Morocco and then having repressed the Asturias revolt in October 1934 in Spain, were well placed to serve as the core of the rebel force in 1936.[28] This risk need not respect national borders either: just as JN, ISIS, and the Yekîneyên Parastina Gel and Yekîneyên Parastina Jin (YPG/YPJ) carried legacies from conflicts in Iraq and Turkey, Rwandans who fought in the National Resistance Army in Uganda from 1981 to 1986 gained valuable experience for launching the Rwandan Patriotic Front rebellion in 1990–94.[29] Cohesive armed groups may be especially likely to take up arms again (other things equal), but, in particular, likely to take up arms *as themselves*, along their previous lines. In contrast, armed groups that suffer from cohesion problems during the conflict may well presage new lines of renewed conflict, among subgroups that happened to hold together and to develop lines of trust internal to themselves.[30]

There should also be opportunities for other forms of collective action than just fighting. Ex-combatants appear more willing to participate in common projects. These can be highly positive, such as former child soldiers leading communities in Uganda.[31] In times of crisis, though, these common projects may have terrible consequences: soldiers with combat experience in the Second World War may have drawn on their organizational skills to drive ethnic cleansing in the partition of India.[32] Desertion and cohesion during wartime may help shape this process by specifying which other people one cooperates with in the future. Those who fight together may be more likely to participate in common projects. In contrast, deserters may often be excluded. Indeed, Union deserters in the American Civil War were more likely than non-deserters to leave home once the war was over, living as they did under community-enforced shame. Notably, this effect was especially pronounced for deserters from pro-Lincoln districts, and deserters tended to go to more antiwar states.[33] Further, patterns of mistrust, coercion, and desertion could shape and reshape political identities. In Spain, as we saw in chapter 5, the defection of officers from the Republic helped reinforce the sense that officers were all for Franco in the postwar era. But if the Republic had managed to keep a grip on the violence against officers and target only those who really did switch sides, it might have been able to retain more of them. It may then have been more apparent that the officer corps was split and far from homogeneous. In Syria, sectarian patterns of coercion in the regime army and ethnic divides in the YPG/YPJ seem to have provoked many desertions, and may contribute in their way to driving a wedge among different communities over the long term. Desertion, in other words, shaped who would cooperate with whom. Trust and mistrust, at a micro level, carry on after conflict.

The choice to desert or to fight is one of the many trials that a civil war poses, and not one with an easy solution. And it engages a difficult game of figuring out what others want, and what they think you want. These are judgments that rest on courage, comradeship, violence, and politics. In this book, I have tried to understand how people go through this trial and what they decide to do. Studying desertion in civil wars has led me to try to put myself in the shoes of a soldier thinking about leaving. I hope I have helped explain this decision better. But in the process, I have certainly come to understand that I have little idea of what I would do. It would depend on what I thought everyone around me would do.

Civil wars pass into simplifying myths, and it can be hard for deserters to fit in the myth—as hard as it is for them to fit in their armies.[34] But deserters are very much a part of the story, and in learning about them, we can try to make better sense of the complexity of life in civil wars.

Appendix

Additional Tables for Chapter 4

TABLE A.1. Descriptive statistics, Santander province

	N	MEAN	STD. DEV.	MIN	MAX
INDIVIDUAL LEVEL (TIME-VARIANT)					
Desertion	9038	.020	.139	0	1
INDIVIDUAL LEVEL (TIME-INVARIANT)					
Conscript	3945	.533	.499	0	1
Left-wing affiliation	3945	.810	.392	0	1
COMPANY-PERIOD LEVEL					
Proportion conscripts	111	.507	.364	0	1
Political polarization	111	.662	.204	.031	.930
Social heterogeneity index	111	−.073	1.58	−4.80	2.58

TABLE A.2. Multilevel logit model of desertion in Santander province

	COEFFICIENT ESTIMATE	STANDARD ERROR
Conscript	.658**	.322
Left-wing affiliation	−1.359***	.178
Company proportion conscripts	3.369***	.985
Company social heterogeneity	.772***	.229
Conscription * heterogeneity	−1.443***	.483
Company union polarization	2.882***	1.071
Time since entry: 2 months	.608**	.242
Time since entry: 4 months	.393	.321
Time since entry: 6 months	−.255	.540
Constant	−5.759***	.501
Variance in constants	401	.310
Observations	9038	
Number of groups	111	

*** $p < .01$; ** $p < .05$.

Additional Tables for Chapter 5

TABLE A.3.   Descriptive statistics, officer corps data, cross-sectional time-series

	N	MEAN	STD. DEV.	MIN	MAX
INDIVIDUAL LEVEL, TIME-INVARIANT					
Defected	3414	.228	.419	0	1
Age	3414	41.75	8.29	22	66
Posted to a unit	3414	.915	.278	0	1
Unit leader	3414	.069	.254	0	1
Rank (0 = 2nd Lt, 8 = LtGen)	3414	1.58	1.35	0	8
Career progress[1]	3414	.925	.658	−1.70	2.83
Fired	3414	.345	.476	0	1
INDIVIDUAL LEVEL, TIME-VARYING					
Defected in quarter	27440	.025	.156	0	1
Fired in quarter	27440	.017	.129	0	1
Fired previously	27440	.281	.449	0	1
Time elapsed, in quarters	27440	5.18	2.88	1	10
PROVINCE-CORPS GROUP LEVEL, TIME-INVARIANT					
Coup participation rate	81	.167	.165	0	.76
PROVINCE-CORPS GROUP LEVEL, TIME-VARYING					
Execution rate, cumulative	593	.167	.144	0	.645

[1] For details on how this variable is calculated, see the appendix to McLauchlin and La Parra-Pérez 2018.

TABLE A.4. Over-time influence of coercion on defection

VARIABLE	(1) WHOLE SAMPLE, BY PROVINCE-CORPS	(2) WHOLE SAMPLE, BY PROVINCE-CORPS	(3) LOWEST-QUARTILE COUP PROPENSITY; BY PROVINCE-CORPS	(4) HIGHEST-QUARTILE COUP PROPENSITY; BY PROVINCE-CORPS	(5) WHOLE SAMPLE, BY PROVINCE, WITH CORPS FIXED EFFECTS
Execution rate, cumulative	1.248	2.693**	4.694**	2.037	1.202
	(0.838)	(1.262)	(2.362)	(1.322)	(1.414)
Coup participation rate	0.873	2.086*	5.608***	0.576	1.473
	(0.809)	(1.109)	(1.752)	(1.117)	(1.055)
Execution rate, cumulative * coup participation rate	-7.562	-7.562	-12.493	-3.294	-5.949
	(5.037)	(5.037)	(10.258)	(4.846)	(4.652)
Age	-0.047***	-0.047***	-0.036*	-0.042**	-0.044***
	(0.006)	(0.006)	(0.021)	(0.017)	(0.006)
Posted to a unit	0.107	0.100	-1.898**	0.265	0.028
	(0.174)	(0.174)	(0.881)	(0.237)	(0.164)
Unit leader	-0.691***	-0.686***	-0.946***	-0.848***	-0.848***
	(0.238)	(0.237)	(0.364)	(0.225)	(0.225)
Rank	0.227***	0.224***	0.100	0.165	0.223***
	(0.044)	(0.044)	(0.104)	(0.134)	(0.041)
Career progress	-0.280***	-0.277***	-0.230	-0.149	-0.336***
	(0.076)	(0.075)	(0.184)	(0.175)	(0.071)
Dismissal in current quarter	0.118	0.117	0.019	-0.033	0.003
	(0.341)	(0.341)	(0.780)	(0.551)	(0.334)
Dismissal at any time before current quarter	0.571***	0.575***	0.777***	0.397***	0.474***
	(0.093)	(0.093)	(0.252)	(0.153)	(0.088)

(continued)

TABLE A.4. (continued)

VARIABLE	(1) WHOLE SAMPLE, BY PROVINCE-CORPS	(2) WHOLE SAMPLE, BY PROVINCE-CORPS	(3) LOWEST- QUARTILE COUP PROPENSITY; BY PROVINCE-CORPS	(4) HIGHEST- QUARTILE COUP PROPENSITY; BY PROVINCE-CORPS	(5) WHOLE SAMPLE, BY PROVINCE, WITH CORPS FIXED EFFECTS
Time elapsed	0.735*	0.672*	0.225	1.129**	1.137**
	(0.399)	(0.402)	(0.715)	(0.514)	(0.492)
Spline 1	0.122*	0.116*	0.074	0.203**	0.190**
	(0.063)	(0.064)	(0.113)	(0.083)	(0.078)
Spline 2	−0.100*	−0.097*	−0.084	−0.153**	−0.160**
	(0.052)	(0.052)	(0.093)	(0.070)	(0.064)
Spline 3	0.041*	0.041*	0.053	0.044	0.068***
	(0.021)	(0.021)	(0.039)	(0.030)	(0.026)
Constant	−3.523***	−3.621***	−1.993	−3.683***	−3.255***
	(0.603)	(0.606)	(1.492)	(0.904)	(0.739)
Variance in constants, province-corps level	0.707***	0.607***	0.929	0.141	0.232**
	(0.237)	(0.221)	(0.584)	(0.123)	(0.118)
Variance in constants, province-corps-quarter level	0.736***	0.753***	0.433	0.573***	0.576***
	(0.143)	(0.146)	(0.383)	(0.213)	(0.136)
Observations	26,528	26,528	6,378	6,082	28,324
Number of groups	72	72	69	51	22

Note: Standard errors in parentheses.

*** $p < .01$; ** $p < .05$; * $p < .1$

Additional Tables for Chapter 6

TABLE A.5.   Disappearances and deaths in Republican militias, 1936, by Fifth Regiment affiliation

MILITIA	DEATHS	DISAPPEARANCES	RATIO
Fifth Regiment	1,286	523	2.46
Non–Fifth Regiment	1,755	1,186	1.48
Total	3,041	1,709	1.78

Source: Comandancia Militar de Milicias, "Estadística correspondiente a los combatientes muertos, desaparecidos e inútiles, agrupados según las Unidades Militares a que pertenecieron los mismos" (n.d., after June 1937), Archivo General Militar, Ávila (AGMAV), caja 1165, carpeta 8, documento 1.

TABLE A.6.   Fifth Regiment units included in data

Acero	Frente Rojo
Aida Lafuente	Jaén
Alicante	José Diaz
Alpino	Juventudes Camposinos
Amanecer	Juventudes Socialistas Unificadas
Antigas	La Montaña
Artes Blancas	La Victoria
Asturias	Leal
Balas Rojas	Lenin
Bautista Garcés	Leones Rojas
Bolívar	Lister
Cavada	Luis Carlos Prestes
Campesino "El" y Cª Galán	Madrid
Canarias	Mangada
Capitán Benito	Marina Pineda
Capitán Condés	Matteoti
Catorce Abril	Octubre n°1 y 11
Columna Galán	Quinto Regimiento
Comuneros de Madrid	Algunas Unidades
Diecicies de Febrero	Sargento Vázquez
Dimitroff	Thaelmann
El Aguila	Triana
Extremadura	UHP
Félix Bárzana	Vanguardia Roja
Frente de la Juventud	Vorochiloff
	Zapadores Minadores

Additional Table for Chapter 7

TABLE A.7. Disappearances and deaths in Republican forces, 1936 and 1937, by combatant's date of affiliation to a left-wing party or union

YEAR	DATE OF AFFILIATION	DEATHS	DISAPPEARANCES	RATIO
1936	Before July 18, 1936	394	233	1.69
	After July 18, 1936	83	52	1.60
	Date unknown	2,153	1,347	1.60
	Not affiliated	334	366	0.91
1937	Before July 18, 1936	1,618	390	4.15
	After July 18, 1936	708	333	2.13
	Date unknown	1,360	532	2.55
	Not affiliated	510	263	1.94

Source: Comandancia Militar de Milicias, "Estadística correspondiente a los combatientes muertos, desaparecidos e inútiles, agrupados según fecha de filiación política o sindical de los mismos" (n.d.; certainly after October 31, 1937), AGMAV, caja 1165, carpeta 4, documento 1.

Notes

1. SLIPPING AWAY

1. Montoliú 1999, 215–27. I have been able to confirm some details of Pozuelo's story, but not others. Siro Villas was indeed the brigade's chief medical officer (Prieto 2013). Juan Carrascosa Peñuela was indeed a doctor (death notice in *ABC*, 6 November 1981, p. 78) and had been detained in Valencia, which is where Pozuelo claims he was from (Delegación Nacional de Servicios Documentales, Secretaria General, Fichero de la Secretaria General y de la Sección Político Social, Fichero no. 68). In the brigade's incomplete files, I have not been able to find a record of Pozuelo's membership in the unit, or of his desertion.

2. Salas Larrazábal 2006, III: 2105.

3. Ragin 1987.

4. Skocpol 1979.

5. International Crisis Group 2011.

6. Russell 1974.

7. Connable and Libicki 2010.

8. Staniland 2012.

9. E. Wood 2003, 2008.

10. Peters and Richards 1998; Collier 2000; Collier and Hoeffler 2004; Weinstein 2005; Kalyvas and Kocher 2007; Humphreys and Weinstein 2008; Collier, Hoeffler, and Rohner 2009; Cederman, Wimmer, and Min 2010; Beber and Blattman 2013; Eck 2014. For the exceptions, see Gates 2002; Costa and Kahn 2008; Staniland 2014; Oppenheim et al. 2015; Koehler, Ohl, and Albrecht 2016; Albrecht and Koehler 2018; J. Richards 2018.

11. On fragmentation, see Christia 2012; McLauchlin and Pearlman 2012; Asal, Brown, and Dalton 2012; Fjelde and Nilsson 2012; Staniland 2014; Seymour 2014; Seymour, Bakke, and Cunningham 2016.

12. Mironova (2019) builds an account of defection and desertion in Syria that draws to an important degree on these issues. Holmes 1986 is an important guide to these matters in army life generally: on daily life, 109–30; on deserters as those who just have trouble dealing with these conditions, 84–85. Holmes similarly argues that much "desertion" is really just apathy arising from battle fatigue or shell shock (256). On drugs, see Andreas 2020.

13. This distinction is found in Lehmann and Zhukov's (2019) work on surrender across battles: a high rate of prisoners of war and commander surrenders produces more of the same, but a high rate of losses does not produce a higher rate of subsequent surrender. Behavior, not results, sends the relevant signal.

14. Costa and Kahn 2008.

15. Stouffer et al. 1949; Shils and Janowitz 1948; Marshall 1947.

16. Kier 1998.

17. On fragging, see Bond 1976, cited in Kier 1998: 16.

18. Bearman 1991, cited in Kier 1998:16.

19. Kaufmann 1996.

20. Ugarriza and Craig 2013; Costalli and Ruggeri 2015.

21. Oppenheim et al. 2015.

22. Bartov 1991. See also Barber and Miller 2019.

23. Kalyvas 2008.

24. McPherson 1997.

25. Moskos 1970; Wesbrook 1980.

26. Kier 1998; MacCoun, Kier, and Belkin 2006; MacCoun 1993.

27. King 2013; Cohen 2016; Barkawi 2017; Checkel 2017; Hoover Green 2018.

28. Manekin 2017.

29. Barkawi 2017, 191.

30. Gates 2002; Collier and Hoeffler 2004; Beber and Blattman 2013; Oppenheim et al. 2015.

31. Weinstein 2007; Ardant du Picq 2017; Lyall 2017.

32. Ganin 2013.

33. Posen 1993b; Kaufmann 1996.

34. Kalyvas 1999; Fearon and Laitin 2003; Collier and Hoeffler 2004; Valentino, Huth, and Balch-Lindsay 2004; Kalyvas 2006; Christia 2012.

35. Collier and Hoeffler 2004; Kalyvas 2003; Kalyvas 2006; Seymour 2014.

36. Cederman, Gleditsch, and Buhaug 2013; Ugarriza and Craig 2013; Gutiérrez Sanín and Wood 2014; Leader Maynard 2014; Oppenheim et al. 2015; Costalli and Ruggeri 2015; Walter 2017a; Leader Maynard 2019.

37. Lyall 2020.

38. Pearlman and Cunningham 2012.

39. Mobilize: Petersen 2001; E. Wood 2003; Parkinson 2013; Shesterinina 2016; search for resources: Szekely 2016; cohesion and conflict: Bakke, Cunningham, and Seymour 2012; Parkinson 2017; Mosinger 2018; members' behavior: Weinstein 2007; Mampilly 2015; Cohen 2016; Checkel 2017; Hoover Green 2018.

40. Parkinson and Zaks 2018; though see Mironova 2019.

41. Mironova 2019, 272–73.

42. Gould 1995; Shesterinina 2016.

43. This is not the only possible relationship between interpersonal trust and ideologies: Aisha Ahmad (2017), for example, shows how adopting an Islamist identity allows actors in war economies to build trust among each other. In her analysis, the content of the ideology is at first strategically adopted in order to solve trust problems, rather than the other way around, as in my work.

2. TRUST, MISTRUST, AND DESERTION IN CIVIL WARS

1. Henderson 1976, 117.

2. Quoted in Henderson 1976, 111–12.

3. Kalyvas 2006, 17; Sambanis 2004, 829.

4. Balcells 2017.

5. Lewis 2020; Bakke, Cunningham and Seymour 2012.

6. Moskos 1970; King 2013, 85; Lynn 1984.

7. Consistent with this, Lyall (2020, 191) finds that the incidence of mass desertion is higher in civil than in international conventional wars.

8. On coercion in both civil and international wars, see Lyall 2017.

9. Tilly 2001.

10. Oppenheim et al. 2015.

11. Lynn 1984, 35–36.

12. This can certainly vary, however; many armed groups are deeply intertwined with civilian support networks. See Petersen 2001; Parkinson 2013.

13. Ardant du Picq 2017; Marshall 1947; Shils and Janowitz 1948; King 2013.

14. Lynn 1984, 35.

15. Koehler, Ohl, and Albrecht 2016.

16. Corral 2007, 34.

17. Malešević 2010, 3.
18. Schelling 1973; Taylor 1987.
19. Levi 1997, 24.
20. E. Wood 2003, 235–36.
21. Marshall 1947; Shils and Janowitz 1948; Stouffer et al. 1949; Costa and Kahn 2008.
22. Costa and Kahn 2008, 215. Bracketed note is Costa and Kahn's. Errors in the quotation are as Costa and Kahn quote it.
23. Siebold 2007; King 2013, 13.
24. King 2013, 67; Marshall 1947, 148–49, 153.
25. Rousseau et al. 1998, 395.
26. Coleman 1990, 91.
27. Hardin 2002, 94.
28. Olson 1971; Taylor 1987, 1988; Levi 1997.
29. Coleman 1990, 188–94.
30. Gould 1995; Shesterinina 2016; Checkel 2017.
31. For example, a young Parisian who in 1871 marched with the Communards not because he wanted to but so he would not be shot by those who did. Gould 1995, 178.
32. Checkel 2017; Barkawi 2017.
33. Manekin 2017.
34. Wesbrook 1980, 258.
35. Helmer 1974, 47; Moskos 1970.
36. Bond 1976.
37. Peters and Richards 1998; Humphreys and Weinstein 2004; Arjona and Kalyvas 2006.
38. Enloe 1980; Barkawi 2015, 30–31. For contrasting cases of groups regarded as inherently antimilitarist, valorizing resistance to military service, see Scott 2009, 30, 148.
39. Humphreys and Weinstein 2008; Kalyvas and Kocher 2007.
40. Weinstein 2007; Oppenheim et al. 2015.
41. King 2013, 117–19; Henriksen 2007; Bilefsky 2018.
42. Quoted in King 2013, 56. For a similar note in the Korean War, see Little 1964, 202–3.
43. Quoted in Henderson 1976, 116.
44. Gutiérrez Sanín and Wood 2014, 215.
45. Ugarriza and Craig 2013.
46. Converse 1964.
47. Achen and Bartels 2017.
48. Leader Maynard 2019, 637–38.
49. Shesterinina 2016.
50. McPherson 1997, 97.
51. Peters and Richards 1998, 197.
52. E. Wood 2003, 228.
53. Barber and Miller 2019.
54. Castillo 2014; Lyall 2020.
55. Balcells 2017.
56. DeNardo 1985; Lichbach 1995; Kalyvas 2006, 103.
57. Weinstein 2007, 116–25.
58. Beber and Blattman 2013; see also Eck 2014.
59. Bakke, Cunningham, and Seymour 2012.
60. Christia 2012, 149–96.
61. McLauchlin and Pearlman 2012.
62. Snyder 1997, 165; Christia 2012.

63. Christia 2012, 173–74; for the theoretical argument, 33–34 and ff.

64. Oppenheim et al. 2015.

65. Dandeker 1990.

66. Ardant du Picq 2017, 56.

67. King 2013, 49, quoting Marshall 1962, 334. Bowdlerization is in Marshall.

68. Weinstein 2007, 130–31.

69. Kuran 1995. Kalyvas (2006, 93) makes the link between Kuran's concept of preference falsification and civil wars.

70. Koehler, Ohl, and Albrecht 2016, 446.

71. Koehler, Ohl, and Albrecht 2016, 447.

72. Bou Nassif 2015, 643.

73. George 1967, 89.

74. Spence 1974. Game-theoretic proof that such signals can underpin cooperation is found in Gintis, Smith, and Bowles 2001.

75. Staniland 2014, 18–20.

76. Staniland 2014, 67, quoting Gauhar 2007, 81.

77. Weinstein 2007.

78. King 2013; Ben-Shalom, Lehrer, and Ben-Ari 2005.

79. Keegan 1976, 15; Grossman 1996.

80. In line with this, Shesterinina (2019) argues that spontaneous groups of insurgents build cohesion through demonstrations of self-sacrifice.

81. Carey and Mitchell 2017.

82. Coleman 1990, chapter 12.

83. Wesbrook 1980, 267; McPherson, Smith-Lovin, and Cook 2001, 435; Habyarimana et al. 2007.

84. Costa and Kahn 2008, 220.

85. Costa and Kahn 2008, 104.

86. Bearman 1991.

87. I include the rider "somewhat costly" because evidence from extremely professional armed forces suggests that when combatants continually send very costly signals of their willingness to fight—joining up voluntarily with tight selection criteria and undergoing rigorous, realistic training scenarios, above all—the signals may be so strong that social homogeneity does not matter anymore (King 2013, 294–96, 331–32). If you learn enough from behavior, you do not need a social tie. However, the small, highly selective armies of career soldiers that can insist on such costly signals are far from a typical force in civil war armies, and are outside the empirical scope of this book.

88. Enloe 1980, 15.

89. Kalyvas 2008, 1047.

90. De Bruin 2018.

91. Parkinson 2017.

92. Kalyvas 2003.

93. Phillips 2015, 361.

94. Chandra and Wilkinson 2008; Caselli and Coleman 2006.

95. Quoted in Palmer 1986, 99.

96. Lyall 2017.

97. Albrecht and Ohl 2016, 38.

98. J. Richards 2018.

99. Strachan 1997, 374–375; 2006, 215.

100. King 2013, 363; Henderson 1976, 2–3; Wesbrook 1980, 250.

101. Wesbrook 1980, 249.

102. Posen 1993a; Biddle 2004; King 2013; Talmadge 2015.

103. Lyall 2017.

104. Lonn 1928, 63–65; Giuffre 1997; Weitz 2005, 20–21.

105. McLauchlin 2014; Scott 2009.

106. J. Richards 2018.

107. Schelling 1966, 4; for civil war applications, see Saideman and Zahar 2008.

108. This is much like the problem that indiscriminate violence against civilians tends to backfire, pushing them to support the other side. Kalyvas 2006, 114. See also Goodwin 2001.

109. Lyall 2017.

3. STUDYING DESERTION IN THE SPANISH CIVIL WAR

1. Balcells 2017.

2. Derriennic 2001, chap. 5; Kalyvas and Balcells 2010.

3. For more on this kind of distinction, see Gutiérrez Sanín and Giustozzi 2010; Petersen 2001.

4. Preston 1994a.

5. Balcells 2017.

6. Ohl, Albrecht, and Koehler 2015; Koehler, Ohl, and Albrecht 2016; Albrecht and Koehler 2018; Oppenheim et al. 2015; J. Richards 2018; Mironova 2019.

7. Alpert 2004; Casanova 2010, 335–39.

8. This summary draws on Payne 1967; Salas Larrazábal 2006; Thomas 1994; Graham 2002; Preston 2007. The last is an excellent one-volume overview of the Spanish Civil War.

9. On these factions see Navajas Zubeldía 2011, 75, 111, 119.

10. Cruells 1974, 11–14; Mainar Cabanes 1998, 17–18; Salas Larrazábal 2006, I: 198.

11. Salas Larrazábal 2006, I: 264; Engel 2008, 49.

12. Alpert 2013, 25.

13. Alpert 2013, 20–24; Bolloten 1991, 48.

14. McLauchlin 2014.

4. COOPERATION AND SOLDIERS' DECISIONS

1. Matthews 2012.

2. Corral 2007, 325–26. Corral notes that desertion in calm fronts appears likelier to generate records than desertion during combat (195).

3. The following account draws on Salas Larrazábal 2006; Saíz Viadero 1979; Martínez Bande 1972, 1980; Solar 1996; Solla Gutiérrez 2005, 2006.

4. Linz and de Miguel 1977, 43.

5. Solla Gutiérrez 2005, 89–91, 112–21.

6. Saíz Viadero 1979, 33–34.

7. Solla Gutiérrez 2006, 385.

8. Gutiérrez Flores and Gudín de la Lama 2005, 212–13.

9. Solla Gutiérrez 2005, 133–35.

10. Salas Larrazábal 2006, I: 503.

11. Solla Gutiérrez 2006, 152.

12. Solla Gutiérrez 2006, 385.

13. Solla Gutiérrez 2006, 385–86.

14. "Instrucciones para el combate," Editorial Montañesa, Santander, 1936, Centro Documental de la Memoria Histórica (CDMH), PS Santander L, caja 273, carpeta 4, p. 2.

15. Gutiérrez Flores and Gudín de la Lama 2005, 181, 215.

16. *Boletín Oficial de la Provincia de Santander*, October 12, 1936; October 29, 1936; February 17, 1937; May 16, 1937; Solla Gutiérrez 2006, 387. For example, Consejo Municipal de Rionansa, "Relación de soldados de los reemplazos de 1921, 22 y 39, residentes

en este término que deben efectuar su presentacion en Santander," June 19, 1937, CDMH, PS Santander L, caja 443, carpeta 7, p. 41.

17. CDMH, PS Santander L, caja 444, carpeta 8, expediente 7; CDMH, PS Santander L, caja 444, carpeta 10, expediente 2.

18. Martínez Bande 1980, 183.

19. Matthews 2012, 26–27.

20. Costa and Kahn 2008.

21. Corral 2007, 195–97, 297.

22. Expediente, CDMH, PS Santander L, caja 443, carpeta 9, expediente 4.

23. Costa and Kahn 2008, 95.

24. Solla Gutiérrez 2006, 71, 97.

25. I used the same formula as Montalvo and Reynal-Querol 2005.

26. Beck, Katz, and Tucker 1998.

27. On hunger and ration cuts, see Martínez Bande 1980, 165; Solla Gutiérrez 2006, 343; on an argument linking this to desertion, see Solar 1996, 85–86.

28. Seidman 2002, 197, 218–21.

29. In all cases I excluded hospitalizations for gunshot and shrapnel wounds and sexually transmitted infections. The former could indicate either self-sacrifice or self-injury, while the latter could be subject to punishment and therefore could indicate discipline problems. Either way, they would be problematic indicators of maladies caused by a lack of supply.

30. Obregón Goyarrola 2007, 114–15. My dataset includes Third Company, Battalion 105. Ninety-five percent of this company was conscripts in my data.

31. Jefe de Operaciones to Srs. Jefes de la 1a, 2a, 3a Divisiones and 11a Brigada, Santander, May 8, 1937, Archivo General Militar, Ávila (AGMAV), caja 686, carpeta 1, documento 1, p. 1.

32. Unknown [Jefe de Operaciones?] to Srs. Jefes de la 1a, 2a, 3a Divisiones and 11a Brigada, Santander, May 18, 1937, AGMAV, caja 686, carpeta 1, documento 1, p. 2.

33. Jefe de Operaciones to Sr. Jefe de E.M. del Ejército del Norte—Bilbao, n.d. [May 1937?], AGMAV, caja 686, carpeta 1, documento 3, p. 2.

34. Saíz Viadero 1979, 40–41.

35. Rivero Solozábal 1941, 19–20, 30.

36. Obregón Goyarrola 2007, 114.

37. Comisario General de Guerra to Jefe del Batallón Disciplinario, April 6, 1937, CDMH, PS Santander L, caja 562, carpeta 6, p. 19; Agente de Movilización y Control, n.d., CDMH, PS Santander L, caja 436, carpeta 17, expediente 3–5; soldier file, CDMH, PS Santander L, caja 412, carpeta 21, expediente 3.

38. For example, representatives of Popular Front Organizations of Riotuerto to Jefe del Estado Mayor, Ejército del Norte, April 27, 1937, CDMH, PS Santander L, caja 444, carpeta 4, p. 1; PSOE, Agrupación de San Salvador, to Comité Ejecutivo del Federación Socialista, May 27, 1937, CDMH, PS Santander L, caja 444, carpeta 13, expediente 10.

39. "Organización del comisariado y actuación del comisario," no author, n.d., n.p., CDMH, PS Santander L, caja 544, carpeta 5, pp. 1–4.

40. Soldier case file, CDMH, PS Santander L, caja 406, carpeta 6, pp. 42–46.

41. Soldier case file, CDMH, PS Santander L, caja 406, carpeta 8, expediente 6.

42. Gutiérrez Flores and Gudín de la Lama 2005, 215.

43. Obregón Goyarrola 2007, 122. Confirming this, the First Company of this battalion, which appears in my dataset, recorded seventeen Lebaniégo soldiers: fifteen volunteers, two conscripts.

44. Agente de Movilización y Control, n.d., CDMH, PS Santander L, caja 436, carpeta 17, expediente 3–5.

45. Letter from Comisario Delegado, 1st Division to Comisario General de Guerra, Santander, June 16, 1937, CDMH, PS Santander L, caja 406, carpeta 7, expediente 3; trial record, Tomas Cosio Gonzalez, April 1, 1937, CDMH, PS Santander L, caja 406, carpeta 8, expediente 5.

46. Oficial informador 3 Division to Jefe 2 Secn EM, July 23, 1937, Reinosa, CDMH, PS Santander L, caja 406, carpeta 5, p. 101.

47. Comandante Jefe and Capitán Ayudante, n.d., recipient unknown, CDMH, PS Santander L, caja 436, carpeta 14, expediente 1–2.

48. Letter from Mayor Jefe, Batallon 131, to Jefe, Estado Mayor, June 24, 1937, CDMH, PS Santander L, caja 406, carpeta 7, expediente 11.

49. Letter to Brigada de Documentación del Batallón 136, Compañía de Capitán Maroto, n.d., CDMH, PS Santander L, caja 436, carpeta 17, expediente 2.

50. Gutiérrez Flores and Gudín de la Lama 2005, 186.

51. E.g., "Relación de Comisarios Políticos de Batallón de la UGT y Partido Socialista de la Provincia de Santander," about July 1937, CDMH, PS Santander D, caja 31, carpeta 9, p. 4; Solla Gutiérrez 2006, 389.

52. Mueller 2000; Kaldor 2006. Outside observers seem to be more willing to accept the ideological character of the "new new civil wars" in Nigeria, Syria, and Iraq, particularly with the rise of ISIS (Walter 2017b), but I think this may simply be because the ideologies are, as in Spain and again during the Cold War, very easy to interpret in terms of struggles that are transnational and easy to see (see Kalyvas 2001).

53. Seidman 2002; Corral 2007; Matthews 2012.

54. Kalyvas 2001.

55. McLauchlin and Reiss 2018.

56. Eck 2014, 377.

57. Eck 2014, 386–88.

58. Asal, Conrad, and Toronto 2017, 1467–68.

59. Perri 2008; Figes 1990; Pepper 1999, 163; Koehler, Ohl, and Albrecht 2016; Abdulrahim 2016.

60. Leech 2011, chap. 4.

5. COERCION AND SOLDIERS' DECISIONS

1. Martín Blázquez 1939, 111.

2. Fraser 1979, 69.

3. Salas Larrazábal 2006, I: 176–77.

4. Mainar Cabanes 1998, 19–20.

5. Montoliú 1999, 183.

6. Engel 2008.

7. On inflation in Francoist records, see Ruiz 2017, 11.

8. Fraser 1979, 71–72.

9. Graham 2002, 161.

10. Preston 2012, 361.

11. Preston 2012, 268–69.

12. Fraser 1979, 120.

13. Martínez Reverte 2004, 56.

14. Arcarazo García 2004, 97–101.

15. García Oliver 1978, 269.

16. Preston 2012, 268.

17. Ruiz 2017, 140; see also 28–29.

18. Ruiz 2017, 24.

19. Preston 2012; Ruiz 2017.

20. Ruiz 2017, 145, citing Carrillo 2012, 114.
21. Martín Blázquez 1939, 116.
22. Fraser 1979, 78.
23. Martín Blázquez 1939, 135.
24. Preston 2012, 269.
25. Ruiz 2017, 49–50.
26. McLauchlin and La Parra-Pérez 2018.
27. Cordón 2008, 410.
28. Cordón 2008, 427.
29. Fraser 1979, 117.
30. Alpert 2013, 21.
31. Fraser 1979, 118.
32. Pérez Salas 1947, 106.
33. Navajas Zubeldía 2011, 137–38.
34. Navajas Zubeldía 2011, 137, citing Álvarez del Vayo 1940.
35. Cordón 2008, 427.
36. Engel 2008.
37. Martín Blázquez 1939, 135.
38. Solé i Sabaté and Villaroya Font 1990; Casas de la Vega 1994; McLauchlin and La Parra-Pérez 2018.
39. Alpert 2013, 87; Payne 1967, 320–21.
40. La Parra-Pérez 2020.
41. La Parra-Pérez (2020) cites shorter tenure instead, but this correlates with age at 0.95 for obvious reasons.
42. Gutiérrez Sanín and Wood 2014; Leader Maynard 2019.
43. Martínez Reverte 2012.
44. Martínez Reverte 2012, 24.
45. Schmidt 2018, 14.
46. Marks 2013, 369–72.
47. McLauchlin and Reiss 2018; Humphreys and Weinstein 2004.
48. McLauchlin and La Parra-Pérez 2018, 1029; data are from Sudduth 2017.
49. Lynn 1984, 81.
50. Lynn 1984, 83–84.
51. Six 1947, 196.
52. Ganin 2013.
53. Argenbright 1991, 174–75; Ganin 2013, 263, 304–7; Kotkin 2015, 300–310.
54. Giustozzi 2015, 119.
55. International Crisis Group 2017a, 3–6; Gramajo et al. 2016, paras. 33–36.
56. Albrecht and Ohl 2016.
57. Sanborn 2003, 125.
58. Sanborn 2003, 125–26.
59. Sanborn 2003, 94.
60. Kaufmann 1996.
61. Kalyvas 2008.
62. Fearon and Laitin 2000; Bergholz 2016.
63. Enloe 1980; Horowitz 2000.
64. Caselli and Coleman 2006; Chandra and Wilkinson 2008.
65. McLauchlin 2010.
66. Harkness 2016; Roessler 2011; Morency-Laflamme and McLauchlin, forthcoming.

6. MILITIAS IN THE SPANISH REPUBLIC, SUMMER–FALL 1936

Epigraph: Fraser 1979, 293.

1. Communist: Líster 2007, 99; Blanco Rodríguez 1993, 26–28; Fraser 1979, 49; Alpert 2013, 13–15; socialist: Zugazagoitia 1977, 58–59; anarchist: Fraser 1979, 62–63.

2. Cruells 1974, 11–14; Fraser 1979, 64, 106.

3. Blanco Rodríguez 1993, 26–28; Fraser 1979, 107.

4. Staniland 2014, 18–19.

5. Blanco Rodríguez 1993, 28–29; Modesto 1969, 25.

6. Montoliú 1998, 61; de Guzmán 2004, 67 (quote).

7. Bolloten 1991, 39–40; Graham 2002, 24; Montoliú 1998, 54; Salas Larrazábal 2006, I: 194; Thomas 1994, 227; Zugazagoitia 1977, 57; Fraser 1979, 62–63; Martín Blázquez 1939, 112; García Venero 1973, 382–83.

8. Fraser 1979, 72; see also Mera 1976, 17–18.

9. Maldonado 2007, 70; Salas Larrazábal 2006, I: 548.

10. Martín Blázquez 1939, 122; Alpert 2013, 35.

11. Martín Blázquez 1939, 128.

12. Fraser 1979, 110.

13. Ruiz 2014, 88–90.

14. Casanova 1985.

15. Bolloten 1991, chap. 7.

16. Quoted in Bolloten 1991, 48–49.

17. Juliá 1999.

18. Balcells 2017.

19. Martín Blázquez 1939, 175–76, 128 (quote).

20. "Barricadas," *Solidaridad Obrera* (Barcelona), July 24, 1936.

21. Fraser 1979, 134.

22. Alpert 2013, 52.

23. Seidman 2002, 34.

24. Fraser 1979, 119.

25. Fraser 1979, 120.

26. Montoliú 1999, 64–65.

27. Montoliú 1999, 253–54.

28. Thomas 1994, 434.

29. García Oliver 1978, 261–62.

30. "El importante acto de la C.N.T. en el Principal," *Fragua Social* (Valencia), October 10, 1936, pp. 2–4. On desertions in the Uribarry column, see Cardona 1996, 49; Mainar Cabanes 1998, 33–35.

31. Montoliú 1999, 254.

32. Corral 2007, 86–87.

33. Orwell 1989, 10.

34. Gutiérrez Rueda and Gutiérrez Rueda 2003, 60.

35. Seidman 2002, 35; Martín Blázquez 1939, 209–10.

36. Martín Blázquez 1939, 125–26.

37. Casanova 1985, 110–11; Seidman 2002, 36; Modesto 1969, 33–34.

38. Bolloten 1991, 333–34.

39. Creveld 2004; Graham 2002, 352–53.

40. "¡Alerta! Hay fascistas enrolados en las milicias," *Solidaridad Obrera* (Barcelona), August 1, 1936, p. 6.

41. Cirre Jiménez 1937, 92–93.

42. Mainar Cabanes 1998, 19–20.

43. Montoliú 1999, 209.

44. Seidman 1990, 94.

45. Fraser 1979, 352–53.

46. For example, *Solidaridad Obrera* (Barcelona), July 27, 1936; July 29, 1936; August 2, 1936; Graham 2002, 87; Cervera 2006, 112; Montoliú 1999, 139, 149.

47. Bolloten 1991, chap. 5; "¡Ni pillaje, ni saqueo, camaradas!" *Solidaridad Obrera* (Barcelona), July 24, 1936, p. 1; "Un caso bochornoso de pillaje," *Solidaridad Obrera* (Barcelona), July 29, 1936, p. 1.

48. Bolloten 1991, 773n73, citing Pons Prades 1977, 141–45.

49. Mera 1976, 28.

50. *Milicia Popular* (Madrid), August 4, 1936.

51. de Frutos 1967, 18, 35, 45, 57.

52. Blanco Rodríguez, Fernández Cuadrado, and Martínez Martín 1988, 330.

53. Blanco Rodríguez, Fernández Cuadrado, and Martínez Martín 1988, 330–31, 333.

54. Aroca Sardagna 1972, 11, 13.

55. Fraser 1979, 256.

56. Blanco Rodríguez 1993, 242.

57. de Frutos 1967, 18.

58. de Frutos 1967, 73.

59. de Frutos 1967, 53–54.

60. Aroca Sardagna 1972, 20–21, 27.

61. Arcarazo García 2004, 111.

62. Fraser 1979, 134.

63. Fraser 1979, 134.

64. For example, see de Frutos 1967, 37–40.

65. Montoliú 1999, 61.

66. Fraser 1979, 267–68.

67. Montoliú 1999, 65.

68. Fraser 1979, 293.

69. de Frutos 1967, 37–46.

70. Comité de la Confederación Nacional de Trabajo de Cataluña, "La actitud de la organización obrera ante la llamada a filas de los reemplazos," *Solidaridad Obrera* (Barcelona), August 5, 1936, pp. 1–2. This claim was reprinted verbatim, suggesting José Peirats's authorship, in Peirats 1971, 186–87.

71. Bolloten 1991, 261, quoting *Fragua Social*, November 18, 1936.

72. Alpert 2013, 5.

73. Fraser 1979, 120.

74. de Frutos 1967, 27–28.

75. Seidman 2002, 56.

76. Cirre Jiménez 1937, 37–38.

77. García Oliver 1978, 266; Brusco 2003, 71–73.

78. Martínez Reverte 2004, 10.

79. Thomas 1994, 325; see also Salas Larrazábal 2006, I: 547.

80. Fraser 1979, 117.

81. Broué and Témime 1970, 174.

82. de Frutos 1967, 28–29.

83. Mera 1976, 30–32.

84. Matthews 2012, 21.

85. de Frutos 1967, 42.

86. de Frutos 1967, 56–58.

87. Seidman 2002, 50.

88. de Guzmán 2004, 83.

89. de Guzmán 2004, 84.

90. Colodny 1958, 158.

91. Blanco Rodríguez 1993, 236–37.

92. Fraser 1979, 258.

93. "La instrucción militar," de "Documentos históricos" del 5º Regimiento, no. 1, p. 29, reprinted in Vidali 1975, 98.

94. "Camaradería y Disciplina," de "Documentos históricos" del 5º Regimiento, no. 1, p. 14, reprinted in Vidali 1975, 94–96.

95. Vidali 1975, 19–20, 28.

96. *Milicia Popular* (Madrid), August 4, 1936.

97. Bolloten 1991, 268.

98. Reprinted in Vidali 1975, 109–10.

99. Blanco Rodríguez 1993, 235–36.

100. Blanco Rodríguez 1993, 241.

101. Montoliú 1999, 253.

102. *Milicia Popular* (Madrid), August 4, 1936.

103. *Milicia Popular* (Madrid), August 6, 1936.

104. *Milicia Popular* (Madrid), September 20, 1936.

105. Bolloten 1991, 269–70, citing Martín Blázquez 1939, 205.

106. Martínez Reverte 2004, 65.

107. Blanco Rodríguez 1993, 242.

108. Montoliú 1999, 39.

109. Martínez Reverte 2004, 9–10.

110. Salas Larrazábal 2006, I: 613.

111. Salas Larrazábal 2006, I: 616; Matthews 2012, 21.

112. Comandancia Militar de Milicias, "Estadística correspondiente a los combatientes muertos, desaparecidos e inútiles, agrupados según las Unidades Militares a que pertenecieron los mismos" (n.d., after June 1937), Archivo General Militar, Ávila [AGMAV], caja 1165, carpeta 8, documento 1.

113. Full results and a list of units coded as belonging to the Fifth Regiment are in the appendix, tables A.5 and A.6.

114. Smyth 1996, 90–93; Alpert 2004, 76; Howson 1998, 28, 142; Martín Blázquez 1939, 124–125.

115. Matthews 2012, 21.

116. Fraser 1979, 120.

117. Fraser 1979, 135.

118. Bolloten 1991, 257.

119. Bolloten 1991, 257.

120. Aroca Sardagna 1972, 114–15.

121. Fraser 1979, 133.

122. Montoliú 1999, 76; Modesto 1969, 13–14.

123. Líster 2007, 102.

124. Graham 2002, 145.

125. Vidali 1975, 28.

7. THE POPULAR ARMY OF THE REPUBLIC, FALL 1936–39

1. Mera 1976, 28.

2. Mera 1976, 28–35.

3. Mera 1976, 30–31, 35.

4. Fraser 1979, 266.

5. G. Séguero, "Impresiones de un viaje al frente de Bujaraloz," *Solidaridad Obrera* (Barcelona), August 28, 1936. See also Alfonso Martínez Rizo, "De Barcelona a Zaragoza: Una asemblea de milicianos," *Solidaridad Obrera* (Barcelona), August 8, 1936.

6. Anonymous 1997, "Barracks and prisons . . .", 14; "Who can claim . . .", 21.

7. Bolloten 1991, 250; Azaña 1967, 488; Salas Larrazábal 2006, I: 540–45.

8. Kowalsky 2001, paras. 591–92.

9. Radosh, Habeck, and Sevostianov 2001, document 15, 41–42.

10. Alpert 2013, 60–63.

11. Salas Larrazábal 2006, I: 634.

12. Alpert 2013, 68.

13. Salas Larrazábal 2006, I: 649.

14. Salas Larrazábal 2006, I: 652–55.

15. Brusco 2003, 111; Aroca Sardagna 1972, 39–40.

16. Graham 2002, 138–39.

17. Smyth 1996, 90–93; Alpert 2004, 76; Howson 1998, 28, 142.

18. Orwell 1989; Bolloten 1991; Graham 2002.

19. Bolloten 1991, 264.

20. De Guzmán 2004, 117–18. The same decree was published in Aragón on October 11. Núñez Díaz-Balart 2013, para. 14.

21. Fraser 1979, 133.

22. Fraser 1979, 133.

23. E. Gimeno Ortells, "Los Cobardes en la Vanguardia y los Derrotistas en la Retaguardia," *Fragua Social* (Valencia), October 29, 1936, p. 13.

24. Matthews 2012, 26–27.

25. MacMaster 1990, 66.

26. Bolloten 1991, 264; see also de Guzmán 2004, 117–18.

27. Núñez Díaz-Balart 2013, quoting *El Combate*, no. 20, October 28, 1936.

28. Núñez Díaz-Balart 2013, quoting "Recientes declaraciones," *Línea de Fuego*, no. 26, October 9, 1936, p. 1.

29. Pedro Lopez Calle, "Disciplina," *Libertad*, no. 1 (n.d., around June 1937), p. 12.

30. E. Gil, "La disciplina garantía del Ejército," *Libertad*, no. 2 (n.d., around June 1937), p. 15.

31. MacMaster 1990, 66.

32. Fraser 1979, 258.

33. Estadillo de altas y bajas, Centro Documental de la Memoria Histórica (CDMH), Serie Militar (SM), caja 776.

34. The documents available on this unit are indeed "exceptionally rich." Blanco Rodríguez, Fernández Cuadrado, and Martínez Martín 1988, 330n.

35. For example, Milicias Castellanas, Solicitud de Ingreso, August 27, 1936, CDMH, SM, caja 716, folio 114.

36. Milicias Castellanas, Solicitud de Ingreso, August 27, 1936, CDMH, SM, caja 716, folio 114.

37. For example, Milicias Castellanas Antifascistas, expediente, October 11, 1936, CDMH, SM, caja 716, folio 114.

38. Following my practice elsewhere in this book, here I count thirty-one disappearances whose dates were known as desertions, alongside forty-six desertions or defections clearly labeled as such. Not counting these disappearances as desertions does not change the overall trend, and in fact the cohesion of the unit in the aftermath of militarization is even more strongly indicated.

39. El Comandante Jefe, no title, Madrid, November 21, 1936, Archivo General Militar, Ávila [AGMAV], caja 1165, carpeta 2, document 1. This document lists available mi-

litia units on the Madrid front. Los Comuneros is indicated as being rested and ready on November 21, 1936; this is consistent with the registry book, which lists a death on November 14 and then not another until the 23rd. University City: Blanco Rodríguez, Fernández Cuadrado, and Martínez Martín 1988, 333.

40. Blanco Rodríguez, Fernández Cuadrado, and Martínez Martín 1988, 333–34.

41. Blanco Rodríguez, Fernández Cuadrado, and Martínez Martín 1988, 329–30.

42. Seidman 2002, 59, 83.

43. 1 Cuerpo de Ejército, "Estado numérico," n.d., CDMH, SM, caja 5379. This is an estimate. For the tables covering this period, desertions and defections are lumped together. I used the same proportion of defections in this period as occurred in the next period (41%). For December 1937–March 1938: 69 División, "Relación numérica," April 8, 1938; 2 División, "Relación numérica," April 13, 1938; 1 División, "Relación de bajas habidas," CDMH, SM, caja 5379.

44. "Información: Deserciones," CDMH, SM, September 3, 1938, through March 18, 1939, caja 421, folios 1–208; and "Información: Deserciones," March 22, 1939, CDMH, SM, caja 781, folios 1–9.

45. Reconstructed from Engel 1999, 40–47, 181, 198–99, 202.

46. As noted in the previous chapter, the difficulty of distinguishing disappearance from desertion makes these statistics a good rough indicator of desertion, in the absence of more specific statistics across the army.

47. Comandancia Militar de Milicias, "Estadística correspondiente a los combatientes muertos, desaparecidos e inútiles, agrupados según fecha de filiación política o sindical de los mismos" (n.d.; certainly after October 31, 1937), AGMAV, caja 1165, carpeta 4, documento 1. Summary figures are given in the appendix, table A.7.

48. Matthews 2012, 161–64.

49. Matthews 2012, 28.

50. Corral 2007, 98, 109, 110.

51. Corral 2007, 125.

52. Graham 2002, 344–45, 375; Corral 2007, 119–20.

53. Corral 2007, 157–58.

54. Matthews 2012, 140.

55. Corral 2007, 158–59.

56. Seidman 2002, 202.

57. Matthews 2012, 10.

58. "Los incoregibles," Libertad, no. 1 (n.d., around June 1937), p. 6.

59. Matthews 2012, 173.

60. Corral 2007, 194.

61. Seidman 2002, 220–21.

62. Matthews 2012, 142.

63. "Desertores," 1 Cuerpo, February 10, 1939, CDMH, SM, caja 421, folios 74–81.

64. Corral 2007, 198.

65. Seidman 2002, 75.

66. Corral 2007, 155.

67. Corral 2007, 158.

68. Seidman 2002, 159.

69. Seidman 2002, 197, 218–21.

70. Corral 2007, 236.

71. Corral 2007, 37.

72. Corral 2007, 30–31, 37–40.

73. "Desertores," 1 Cuerpo, February 10, 1939, CDMH, SM, caja 421, folios 74–81; "Desertores," 1 Cuerpo, September 16, 1938, CDMH, SM, caja 421, folios 181–83.

74. "Desertores," 1 Cuerpo, October 15, 1938, CDMH, SM, caja 421, folios 29–31; "Desertores," 1 Cuerpo, February 10, 1939, CDMH, SM, caja 421, folios 74–81.
75. Corral 2007, 285.
76. Almendral Parra, Flores Velasco, and Valle Sánchez 1990, 191; Murillo Pérez 1990, 206.
77. Corral 2007, 293.
78. Graham 2002, chap. 5.
79. Graham 2002, 254–61.
80. Bolloten 1991, 83–84.
81. Abad de Santillán 1975, 195.
82. Graham 2002, 278.
83. Quoted in Bolloten 1991, 419.
84. Bolloten 1991, 338; Casanova 2005, 125.
85. Bolloten 1991, 420.
86. Graham 2002, 274–75.
87. Fraser 1979, 380.
88. Graham 2002, 272–73.
89. Fraser 1979, 380.
90. "Hombres de la victoria: Los forjadores de la ofensiva de Aragón," *Libertad*, no. 7, p. 3 (no publication date but article dated to September 15, 1937).
91. Bolloten 1991, 337–42.
92. Bolloten 1991, 330–31.
93. Abad de Santillán 1975, 208–9.
94. Graham 2002, 235.
95. Graham 2002, 274.
96. Bolloten 1991, 500–1.
97. Ruiz 2017, 131.
98. Bolloten 1991, 502.
99. Alba and Schwarz 1988, 230–31, 243.
100. Graham 2002, 274.
101. Bolloten 1991, 452, 875.
102. Orwell 1989, 162.
103. Bolloten 1991, 452, 875.
104. Alba and Schwarz 1988, 228.
105. Orwell 1989, 168–69.
106. Orwell 1989, 165.
107. Alba and Schwarz 1988, 229.
108. Alba and Schwarz 1988, 230–31.
109. Fraser 1979, 386.
110. Bolloten 1991, 600.
111. Graham 2002, 375–77.
112. Corral 2007, 334–36.
113. Corral 2007, 314.
114. Corral 2007, 338.
115. Corral 2007, 119.
116. McLauchlin 2014.
117. Corral 2007, 54, 295.
118. Graham 2002, 331–32; Seidman 2002, 157–59; Alpert 2013, 189.
119. "Desertores," 1 Cuerpo, October 15, 1938, folio 30, CDMH, SM, caja 421, folios 29–31.

120. "Desertores," 1 Cuerpo, February 10, 1939, folio 77, CDMH, SM, caja 421, folios 74–81.

121. "Filiación e informe," 26 Brigada Mixta, September 24, 1938, CDMH, SM, caja 607, folios 3–4.

122. Matthews 2012, 142.

123. "Desertores," 1 Cuerpo, October 15, 1938, folio 30, CDMH, SM, caja 421, folios 29–31.

124. "Desertores," 1 Cuerpo, October 14, 1938, folio 34, CDMH, SM, caja 421, folios 32–35.

125. For example, a commissar in Santander was ordered to proceed in his vigilance over a particular soldier with "maximum discretion so as to avoid a lamentable mistake." Jefe, Sección Segunda, Estado Mayor, to Jefe del Batallón 115, January 20, 1937, CDMH, Serie Político-Social [PS] Santander L, caja 436, carpeta 13, expediente 19.

126. Montoliú 1999, 45.

127. Seidman 2002, 159; Corral 2007, 219.

128. Graham 2002, 374.

8. THE NATIONALIST ARMY, 1936–39

1. Salas Larrazábal 2006, III: 2105.

2. Preston 1994b.

3. Payne 1967, 155–57.

4. Gárate Córdoba 1991, 9.

5. de Madariaga 1992.

6. Gárate Córdoba 1991, 25; Alpert 2013, 19.

7. Ellwood 1987, 30–31; Payne 1961, 114–15.

8. Payne 1961, 115–20; Blinkhorn 1975, 252–54; Fraser 1979, 55.

9. Blinkhorn 1975, 256; Ellwood 1987, 33, citing Casas de la Vega 1974; Payne 1961, 146.

10. Corral (2007, 432), however, notes that some Regulares were, exceptionally, forced to fight by local authorities who sought a better relationship with the Nationalists.

11. Balfour 2002, 260–64; Ruiz 2014, 38.

12. Preston 1993, 146.

13. Balfour 2002, 312–13.

14. Balfour 2002, 291.

15. Whitaker 1942, 115.

16. Balfour 2002, 313.

17. Corral 2007, 431.

18. Corral 2007, 90.

19. Seidman 2011, 40–41.

20. Balfour 2002, 181.

21. Seidman 2011, 41, 47–48, 167, 228.

22. Balfour 2002, 19–20, 84, 116–17.

23. Payne 1967, 156–57; Preston 1993, 28.

24. Balfour 2002, 175.

25. Seidman 2011, 43.

26. Preston 1993, 192.

27. Preston 1993, 28.

28. Preston 1998, 69–72; Jensen 2002, 146–47.

29. Preston 1993, 17.

30. Balfour 2002, 278.

31. Balfour 2002.
32. Balfour 2002, 277.
33. Balfour 2002, 176.
34. Balfour 2002, 275.
35. Preston 1993, 26–28; 1998, 69–72.
36. Balfour 2002, 104.
37. Seidman 2011, 52.
38. Corral 2007, 108–9.
39. Matthews 2012, 194–95.
40. Matthews 2012, 442.
41. *Fragua Social* (Valencia), October 4, 1936, p. 6.
42. Corral 2007, 446.
43. Thomas 1994, 239; see also Caspistegui 2009, 186.
44. Caspistegui 2009, 183–84.
45. Caspistegui 2009, 184.
46. Caspistegui 2009, 179.
47. Seidman 2011, 26.
48. Blinkhorn 1975, 259.
49. Blinkhorn 1975, 259. See also Caspistegui 2009, 185.
50. Caspistegui 2009, 187.
51. Blinkhorn 1975, 257–59.
52. Blinkhorn 1975, 254–55.
53. Seidman 2002, 53.
54. Payne 1961, 143.
55. Payne 1961, 145; Seidman 2011, 232.
56. Corral 2007, 121.
57. Fraser 1979, 145.
58. Payne 1961, 145.
59. Ellwood 1987, 32; Payne 1961, 142.
60. Corral 2007, 121.
61. Corral 2007, 116–17; quotation is at 117.
62. Fraser 1979, 284.
63. Corral 2007, 158–59.
64. Seidman 2011, 52.
65. Seidman 2011, 55, 74.
66. Corral 2007, 30–32.
67. Fraser 1979, 465–66.
68. Corral 2007, 214–15; see also Seidman 2011, 239.
69. Juliá 1999; M. Richards 1998.
70. Ruiz 2014, 6–8; Payne 1987, 211–12.
71. "Top Priority Orders by the Junta de Gobierno," in del Castillo and Álvarez 1958, 164–65, quoted by Raguer 2007, 130.
72. Sánchez 1987, 111–12.
73. Raguer 2007, 132.
74. Payne 1987, 211.
75. Raguer 2007, 143.
76. Payne 1987, 215.
77. M. Richards 1998, 34–35.
78. Rodrigo 2008, 137.
79. Rodrigo 2008, 139; see also Rodrigo 2012.
80. Espinosa Maestre 2003, 6–7.

81. Preston 2004, 286, quoting Foltz 1948, 116. The biography of Aguilera by Luis Arias González (2013, 165–66), which explores several myths about the count, accepts that he probably said this. I am grateful to an anonymous reviewer for pointing this reference out.

82. Balcells 2017, 113.

83. Balcells 2017, 111.

84. Matthews 2010, 352–53. See also Seidman 2011, 237–39.

85. Matthews 2010, 353–54.

86. Matthews 2010, 353.

87. Fraser 1979, 315–16.

88. Payne 1961, 146.

89. Corral 2007, 268–72.

90. Corral 2007, 245–46.

91. Matthews 2010, 350–51.

92. Corral 2007, 214–15, 270.

93. Corral 2007, 286, 288.

94. Seidman 2011, 238.

95. Fraser 1979, 284.

96. Corral 2007, 319–20.

97. Corral 2007, 116–17; Nieto 2007, 31.

98. Seidman 2011, 239; on desertion in mountainous terrain on the Republican side, see McLauchlin 2014.

99. Seidman 2011, 213.

100. Seidman 2011, 27.

101. Corral 2007, 145.

102. Corral 2007, 286–87.

103. Seidman 2011, 74.

104. Corral 2007, 52.

105. Seidman 2011, 59.

106. Matthews 2010, 348.

107. Matthews 2010, 356–59.

108. Fraser 1979, 203.

109. Payne 1961, 109–10; Ellwood 1987, 41, 45.

110. Preston 1993; Payne 1987.

111. Blinkhorn 1975, 167; Payne 1961, 152.

112. Blinkhorn 1975, 242–45; Payne 1961, 110.

113. Fraser 1979, 318–19.

9. THE CRUMBLING OF ARMIES IN CONTEMPORARY SYRIA

1. Walter 2017a.

2. Walter 2017b.

3. Kaldor 2006.

4. Pettersson and Eck 2018.

5. Mironova 2019.

6. Mironova 2019, 33–35.

7. Christia 2012; Fjelde and Nilsson 2012; Staniland 2014; Seymour, Bakke, and Cunningham 2016; on factions in Syria specifically, see Gade et al. 2019.

8. For example, C. Lister 2015, 2016a; Lund 2014, 2017.

9. Batatu 1999; Van Dam 2011.

10. Abboud 2015, 40–46. On the everyday domination of the Hafiz al-Asad regime, see Wedeen 1999.

11. Abboud 2015, 36–39; Haddad 2012.

12. Phillips 2015; McLauchlin 2010.

13. Batatu 1999, 227–28; 1981; Van Dam 2011; Nakkash 2013; Paoli 2013; Goldsmith 2015.

14. Abboud 2015, 56–57; Pearlman 2017, 80.

15. Abboud 2015, 87–89.

16. UNHCR 2017.

17. Koehler, Ohl, and Albrecht 2016, 440, 448; Hokayem 2013, 60.

18. Gaub 2014.

19. Sorenson 2016, 41; Samaan and Barnard 2015.

20. Bou Nassif 2015, 644.

21. McLauchlin 2018; Khaddour 2016, 6; Phillips 2016, 148.

22. Hokayem 2013, 53, 58–59; Semenov 2017.

23. Khaddour 2016, 2; Dalle and Glasman 2016, 111–12.

24. Ohl, Albrecht, and Koehler 2015, 5.

25. Kozak n.d.; Dalle and Glasman 2016, 115.

26. Kuhn 2012; Holliday 2013; Pfeffer 2012.

27. Khaddour 2016, 2, 8.

28. Gaub 2014; Holliday 2013; Pfeffer 2012; Semenov 2017.

29. Bou Nassif 2015, 644; Khaddour 2016, 8.

30. Koehler, Ohl, and Albrecht 2016, 449–51.

31. Khaddour 2015.

32. Ohl, Albrecht, and Koehler 2015, 6.

33. Albrecht and Koehler 2018.

34. Bou Nassif 2015, 639.

35. Khaddour 2016, 2; 2015, 8.

36. Bou Nassif 2015, 637.

37. Bou Nassif 2015, 637–38.

38. Kuhn 2012.

39. Dalle and Glasman 2016, 113.

40. Ohl, Albrecht, and Koehler 2015, 4. However, according to Aron Lund, the regime stopped losing support among its Sunni combatants after about 2013. Lund is quoted in Cambanis 2015.

41. Bou Nassif 2015, 634–35, 642.

42. Khaddour 2015, 2, 6.

43. Koehler, Ohl, and Albrecht 2016, 447.

44. Koehler, Ohl, and Albrecht 2016, 451–52. This key finding is replicated in Baczko, Dorronsoro, and Quesnay 2018, 105.

45. Koehler, Ohl, and Albrecht 2016, 447.

46. Khaddour 2015, 5–6.

47. Bou Nassif 2015, 640.

48. Koehler, Ohl, and Albrecht 2016, 447; Bou Nassif 2015, 642.

49. Koehler, Ohl, and Albrecht 2016, 447.

50. Ohl, Albrecht, and Koehler 2015, 4.

51. Ohl, Albrecht, and Koehler 2015, 4.

52. Baczko, Dorronsoro, and Quesnay 2018, 105.

53. The desertion problem stabilized somewhat after about 2013: the soldiers who remained after this huge wave of desertion were especially loyal and effective. Dalle and Glasman 2016, 112; Hokayem 2013, 61; Gaub 2014.

54. McLauchlin 2010, 2018.

55. Abboud 2015, 88–89.

56. O'Bagy 2013, 10; Abboud 2015, 91.

57. Gade, Hafez, and Gabbay 2019.

58. Mahmood and Black 2013; Abdulrahim 2014; Lucente and Al Shimale 2015; Baczko, Dorronsoro, and Quesnay 2018, 110.

59. Abdulrahim 2014; Lucente and Al Shimale 2015.

60. Baczko, Dorronsoro, and Quesnay 2018, 104, 106, 107–8.

61. Koehler, Ohl, and Albrecht 2016.

62. Baczko, Dorronsoro, and Quesnay 2018, 104, 107.

63. Finnish Immigration Service 2016, 20.

64. Baczko, Dorronsoro, and Quesnay 2018, 106; Elshayyal 2013; Black 2013.

65. Baczko, Dorronsoro, and Quesnay 2018, 109.

66. Ohl, Albrecht, and Koehler 2015, 8.

67. al-Abdeh 2013; Abdul-Ahad 2013a.

68. al-Abdeh 2013.

69. Abdul-Ahad 2013a; Abboud 2015, 92.

70. Mironova, Mrie, and Whitt 2014b.

71. Abdulrahim 2014; Sorenson 2016, 48.

72. Mironova, Mrie, and Whitt 2014b.

73. Mironova 2019, 73.

74. Ohl, Albrecht, and Koehler 2015, 8; al-Abdeh 2013; Mironova, Mrie, and Whitt 2014b; Pearlman 2017, 157, 189; Samaha 2017.

75. Mironova 2019, 73.

76. Abdul-Ahad 2013a; Khatib 2015, 9.

77. Lucente and Al Shimale 2015; Ohl, Albrecht, and Koehler 2015, 8.

78. Mahmood and Black 2013; Baczko, Dorronsoro, and Quesnay 2018, 110.

79. Mironova 2019, 72–73.

80. Pearlman 2017, 151, 205.

81. Mironova, Mrie, and Whitt 2014a, 21–22, 25.

82. C. Lister 2016b, 9–11; 2015, 56–60; Benotman and Blake 2013; Wright et al. 2016, 22.

83. Anzalone 2016, 41; Cafarella 2014; Dalle and Glasman 2016, 131.

84. C. Lister 2016b, 11; 2015, 93–94.

85. C. Lister 2015, 80, 86, 98; Pearlman 2017, 163.

86. Cafarella 2014; C. Lister 2016b, 33.

87. Gerges 2016, 185.

88. Mironova 2019, 48.

89. Mironova, Mrie, and Whitt 2014c; Mironova, Mrie, and Whitt 2014a.

90. C. Lister 2016b, 5, 9–10; 2015, 56–59.

91. Cafarella 2014, 14.

92. Cafarella 2014, 25; Lister 2016b, 35; Cafarella 2014, 16.

93. One month: Cafarella 2014, 26; six to eight weeks: C. Lister 2016b, 35; several months: Finnish Immigration Service 2016, 20; Mironova 2019, 75.

94. Cafarella 2014, 25; Hokayem 2013, 92.

95. Cafarella 2014, 16.

96. C. Lister 2016b, 12–13, 31–32; Abdul-Ahad 2013b.

97. Khatib 2015, 9.

98. Abdul-Ahad 2013b; Cafarella 2014, 16. On the importance of centrally directing financing, see Worsnop 2017.

99. Cafarella 2014, 16; Baczko, Dorronsoro, and Quesnay 2018, 109.

100. C. Lister 2016b, 11–13; Abboud 2015, 177.

101. Gerges 2016, 254.

102. C. Lister 2016b, 24.

103. C. Lister 2016b, 13.

104. Abboud 2015, 107.

105. Lund 2015a; Gerges 2016, 254.

106. C. Lister 2014, 2.

107. Gerges 2016, 275–77.

108. Gerges 2016, 275.

109. Speckhard and Yayla 2015, 106.

110. Al-Arabiya 2014; Speckhard and Yayla 2015; Neumann 2015, 5; P. Wood 2016.

111. Browne 2016; Chulov 2017.

112. Gerges 2016, 133; Weiss and Hassan 2015, 86, 145–47.

113. Speckhard and Yayla 2015, 104–5; C. Lister 2014, 17; Khatib 2015, 18.

114. Khatib 2015, 18.

115. Byman 2016, 141–42; Khatib 2015, 9; Speckhard and Yayla 2015, 102–3.

116. Byman 2016, 149–50; Gerges 2016, 193–94.

117. C. Lister 2014, 24; Byman 2016, 141; Khatib 2015, 9; Gerges 2016, 178–79.

118. Byman 2016, 141.

119. Gerges 2016, 269; Speckhard and Yayla 2015, 102.

120. Khatib 2015, 17–18; Speckhard and Yayla 2015, 101–2.

121. Khatib 2015, 18.

122. Alami 2015; Gerges 2016, 270; Byman 2016.

123. Khatib 2015, 22; Neumann 2015.

124. Byman 2016, 151; Khatib 2015, 21–22.

125. Byman 2016, 151; Khatib 2015, 22; Gerges 2016, 245.

126. Neumann 2015, 11.

127. Lyall 2017, 88.

128. Neumann 2015, 12.

129. Speckhard and Yayla 2015, 100; Weiss 2016.

130. Lund 2015c; Perry 2017.

131. Caves 2012, 4; International Crisis Group 2013, 26; 2014, 5.

132. Abboud 2015, 103; Gunter 2014, 110–11.

133. Gunter 2017, 120–23, 129–31; International Crisis Group 2017b; Savelsberg and Tejel 2013, 211.

134. Lund 2015c; Congressional Research Service 2016.

135. Stephens 2014; Congressional Research Service 2016, 13–14; Lister and Ward 2015.

136. Lund 2015b.

137. Lund 2015c; Congressional Research Service 2016.

138. *Economist* 2017; Zaman al-Wasl 2017.

139. Drott 2014a; Lister and Ward 2015.

140. International Crisis Group 2014, 1.

141. International Crisis Group 2014, 1; Gunter 2014, 110.

142. Allsopp 2014, 189–90; International Crisis Group 2014, 4.

143. International Crisis Group 2013, 2.

144. Danish Immigration Service 2015, 18; Drott 2015.

145. International Crisis Group 2014, 13–14.

146. Zaman 2017; NBC News 2014; Öğür and Baykal 2018, 54.

147. Drott and Di Stefano Pironti 2014; Geneva Call 2016; International Crisis Group 2017c, 6.

148. Wilgenburg 2014; Danish Immigration Service 2015; Baczko, Dorronsoro, and Quesnay 2018, 171.

149. Danish Immigration Service 2015, 17; Baczko, Dorronsoro, and Quesnay 2018, 171; ARA News 2016, 2017.

150. Danish Immigration Service 2015, 30; ARA News 2017.

151. Allsopp 2013, 237; 2014, 204–5; Abboud 2015, 170; International Crisis Group 2014, 14; Caves 2012, 4.

152. Savelsberg and Tejel 2013, 214.

153. International Crisis Group 2014, 14.

154. Drott 2014b.

155. Lund 2016.

156. International Crisis Group 2017b, 4.

157. McLauchlin 2018.

158. Walter 2017a.

159. Mironova 2019, 89–90.

160. Walter 2017b, 22.

161. Abrahms in Abrahms, Leader Maynard, and Thaler 2018.

CONCLUSION

1. Thomas 1994, 613, 691–92; Martínez Bande 1980, 221; Solar 1996, 85–86; Seidman 2002, 111–15, 190–93.

2. Posen 1993b; Kaufmann 1996.

3. Olson 1971; Tullock 1971; Blattman and Miguel 2010.

4. Collier 2001; Collier and Hoeffler 2004.

5. Taylor 1988; Lichbach 1995; E. Wood 2003.

6. Costa and Kahn 2008; Gould 1995; Staniland 2014.

7. Kalyvas and Kocher 2007; Kalyvas 2006, 103.

8. Kalyvas 2006, 113.

9. This is not just a property of "ethnic conflict" either: ideologies in general tend to define social groups to defend and to target. Consider the kulaks in the Soviet Union, for instance. For more: Gutiérrez Sanín and Wood 2014; Leader Maynard 2019.

10. Checkel 2017.

11. Gates 2017.

12. Manekin 2017.

13. Kalyvas 2006, 93–100; 2008.

14. McLauchlin 2010, 2018.

15. Corral 2007, 146–47, 236–38.

16. Fraser 1979, 466–67.

17. Centro Documental de la Memoria Histórica (CDMH), Serie Militar (SM), caja 700, folio 19.

18. Corral 2007, 148–49.

19. Costalli and Ruggeri 2015; Cederman, Gleditsch, and Buhaug 2013; Leader Maynard 2019; Oppenheim et al. 2015.

20. Gates 2002; Johnston 2008; McLauchlin 2014.

21. Jaffe and Morris 2015.

22. International Crisis Group 2010, 29, 34.

23. Eck 2014; Weinstein 2007.

24. J. Richards 2018, 44.

25. Staniland 2014.

26. McLauchlin and Pearlman 2012; Bakke, Cunningham, and Seymour 2012. See also Parkinson 2017.

27. E. Wood 2008.

28. Balfour 2002.
29. Otunnu 1999.
30. Rudloff and Findley 2016.
31. Blattman 2009.
32. Jha and Wilkinson 2012.
33. Costa and Kahn 2008, 160–86.
34. Lonn 1928; Corral 2007.

References

Abad de Santillán, Diego. 1975. *Por Qué Perdimos la Guerra: Una Contribución a la Historia de la Tragedia Española*. Madrid: G. del Toro.

Abboud, Samer N. 2015. *Syria*. Cambridge: Polity.

Abdul-Ahad, Ghaith. 2013a. "How to Start a Battalion (in Five Easy Lessons)." *London Review of Books*, February 21, 2013. https://www.lrb.co.uk/v35/n04/ghaith-abdul-ahad/how-to-start-a-battalion-in-five-easy-lessons.

———. 2013b. "Syria's al-Nusra Front—Ruthless, Organised and Taking Control." *The Guardian*, July 10, 2013. http://www.theguardian.com/world/2013/jul/10/syria-al-nusra-front-jihadi.

Abdulrahim, Raja. 2014. "Hundreds of Fatigued Syrian Rebels Give Up the Fight." *Los Angeles Times*, July 18, 2014. http://www.latimes.com/world/middleeast/la-fg-syria-former-rebels-20140718-story.html.

———. 2016. "Syria Regime Drafts Prisoners, Teachers to Bolster Depleted Army." *Wall Street Journal*, August 5, 2016. http://www.wsj.com/articles/syria-strains-to-bolster-depleted-military-1470413365.

Abrahms, Max, Jonathan Leader Maynard, and Kai Thaler. 2018. "Correspondence: Ideological Extremism in Armed Conflict." *International Security* 43 (1): 186–90. https://doi.org/10.1162/isec_c_00324.

Achen, Christopher H., and Larry M. Bartels. 2017. *Democracy for Realists: Why Elections Do Not Produce Responsive Government*. Princeton, NJ: Princeton University Press.

Ahmad, Aisha. 2016. "Going Global: Islamist Competition in Contemporary Civil Wars." *Security Studies* 25 (2): 353–84. https://doi.org/10.1080/09636412.2016.1171971.

———. 2017. *Jihad & Co: Black Markets and Islamist Power*. Oxford: Oxford University Press.

al-Abdeh, Malik. 2013. "Rebels, Inc." *Foreign Policy* (blog). November 21, 2013. https://foreignpolicy.com/2013/11/21/rebels-inc/.

Alami, Mona. 2015. "ISIS Recruitment Tactics Stumble." *Atlantic Council* (blog). February 26, 2015. http://www.atlanticcouncil.org/blogs/menasource/dispatch-isis-recruitment-tactics-stumble.

Al-Arabiya. 2014. "ISIS 'Executes 100 Deserters' in Syria's Raqqa." December 20, 2014. http://english.alarabiya.net/en/News/middle-east/2014/12/20/ISIS-executes-100-deserters-in-Syria-s-Raqqa-report.html.

Alba, Victor, and Stephen Schwartz. 1988. *Spanish Marxism versus Soviet Communism: A History of the P.O.U.M.* New Brunswick, NJ: Transaction Publishers.

Albrecht, Holger, and Kevin Koehler. 2018. "Going on the Run: What Drives Military Desertion in Civil War?" *Security Studies* 27 (2): 179–203. https://doi.org/10.1080/09636412.2017.1386931.

Albrecht, Holger, and Dorothy Ohl. 2016. "Exit, Resistance, Loyalty: Military Behavior during Unrest in Authoritarian Regimes." *Perspectives on Politics* 14 (1): 38–52. https://doi.org/10.1017/S1537592715003217.

Allsopp, Harriet. 2013. "The Kurdish Autonomy Bid in Syria: Challenges and Reactions." In *The Kurdish Spring: Geopolitical Changes and the Kurds*, 218–49. Costa Mesa, CA: Mazda Publishers.

——. 2014. *The Kurds of Syria: Political Parties and Identity in the Middle East*. London: I. B. Tauris.

Almendral Parra, Cristina, Teresa Flores Velasco, and David Valle Sánchez. 1990. "Auditoría de Guerra de Gijón: Causas Instruidas por los Jueces Militares de Gijón." In *Justicia en Guerra: Jornadas sobre la Administración de Justicia Durante la Guerra Civil Española: Instituciones y Fuentes Documentales*, edited by Archivo Histórico Nacional Sección Guerra Civil, 189–204. Madrid: Ministerio de Cultura.

Alpert, Michael. 2004. *A New International History of the Spanish Civil War*. 2nd ed. Houndmills, UK: Palgrave Macmillan.

——. 2013. *The Republican Army in the Spanish Civil War, 1936–1939*. Cambridge: Cambridge University Press.

Álvarez del Vayo, Julio. 1940. *Freedom's Battle*. New York: Knopf.

Andreas, Peter. 2020. *Killer High: A History of War in Six Drugs*. Oxford: Oxford University Press.

Anonymous. 1997. *Un "Incontrolado" de la Columna de Hierro: Marzo 1937*. Barcelona: Etcetera.

Anzalone, Christopher. 2016. "The Multiple Faces of Jabhat Al-Nusra/Jabhat Fath al-Sham in Syria's Civil War." *Insight Turkey* 18 (2): 41–50. https://www.insightturkey.com/the-multiple-faces-of-jabhat-al-nusrajabhat-fath-al-sham-in-syrias-civil-war/articles/10514.

ARA News. 2016. "Kurds Launch Conscription Campaign to Protect Kobane from ISIS Attacks." June 21, 2016. http://aranews.net/2016/06/kurds-launch-conscription-campaign-to-protect-kobane-from-isis-attacks/.

——. 2017. "Increased Conscription of Kurdish Youth in Kobane Facing Widespread Criticism." March 1, 2017. http://aranews.net/2017/03/increased-conscription-of-kurdish-youth-in-kobane-facing-widespread-criticism/.

Arcarazo García, Luis. 2004. "El 'Sector Huesca' Del Frente de Aragón: Los Combates Entre 1936 y 1938." In *Guerra Civil Aragón*, edited by Fernando Martínez de Baños Carrillo, I:95–188. Zaragoza: Editorial Delsan.

Ardant du Picq, Charles Jean Jacques Joseph. 2017. *Battle Studies*. Translated by Roger J. Spiller. Modern War Studies. Lawrence: University Press of Kansas.

Argenbright, Robert. 1991. "Red Tsaritsyn: Precursor of Stalinist Terror." *Revolutionary Russia* 4 (2): 157–83. https://doi.org/10.1080/09546549108575569.

Arias González, Luis. 2013. *Gonzalo de Aguilera Munro, XI Conde de Alba de Yeltes (1886–1965): Vidas y Radicalismo de un Hidalgo Heterodoxo*. Salamanca, Spain: Ediciones Universidad de Salamanca.

Arjona, Ana M., and Stathis N. Kalyvas. 2006. "Preliminary Results of a Survey of Demobilized Combatants in Colombia." Unpublished manuscript, Yale University.

Aroca Sardagna, José María. 1972. *Las Tribus*. Barcelona: Ediciones Acervo.

Asal, Victor, Mitchell Brown, and Angela Dalton. 2012. "Why Split? Organizational Splits among Ethnopolitical Organizations in the Middle East." *Journal of Conflict Resolution* 56 (1): 94–117. https://doi.org/10.1177/0022002711429680.

Asal, Victor, Justin Conrad, and Nathan Toronto. 2017. "I Want You! The Determinants of Military Conscription." *Journal of Conflict Resolution* 61 (7): 1456–81. https://doi.org/10.1177/0022002715606217.

Azaña, Manuel. 1967. *Obras Completas*. Vol. 3. Mexico City: Ediciones Oasis.

Baczko, Adam, Gilles Dorronsoro, and Arthur Quesnay. 2018. *Civil War in Syria: Mobilization and Competing Social Orders*. Cambridge: Cambridge University Press.

Bakke, Kristin M., Kathleen Gallagher Cunningham, and Lee J. M. Seymour. 2012. "A Plague of Initials: Fragmentation, Cohesion, and Infighting in Civil Wars." *Perspectives on Politics* 10 (2): 265–83. https://doi.org/10.1017/S1537592712000667.

Balcells, Laia. 2017. *Rivalry and Revenge: The Politics of Violence during Civil War*. Cambridge: Cambridge University Press.

Balfour, Sebastian. 2002. *Deadly Embrace: Morocco and the Road to the Spanish Civil War*. Oxford: Oxford University Press.

Barber, Benjamin, and Charles Miller. 2019. "Propaganda and Combat Motivation: Radio Broadcasts and German Soldiers' Performance in World War II." *World Politics* 71 (3): 457–502. https://doi.org/10.1017/S0043887118000345.

Barkawi, Tarak. 2015. "Subaltern Soldiers: Eurocentrism and the Nation-State in the Combat Motivation Debate." In *Frontline: Combat and Cohesion in the Twenty-First Century*, edited by Anthony King, 24–45. Oxford: Oxford University Press.

———. 2017. *Soldiers of Empire: Indian and British Armies in World War II*. Cambridge: Cambridge University Press.

Bartov, Omer. 1991. *Hitler's Army: Soldiers, Nazis, and War in the Third Reich*. Oxford: Oxford University Press.

Batatu, Hanna. 1981. "Some Observations on the Social Roots of Syria's Ruling, Military Group and the Causes for Its Dominance." *Middle East Journal* 35 (3): 331–44. https://www.jstor.org/stable/4326249

———. 1999. *Syria's Peasantry, the Descendants of Its Lesser Rural Notables, and Their Politics*. Princeton, NJ: Princeton University Press.

Bearman, Peter S. 1991. "Desertion as Localism: Army Unit Solidarity and Group Norms in the U.S. Civil War." *Social Forces* 70 (2): 321–42. https://doi.org/10.1093/sf/70.2.321.

Beber, Bernd, and Christopher Blattman. 2013. "The Logic of Child Soldiering and Coercion." *International Organization* 67 (1): 65–104. https://doi.org/10.1017/S002081 8312000409.

Beck, Nathaniel, Jonathan N. Katz, and Richard Tucker. 1998. "Taking Time Seriously: Time-Series-Cross-Section Analysis with a Binary Dependent Variable." *American Journal of Political Science* 42 (4): 1260–88. http://dx.doi.org/10.2307/2991857.

Benotman, Noman, and Roisin Blake. 2013. *Jabhat Al-Nusra: A Strategic Briefing*. London: Quilliam Foundation. https://www.quilliaminternational.com/shop/e-publications /jabhat-al-nusra-a-strategic-briefing/.

Ben-Shalom, Uzi, Zeev Lehrer, and Eyal Ben-Ari. 2005. "Cohesion during Military Operations: A Field Study on Combat Units in the Al-Aqsa Intifada." *Armed Forces & Society* 32 (1): 63–79. https://doi.org/10.1177/0095327X05277888.

Bergholz, Max. 2016. *Violence as a Generative Force: Identity, Nationalism, and Memory in a Balkan Community*. Ithaca, NY: Cornell University Press.

Biddle, Stephen D. 2004. *Military Power: Explaining Victory and Defeat in Modern Battle*. Princeton, NJ: Princeton University Press.

Bilefsky, Dan. 2018. "A One-Eyed Québécois 'Rambo' Captures Imaginations in Canada." *New York Times*, May 27, 2018.

Black, Ian. 2013. "Syria Crisis: Saudi Arabia to Spend Millions to Train New Rebel Force." *The Guardian*, November 7, 2013. http://www.theguardian.com/world/2013/nov/07 /syria-crisis-saudi-arabia-spend-millions-new-rebel-force.

Blanco Rodríguez, Juan Andrés. 1993. *El Quinto Regimiento en la Política Militar Del PCE en la Guerra Civil*. Madrid: Universidad Nacional de Educación a Distancia.

Blanco Rodríguez, Juan Andrés, Manuel Fernández Cuadrado, and Jesús A. Martínez Martín. 1988. "Las Milicias Populares Republicanas de Origen Castellano-Leonés." In *Historia y Memoria de la Guerra Civil: Encuentro en Castilla y León*, edited by Julio Aróstegui, II. Investigaciones, 311–40. Valladolid, Spain: Junta de Castilla y León.

Blattman, Christopher. 2009. "From Violence to Voting: War and Political Participation in Uganda." *American Political Science Review* 103 (2): 231–47. https://doi.org/10 .1017/S0003055409090212.

Blattman, Christopher, and Edward Miguel. 2010. "Civil War." *Journal of Economic Literature* 48 (1): 3–57. https://doi.org/doi.org/10.1257/jel.48.1.3.

Blinkhorn, Martin. 1975. *Carlism and Crisis in Spain: 1931–1939*. Cambridge: Cambridge University Press.

Bolloten, Burnett. 1991. *The Spanish Civil War: Revolution and Counterrevolution*. Chapel Hill: University of North Carolina Press.

Bond, T. C. 1976. "The Why of Fragging." *American Journal of Psychiatry* 133 (11): 1328–31. https://doi.org/10.1176/ajp.133.11.1328.

Bou Nassif, Hicham. 2015. "'Second-Class': The Grievances of Sunni Officers in the Syrian Armed Forces." *Journal of Strategic Studies* 38 (5): 626–49. https://doi.org/10.1080/01402390.2015.1053604.

Broué, Pierre, and Émile Témime. 1970. *The Revolution and the Civil War in Spain*. Translated by Tony White. Cambridge, MA: MIT Press.

Browne, Ryan. 2016. "ISIS Docs Show Struggle to Retain Fighters." *CNN* (blog). April 27, 2016. http://www.cnn.com/2016/04/26/politics/isis-documents/index.html.

Brusco, Ramon. 2003. *Les Milícies Antifeixistes i l'Exèrcit Popular a Catalunya (1936–1937)*. Lleida, Spain: Edicions el Jonc.

Byman, Daniel. 2016. "Understanding the Islamic State—A Review Essay." *International Security* 40 (4): 127–65. https://doi.org/10.1162/ISEC_r_00235.

Cafarella, Jennifer. 2014. *Jabhat Al-Nusra in Syria: An Islamic Emirate for al-Qaeda*. Middle East Security Report 25. Washington, DC: Institute for the Study of War.

Cambanis, Thanassis. 2015. "Assad's Sunni Foot Soldiers." *Foreign Policy*, November 5, 2015. https://foreignpolicy.com/2015/11/05/assads-sunni-foot-soldiers-syria/.

Cardona, Gabriel. 1996. "Milicias y Ejércitos." In *Milicias y Ejércitos*, 8–71. La Guerra Civil Española. Barcelona: Folio.

Carey, Sabine C., and Neil J. Mitchell. 2017. "Progovernment Militias." *Annual Review of Political Science* 20 (1): 127–47. https://doi.org/10.1146/annurev-polisci-051915-045433.

Carrillo, Santiago. 2012. *Mi Testamento Político*. Barcelona: Galaxia Gutenberg.

Casanova, Julián. 1985. *Anarquismo y Revolución en la Sociedad Rural Aragonesa, 1936–1938*. Madrid: Siglo XXI.

———. 2005. *Anarchism, the Republic and Civil War in Spain: 1931–1939*. London: Routledge.

———. 2010. *The Spanish Republic and the Civil War*. Cambridge: Cambridge University Press.

Casas de la Vega, Rafael. 1974. *Las Milicias Nacionales en la Guerra de España*. Madrid: Editora Nacional.

———. 1994. *El Terror: Madrid 1936*. Madridejos, Toledo: Editorial Fénix.

Caselli, Francesco, and Wilbur John Coleman. 2006. "On the Theory of Ethnic Conflict." NBER Working Paper 12125, National Bureau of Economic Research, Cambridge, MA.

Caspistegui, Francisco Javier. 2009. "'Spain's Vendée': Carlist Identity in Navarre as a Mobilising Model." In *The Splintering of Spain: Cultural History and the Spanish Civil War, 1936–1939*, edited by Christopher Ealham and Michael Richards, 177–95. Cambridge: Cambridge University Press.

Castillo, Jasen. 2014. *Endurance and War: The National Sources of Military Cohesion*. Stanford, CA: Stanford University Press.

Caves, John. 2012. *Syrian Kurds and the Democratic Unity Party (PYD)*. Washington, DC: Institute for the Study of War.

Cederman, Lars-Erik, Kristian Skrede Gleditsch, and Halvard Buhaug. 2013. *Inequality, Grievances, and Civil War*. Cambridge: Cambridge University Press.

Cederman, Lars-Erik, Andreas Wimmer, and Brian Min. 2010. "Why Do Ethnic Groups Rebel? New Data and Analysis." *World Politics* 62 (1): 87–119.

Cervera, Javier. 2006. *Madrid en Guerra: La Ciudad Clandestina, 1936–1939*. Madrid: Alianza Editorial.

Chandra, Kanchan, and Steven I. Wilkinson. 2008. "Measuring the Effect of 'Ethnicity.'" *Comparative Political Studies* 41 (4–5): 515–63. https://doi.org/10.1177/001041 4007313240.

Checkel, Jeffrey T. 2017. "Socialization and Violence: Introduction and Framework." *Journal of Peace Research* 54 (5): 592–605. https://doi.org/10.1177/0022343317721813.

Chenoweth, Erica, and Maria J. Stephan. 2011. *Why Civil Resistance Works: The Strategic Logic of Nonviolent Conflict*. New York: Columbia University Press.

Christia, Fotini. 2012. *Alliance Formation in Civil Wars*. Cambridge: Cambridge University Press.

Chulov, Martin. 2017. "Hundreds of Isis Defectors Mass on Syrian Border Hoping to Flee." *The Guardian*, September 12, 2017. http://www.theguardian.com/world/2017/sep/12/hundreds-of-isis-defectors-mass-on-syrian-border-hoping-to-flee.

Cirre Jiménez, José. 1937. *De Espejo a Madrid: Con las Tropas del General Miaja (Relato de un Testigo)*. Granada, Spain: Librería Prieto.

Cohen, Dara Kay. 2016. *Rape during Civil War*. Ithaca, NY: Cornell University Press.

Coleman, James S. 1990. *Foundations of Social Theory*. Cambridge, MA: Harvard University Press.

Collier, Paul. 2000. "Rebellion as a Quasi-Criminal Activity." *Journal of Conflict Resolution* 44 (6): 839–53. https://doi.org/10.1177/0022002700044006008.

———. 2001. "Economic Causes of Conflict and Their Implications for Policy." In *Turbulent Peace: The Challenges of Managing International Conflict*, edited by Chester A. Crocker, Fen Osler Hampson, and Pamela Aall, 143–62. Washington, DC: United States Institute of Peace Press.

Collier, Paul, and Anke Hoeffler. 2004. "Greed and Grievance in Civil War." *Oxford Economic Papers* 56 (4): 563–95. https://doi.org/10.1093/oep/gpf064.

Collier, Paul, Anke Hoeffler, and Dominic Rohner. 2009. "Beyond Greed and Grievance: Feasibility and Civil War." *Oxford Economic Papers* 61 (1): 1–27. https://doi.org/10.1093/oep/gpn029.

Colodny, Robert. 1958. *The Struggle for Madrid: The Central Epic of the Spanish Conflict (1936–1937)*. New York: Paine-Whitman.

Congressional Research Service. 2016. *Kurds in Iraq and Syria: U.S. Partners against the Islamic State*. R44153. Washington, DC: Congressional Research Service.

Connable, Ben, and Martin C. Libicki. 2010. *How Insurgencies End*. Santa Monica, CA: RAND Corporation.

Converse, Philip E. 1964. "The Nature of Belief Systems in Mass Publics." In *Ideology and Discontent*, edited by David E. Apter, 206–61. New York: Free Press of Glencoe.

Cordón, Antonio. 2008. *Trayectoria: Recuerdos de un Artillero*. Sevilla, Spain: Ediciones Espuela de Plata.

Corral, Pedro. 2007. *Desertores: La Guerra Civil que Nadie Quiere Contar*. Barcelona: Crítica.

Costa, Dora L., and Matthew E. Kahn. 2008. *Heroes and Cowards: The Social Face of War*. Princeton, NJ: Princeton University Press.

Costalli, Stefano, and Andrea Ruggeri. 2015. "Indignation, Ideologies, and Armed Mobilization: Civil War in Italy, 1943–45." *International Security* 40 (2): 119–57. https://doi.org/10.1162/ISEC_a_00218.

Creveld, Martin van. 2004. *Supplying War: Logistics from Wallenstein to Patton*. Cambridge: Cambridge University Press.

Cruells, Manuel. 1974. *De les Milícies a l'Exèrcit Popular a Catalunya*. Barcelona: Dopesa.

Dalle, Ignace, and Wladimir Glasman. 2016. *Le Cauchemar Syrien*. Paris: Fayard.

Dandeker, Christopher. 1990. *Surveillance, Power and Modernity: Bureaucracy and Discipline from 1700 to the Present Day*. Cambridge: Polity Press.

Danish Immigration Service. 2015. *Syria: Military Service, Mandatory Self-Defence Duty and Recruitment to the YPG*. Copenhagen: Danish Immigration Service.

De Bruin, Erica. 2018. "Preventing Coups d'état: How Counterbalancing Works." *Journal of Conflict Resolution* 62 (7): 1433–58. https://doi.org/10.1177/0022002717692652.

de Frutos, Victor. 1967. *Los que No Perdieron la Guerra: España: 1936–39*. Buenos Aires: Editorial Oberon.

de Guzmán, Eduardo. 2004. *Madrid Rojo y Negro*. Madrid: Oberón.

del Castillo, José, and Santiago Álvarez. 1958. *Barcelona, Objetivo Cubierto*. Barcelona: Timón.

de Madariaga, María Rosa. 1992. "The Intervention of Moroccan Troops in the Spanish Civil War: A Reconsideration." *European History Quarterly* 22 (1): 67–97. https://doi.org/10.1177/026569149202200103.

DeNardo, James. 1985. *Power in Numbers: The Political Strategy of Protest and Rebellion*. Princeton, NJ: Princeton University Press.

Derriennic, Jean Pierre. 2001. *Les guerres civiles*. Paris: Les Presses de Sciences Po.

Drott, Carl. 2014a. "'Extremists' and 'Moderates' in Kobani." *Warscapes* (blog). October 13, 2014. http://www.warscapes.com/reportage/extremists-and-moderates-kobani.

——. 2014b. "Fighting Power in Kobanî." *Le Monde Diplomatique*, September 26, 2014. http://mondediplo.com/outsidein/fighting-power-in-kobani.

——. 2015. "Kobani before the Hurricane Part I." *Utrikespolitiska Föreningen Uppsala* (blog). March 4, 2015. http://www.ufuppsala.se/kobani-before-the-hurricane-part-i/.

Drott, Carl, and Alexandra Di Stefano Pironti. 2014. "Syrian Kurdish Forces Demobilize Child Soldiers." *Rudaw* (blog). July 11, 2014. http://www.rudaw.net/english/middleeast/syria/11072014.

Eck, Kristine. 2014. "Coercion in Rebel Recruitment." *Security Studies* 23 (2): 364–98. https://doi.org/10.1080/09636412.2014.905368.

Economist. 2017. "To the Victors, the Toils." October 21, 2017.

Ellwood, Sheelagh M. 1987. *Spanish Fascism in the Franco Era: Falange Española de las JONS, 1936–76*. Houndmills, UK: Macmillan.

Elshayyal, Jamal. 2013. "Inside Look at Syria Rebels' Tactics and Arms." Al Jazeera. http://www.aljazeera.com/news/middleeast/2013/01/2013120233443473526.html.

Engel, Carlos. 1999. *Historia de las Brigadas Mixtas del Ejército Popular de la República*. Madrid: Almena.

——. 2008. *El Cuerpo de Oficiales en la Guerra de España*. Valladolid, Spain: Alcañiz Fresno's Editores.

Enloe, Cynthia H. 1980. *Ethnic Soldiers: State Security in Divided Societies*. Athens, GA: University of Georgia Press.

Espinosa Maestre, Francisco. 2003. *La Columna de la Muerte: El Avance del Ejército Franquista de Sevilla a Badajoz*. Barcelona: Crítica.

Fearon, James D., and David D. Laitin. 2000. "Violence and the Social Construction of Ethnic Identity." *International Organization* 54 (4): 845–77. https://doi.org/10.1162/002081800551398.

——. 2003. "Ethnicity, Insurgency, and Civil War." *American Political Science Review* 97 (1): 75–90. https://doi.org/10.1017/S0003055403000534.

Figes, Orlando. 1990. "The Red Army and Mass Mobilization during the Russian Civil War 1918–1920." *Past & Present*, no. 129: 168–211. https://doi.org/10.1093/past/129.1.168.

Finnish Immigration Service. 2016. *Syria: Military Service, National Defense Forces, Armed Groups Supporting Syrian Regime and Armed Opposition*. Fact-Finding Mission Report. Helsinki: Finnish Immigration Service.

Fjelde, Hanne, and Desirée Nilsson. 2012. "Rebels against Rebels: Explaining Violence between Rebel Groups." *Journal of Conflict Resolution* 56 (4): 604–28. https://doi.org/10.1177/0022002712439496.

Foltz, Charles, Jr. 1948. *The Masquerade in Spain*. Boston: Houghton Mifflin.

Fraser, Ronald. 1979. *Blood of Spain: The Experience of Civil War, 1936–1939*. London: Allen Lane.

Gade, Emily Kalah, Michael Gabbay, Mohammed M. Hafez, and Zane Kelly. 2019. "Networks of Cooperation: Rebel Alliances in Fragmented Civil Wars." *Journal of Conflict Resolution* 63 (9): 2071–97. https://doi.org/10.1177/0022002719826234.

Gade, Emily Kalah, Mohammed M. Hafez, and Michael Gabbay. 2019. "Fratricide in Rebel Movements: A Network Analysis of Syrian Militant Infighting." *Journal of Peace Research* 56 (3): 321–35. https://doi.org/10.1177/0022343318806940.

Ganin, Andrei Vladislavovich. 2013. "Workers and Peasants Red Army 'General Staff Personalities' Defecting to the Enemy Side in 1918–1921." *Journal of Slavic Military Studies* 26 (2): 259–309. https://doi.org/10.1080/13518046.2013.779877.

Gárate Córdoba, José María. 1991. "Las Tropas de Africa en la Guerra Civil Española." *Revista de Historia Militar* 35 (70): 9–66. https://dialnet.unirioja.es/servlet/articulo?codigo=4171713.

García Oliver, Juan. 1978. *El Eco de los Pasos*. Paris: Ruedo Ibérico.

García Venero, Maximiano. 1973. *Madrid Julio 1936*. Madrid: Tebas.

Gates, Scott. 2002. "Recruitment and Allegiance: The Microfoundations of Rebellion." *Journal of Conflict Resolution* 46 (1): 111–30. https://doi.org/10.1177/0022002702046001007.

———. 2017. "Membership Matters: Coerced Recruits and Rebel Allegiance." *Journal of Peace Research* 54 (5): 674–86. https://doi.org/10.1177/0022343317722700.

Gaub, Florence. 2014. "Syria's Military: Last Man Standing?" Carnegie Europe. July 29, 2014. http://carnegieeurope.eu/strategiceurope/?fa=56274.

Gauhar, G. N. 2007. "Jamat-I-Islami of Jammu and Kashmir." In *Conflict and Politics of Jammu and Kashmir: Internal Dynamics*, edited by Avineet Prashar and Paawan Vivek, 75–84. Jammu, India: Saksham Books International.

Geneva Call. 2016. "A Report from inside Syria: A Visit to Monitor the Prohibition on the Use of Child Soldiers in Kurdish Areas." *Geneva Call* (blog). February 10, 2016. https://genevacall.org/report-inside-syria-visit-monitor-prohibition-use-child-soldiers-kurdish-areas/.

George, Alexander L. 1967. *The Chinese Communist Army in Action: The Korean War and Its Aftermath*. New York: Columbia University Press.

Gerges, Fawaz A. 2016. *ISIS: A History*. Princeton, NJ: Princeton University Press.

Gintis, Herbert, Eric Alden Smith, and Samuel Bowles. 2001. "Costly Signaling and Cooperation." *Journal of Theoretical Biology* 213 (1): 103–19. https://doi.org/10.1006/jtbi.2001.2406.

Giuffre, Katherine A. 1997. "First in Flight: Desertion as Politics in the North Carolina Confederate Army." *Social Science History* 21 (2): 245–63. https://doi.org/10.1017/S0145553200017727.

Giustozzi, Antonio. 2015. *The Army of Afghanistan: A Political History of a Fragile Institution*. London: Hurst.

Goldsmith, Leon T. 2015. *Cycle of Fear: Syria's Alawites in War and Peace*. London: Hurst.

Goodwin, Jeff. 2001. *No Other Way Out: States and Revolutionary Movements, 1945–1991*. Cambridge: Cambridge University Press.

Gould, Roger V. 1995. *Insurgent Identities: Class, Community, and Protest in Paris from 1848 to the Commune*. Chicago: University of Chicago Press.

Graham, Helen. 2002. *The Spanish Republic at War 1936–1939*. Cambridge: Cambridge University Press.

Gramajo, Gaston, Zobel Behalal, Rupert Cook, Michael Sharp, Koenraad de Swaef, and Emmanuel Viret. 2016. *Final Report of the Group of Experts on the Democratic Republic of the Congo*. S/2016/466. New York: United Nations Security Council.

Grossman, Dave. 1996. *On Killing: The Psychological Cost of Learning to Kill in War and Society*. Boston: Little, Brown.

Gunter, Michael M. 2014. *Out of Nowhere: The Kurds of Syria in Peace and War*. London: Hurst.

———. 2017. *The Kurds: A Modern History*. 2nd ed. Princeton, NJ: Markus Wiener Publishers.

Gutiérrez Flores, Jesús, and Enrique Gudín de la Lama. 2005. "Cuatro Derroteros Militares de la Guerra Civil En Cantabria." *Monte Buciero* 11: 18–298. https://dialnet.unirioja.es/servlet/articulo?codigo=1633999.

Gutiérrez Rueda, Laura, and Carmen Gutiérrez Rueda. 2003. *El Hambre en el Madrid de la Guerra Civil (1936–1939)*. Madrid: Ediciones La Librería.

Gutiérrez Sanín, Francisco, and Antonio Giustozzi. 2010. "Networks and Armies: Structuring Rebellion in Colombia and Afghanistan." *Studies in Conflict & Terrorism* 33 (9): 836–53. https://doi.org/10.1080/1057610X.2010.501425.

Gutiérrez Sanín, Francisco, and Elisabeth Jean Wood. 2014. "Ideology in Civil War: Instrumental Adoption and Beyond." *Journal of Peace Research* 51 (2): 213–26. https://doi.org/10.1177/0022343313514073.

Habyarimana, James, Macartan Humphreys, Daniel N. Posner, and Jeremy M. Weinstein. 2007. "Why Does Ethnic Diversity Undermine Public Goods Provision?" *American Political Science Review* 101 (4): 709–25. https://doi.org/10.1017/S0003055407070499.

Haddad, Bassam. 2012. *Business Networks in Syria: The Political Economy of Authoritarian Resilience*. Stanford, CA: Stanford University Press.

Hardin, Russell. 2002. *Trust and Trustworthiness*. New York: Russell Sage Foundation.

Harkness, Kristen A. 2016. "The Ethnic Army and the State: Explaining Coup Traps and the Difficulties of Democratization in Africa." *Journal of Conflict Resolution* 60 (4): 587–616. https://doi.org/10.1177/0022002714545332.

Helmer, John. 1974. *Bringing the War Home: The American Soldier in Vietnam and After*. New York: Free Press.

Henderson, William Darryl. 1976. "Why the Viet Cong Fought: A Study of Motivation and Control." PhD diss., University of Pittsburgh.

Henriksen, Rune. 2007. "Warriors in Combat—What Makes People Actively Fight in Combat?" *Journal of Strategic Studies* 30 (2): 187–223. https://doi.org/10.1080/01402390701248707.

Herreros, Francisco, and Henar Criado. 2009. "Pre-Emptive or Arbitrary: Two Forms of Lethal Violence in a Civil War." *Journal of Conflict Resolution* 53 (3): 419–45. https://doi.org/10.1177/0022002709332208.

Hokayem, Emile. 2013. *Syria's Uprising and the Fracturing of the Levant*. Adelphi Series, no. 438. Abingdon, UK: Routledge for the International Institute for Strategic Studies.

Holliday, Joseph. 2013. "The Syrian Army: Doctrinal Order of Battle." Institute for the Study of War. February 15, 2013. http://www.understandingwar.org/backgrounder/syrian-army-doctrinal-order-battle.

Holmes, Richard. 1986. *Acts of War: The Behavior of Men in Battle*. New York: Free Press.

Hoover Green, Amelia. 2018. *The Commander's Dilemma: Violence and Restraint in Wartime*. Ithaca, NY: Cornell University Press.

Horowitz, Donald. 2000. *Ethnic Groups in Conflict*. 2nd ed. Berkeley: University of California Press.

Howson, Gerald. 1998. *Arms for Spain: The Untold Story of the Spanish Civil War*. New York: St. Martin's Press.

Humphreys, Macartan, and Jeremy M. Weinstein. 2004. "What the Fighters Say: A Survey of Ex-Combatants in Sierra Leone June-August 2003 Interim Report." Columbia University.

———. 2008. "Who Fights? The Determinants of Participation in Civil War." *American Journal of Political Science* 52 (2): 436–55. https://doi.org/10.1111/j.1540-5907.2008.00322.x.

International Crisis Group. 2010. *Loose Ends: Iraq's Security Forces between U.S. Drawdown and Withdrawal*. Middle East Report 99. Brussels: International Crisis Group.

———. 2011. *Popular Protest in North Africa and the Middle East (V): Making Sense of Libya*. Middle East/North Africa Report 107. Brussels: International Crisis Group.

———. 2013. *Syria's Kurds: A Struggle within a Struggle*. Middle East Report 136. Brussels: International Crisis Group.

———. 2014. *Flight of Icarus? The PYD's Precarious Rise in Syria*. Middle East Report 151. Brussels: International Crisis Group.

———. 2017a. *Burundi: The Army in Crisis*. Africa Report 247. Brussels: International Crisis Group.

———. 2017b. *Fighting ISIS: The Road to and beyond Raqqa*. Middle East Briefing 53. Brussels: International Crisis Group.

———. 2017c. *The PKK's Fateful Choice in Northern Syria*. Middle East Report 176. Brussels: International Crisis Group.

Jaffe, Greg, and Loveday Morris. 2015. "Defense Secretary Carter: Iraqis Lack 'Will to Fight' to Defeat Islamic State." *Washington Post*, May 24, 2015.

Jensen, Geoffrey. 2002. *Irrational Triumph: Cultural Despair, Military Nationalism, and the Ideological Origins of Franco's Spain*. Reno: University of Nevada Press.

Jha, Saumitra, and Steven I. Wilkinson. 2012. "Does Combat Experience Foster Organizational Skill? Evidence from Ethnic Cleansing during the Partition of South Asia." *American Political Science Review* 106 (4): 883–907. https://doi.org/10.1017/S000305541200041X.

Johnston, Patrick. 2008. "The Geography of Insurgent Organization and Its Consequences for Civil Wars: Evidence from Liberia and Sierra Leone." *Security Studies* 17 (1): 107–37. https://doi.org/10.1080/09636410801894191.

Juliá, Santos, ed. 1999. *Víctimas de la Guerra Civil*. Madrid: Temas de Hoy.

Kaldor, Mary. 2006. *New & Old Wars: Organized Violence in a Global Era*. 2nd ed. Cambridge: Polity Press.

Kalyvas, Stathis N. 1999. "Wanton and Senseless? The Logic of Massacres in Algeria." *Rationality and Society* 11 (3): 243–85. https://doi.org/10.1177/104346399011003001.

———. 2001. "'New' and 'Old' Civil Wars: A Valid Distinction?" *World Politics* 54 (1): 99–118. https://doi.org/10.1353/wp.2001.0022.

———. 2003. "The Ontology of 'Political Violence': Action and Identity in Civil Wars." *Perspectives on Politics* 1 (3): 475–94. https://doi.org/10.1017/S1537592703000355.

———. 2006. *The Logic of Violence in Civil War*. Cambridge: Cambridge University Press.

———. 2008. "Ethnic Defection in Civil War." *Comparative Political Studies* 41 (8): 1043–68. https://doi.org/10.1177/0010414008317949.

Kalyvas, Stathis N., and Laia Balcells. 2010. "International System and Technologies of Rebellion: How the End of the Cold War Shaped Internal Conflict." *American Political Science Review* 104 (3): 415–29.

Kalyvas, Stathis N., and Matthew Adam Kocher. 2007. "How 'Free' Is Free Riding in Civil Wars? Violence, Insurgency, and the Collective Action Problem." *World Politics* 59 (2): 177–216. https://doi.org/10.1353/wp.2007.0023.

Kaufmann, Chaim. 1996. "Intervention in Ethnic and Ideological Civil Wars: Why One Can Be Done and the Other Can't." *Security Studies* 6 (1): 62–101. https://doi.org /10.1080/09636419608429300.

Keegan, John. 1976. *The Face of Battle*. London: Jonathan Cape.

Khaddour, Kheder. 2015. "Assad's Officer Ghetto: Why the Syrian Army Remains Loyal." Carnegie Middle East Center. November 4, 2015. https://carnegie-mec.org/2015/11 /04/assad-s-officer-ghetto-why-syrian-army-remains-loyal-pub-61449.

———. 2016. "Strength in Weakness: The Syrian Army's Accidental Resilience." Carnegie Middle East Center. March 14, 2016. https://carnegie-mec.org/2016/03/14/strength -in-weakness-syrian-army-s-accidental-resilience-pub-62968.

Khatib, Lina. 2015. *The Islamic State's Strategy: Lasting and Expanding*. Beirut: Carnegie Middle East Center. https://carnegieendowment.org/files/islamic_state_strategy.pdf.

Kier, Elizabeth. 1998. "Homosexuals in the U.S. Military: Open Integration and Combat Effectiveness." *International Security* 23 (2): 5–39. https://doi.org/10.5129/001041 516819197601.

King, Anthony. 2013. *The Combat Soldier: Infantry Tactics and Cohesion in the Twentieth and Twenty-First Centuries*. Oxford: Oxford University Press.

Koehler, Kevin, Dorothy Ohl, and Holger Albrecht. 2016. "From Disaffection to Desertion: How Networks Facilitate Military Insubordination in Civil Conflict." *Comparative Politics* 48 (4): 439–57. https://doi.org/10.5129/001041516819197601.

Kotkin, Stephen. 2015. *Stalin: Paradoxes of Power, 1878–1928*. London: Penguin.

Kowalsky, Daniel. 2001. *Stalin and the Spanish Civil War*. E-book ed. New York: Columbia University Press.

Kozak, Christopher. n.d. "The Assad Regime under Stress: Conscription and Protest among Alawite and Minority Populations in Syria." *Institute for the Study of War* (blog). Accessed August 8, 2017. http://iswresearch.blogspot.com/2014/12/the-assad -regime-under-stress.html.

Kuhn, Anthony. 2012. "Asked to Spy on Rebels, Syrian Soldier Becomes One." *WGBH News* (blog). August 16, 2012. http://news.wgbh.org/post/asked-spy-rebels-syrian -soldier-becomes-one.

Kuran, Timur. 1989. "Sparks and Prairie Fires: A Theory of Unanticipated Political Revolution." *Public Choice* 61 (1): 41–74. https://doi.org/10.1007/BF00116762.

———. 1991. "Now Out of Never: The Element of Surprise in the East European Revolution of 1989." *World Politics* 44 (1): 7–48. https://doi.org/10.2307/2010422.

———. 1995. *Private Truths, Public Lies: The Social Consequences of Preference Falsification*. Cambridge, MA: Harvard University Press.

La Parra-Pérez, Álvaro. 2020. "For a Fistful of Pesetas? The Political Economy of Military Factions in a Failed Democracy: The Second Spanish Republic (1931–1939)." *Economic History Review* 73 (2): 565–94. https://doi.org/10.1111/ehr.12881.

Leader Maynard, Jonathan. 2014. "Rethinking the Role of Ideology in Mass Atrocities." *Terrorism and Political Violence* 26 (5): 821–41. https://doi.org/10.1080/09546553 .2013.796934.

———. 2019. "Ideology and Armed Conflict." *Journal of Peace Research* 56 (5): 635–49. https://doi.org/10.1177/0022343319826629.

Leech, Garry. 2011. *The FARC: The Longest Insurgency*. London: Zed Books.

Lehmann, Todd C., and Yuri M. Zhukov. 2019. "Until the Bitter End? The Diffusion of Surrender across Battles." *International Organization* 73 (1): 133–69. https://doi.org /10.1017/S0020818318000358.

Levi, Margaret. 1997. *Consent, Dissent, and Patriotism*. Cambridge: Cambridge University Press.

Lewis, Janet I. 2020. *How Insurgency Begins: Rebel Group Formation in Uganda and Beyond*. Cambridge: Cambridge University Press.

Lichbach, Mark I. 1995. *The Rebel's Dilemma*. Ann Arbor: University of Michigan Press.

Linz, Juan J., and Jesús M. de Miguel. 1977. "Hacia un Análisis Regional de las Elecciones de 1936 en España." *Revista Española de La Opinión Pública*, no. 48: 27–68. https://doi.org/10.2307/40199476.

Lister, Charles. 2014. "Profiling the Islamic State." Brookings Doha Center Analysis Paper 13. Brookings Doha Center. https://www.brookings.edu/wp-content/uploads/2014/12/en_web_lister.pdf.

———. 2015. *The Syrian Jihad: Al-Qaeda, the Islamic State and the Evolution of an Insurgency*. Oxford: Oxford University Press.

———. 2016a. *The Free Syrian Army: A Decentralized Insurgent Brand*. The Brookings Project on U.S. Relations with the Islamic World. Washington, DC: Brookings Institution. https://www.brookings.edu/research/the-free-syrian-army-a-decentralized-insurgent-brand/.

———. 2016b. *Profiling Jabhat Al-Nusra*. The Brookings Project on U.S. Relations with the Islamic World. Washington, DC: Brookings Institution. https://www.brookings.edu/research/profiling-jabhat-al-nusra/.

Líster, Enrique. 2007. *Nuestra Guerra: Memorias de un Luchador*. Zaragoza, Spain: Silente.

Lister, Tim, and Clarissa Ward. 2015. "Meet the Men Fighting ISIS with Hunting Rifles and Homemade Mortars." *CNN* (blog). October 28, 2015. http://www.cnn.com/2015/10/27/middleeast/inside-syria-front-line-against-isis/index.html.

Little, Roger W. 1964. "Buddy Relations and Combat Performance." In *The New Military: Changing Patterns of Organization*, edited by Morris Janowitz, 195–223. New York: Russell Sage Foundation.

Lohmann, Susanne. 1994. "The Dynamics of Informational Cascades: The Monday Demonstrations in Leipzig, East Germany, 1989–91." *World Politics* 47 (1): 42–101. https://doi.org/10.2307/2950679.

Lonn, Ella. 1928. *Desertion during the Civil War*. New York: Century.

Lucente, Adam, and Zouhir Al Shimale. 2015. "Free Syrian Army Decimated by Desertions." Al Jazeera, November 11, 2015. http://www.aljazeera.com/news/2015/11/free-syrian-army-decimated-desertions-151111064831800.html.

Lund, Aron. 2014. "Politics of the Islamic Front, Part 6: Stagnation?" *Carnegie Middle East Center* (blog). April 14, 2014. http://carnegie-mec.org/diwan/55334?lang=en.

———. 2015a. "The Nusra Front's Internal Purges." *Carnegie Middle East Center* (blog). August 7, 2015. http://carnegie-mec.org/diwan/60967?lang=en.

———. 2015b. "Syria's Kurds at the Center of America's Anti-Jihadi Strategy." *Carnegie Middle East Center* (blog). December 2, 2015. http://carnegie-mec.org/diwan/62158.

———. 2015c. "Why the Victory in Kobane Matters." *Carnegie Middle East Center* (blog). February 13, 2015. http://carnegie-mec.org/diwan/59061.

———. 2016. "Manbij: A Dress Rehearsal for Raqqa?" *Carnegie Middle East Center* (blog). August 10, 2016. http://carnegie-mec.org/diwan/64270.

———. 2017. "The Jihadi Spiral." *Carnegie Endowment for International Peace* (blog). February 8, 2017. http://carnegie-mec.org/diwan/67911.

Lyall, Jason. 2017. "Forced to Fight: Coercion, Blocking Detachments, and Trade-Offs in Military Effectiveness." In *The Sword's Other Edge: Trade-Offs in the Pursuit of Military Effectiveness*, edited by Dan Reiter, 88–125. Cambridge: Cambridge University Press.

———. 2020. *Divided Armies: Inequality and Battlefield Performance in Modern War*. Princeton, NJ: Princeton University Press.

Lynn, John A. 1984. *The Bayonets of the Republic: Motivation and Tactics in the Army of Revolutionary France, 1791–94*. Urbana: University of Illinois Press.

MacCoun, Robert J. 1993. "What Is Known about Unit Cohesion and Military Performance." In *Sexual Orientation and U.S. Military Personnel Policy: Options and Assessment*, 283–331. Santa Monica, CA: RAND Corporation.

MacCoun, Robert J., Elizabeth Kier, and Aaron Belkin. 2006. "Does Social Cohesion Determine Motivation in Combat? An Old Question with an Old Answer." *Armed Forces & Society* 32 (4): 646–54. https://doi.org/10.1177/0095327X05279181.

MacMaster, Neil. 1990. *Spanish Fighters: An Oral History of Civil War and Exile*. Basingstoke, UK: Macmillan.

Mahmood, Mona, and Ian Black. 2013. "Free Syrian Army Rebels Defect to Islamist Group Jabhat Al-Nusra." *The Guardian*, May 8, 2013. http://www.theguardian.com/world/2013/may/08/free-syrian-army-rebels-defect-islamist-group.

Mainar Cabanes, Eladi. 1998. *De Milicians a Soldats: Les Columnes Valencianes en la Guerra Civil Espanyola (1936–1937)*. València, Spain: Universitat de València.

Maldonado, José. 2007. *El Frente de Aragón: La Guerra Civil en Aragón (1936–1938)*. Zaragoza, Spain: Mira Editores.

Malešević, Siniša. 2010. *The Sociology of War and Violence*. Cambridge: Cambridge University Press.

Mampilly, Zachariah Cherian. 2015. *Rebel Rulers: Insurgent Governance and Civilian Life during War*. Ithaca, NY: Cornell University Press.

Manekin, Devorah. 2017. "The Limits of Socialization and the Underproduction of Military Violence: Evidence from the IDF." *Journal of Peace Research* 54 (5): 606–19. https://doi.org/10.1177/0022343317713558.

Marks, Zoe. 2013. "Sexual Violence inside Rebellion: Policies and Perspectives of the Revolutionary United Front of Sierra Leone." *Civil Wars* 15 (3): 359–79. https://doi.org/10.1080/13698249.2013.842749.

Marshall, S. L. A. 1947. *Men against Fire: The Problem of Battle Command*. New York: William Morrow.

——. 1962. *Night Drop: The American Airborne Invasion of Normandy*. Boston: Little, Brown.

Martín Blázquez, José. 1939. *I Helped Build an Army: Civil War Memoirs of a Spanish Staff Officer*. London: Secker and Warburg.

Martínez Bande, José. 1972. *El Final del Frente Norte*. Madrid: Editorial San Martín.

——. 1980. *Nueve Meses de Guerra en el Norte*. 2nd ed. Madrid: Editorial San Martín.

Martínez Reverte, Jorge. 2004. *La Batalla de Madrid*. Barcelona: Crítica.

——. 2012. "Los Militares Españoles en la Segunda República." In *Los Militares Españoles En La Segunda República*, edited by Jorge Martínez Reverte, 7–40. Madrid: Editorial Pablo Iglesias.

Matthews, James. 2010. "'Our Red Soldiers': The Nationalist Army's Management of Its Left-Wing Conscripts in the Spanish Civil War 1936–9." *Journal of Contemporary History* 45 (2): 344–63. https://doi.org/10.1177/0022009409356912.

——. 2012. *Reluctant Warriors: Republican Popular Army and Nationalist Army Conscripts in the Spanish Civil War, 1936–1939*. Oxford: Oxford University Press.

McLauchlin, Theodore. 2010. "Loyalty Strategies and Military Defection in Rebellion." *Comparative Politics* 42 (3): 333–50. https://doi.org/10.5129/001041510X1291 1363509792.

——. 2014. "Desertion, Terrain, and Control of the Home Front in Civil Wars." *Journal of Conflict Resolution* 58 (8): 1419–44. https://doi.org/10.1177/002200271454 7901.

——. 2018. "The Loyalty Trap: Regime Ethnic Exclusion, Commitment Problems, and Civil War Duration in Syria and Beyond." *Security Studies* 27 (2): 296–317. https://doi.org/10.1080/09636412.2017.1386938.

McLauchlin, Theodore, and Álvaro La Parra-Pérez. 2018. "Disloyalty and Logics of Fratricide in Civil War: Executions of Officers in Republican Spain, 1936–1939." *Comparative Political Studies* 52 (7): 1028–58. https://doi.org/10.1177/0010414018774373.

McLauchlin, Theodore, and Wendy Pearlman. 2012. "Out-Group Conflict, In-Group Unity? Exploring the Relationship between Repression and Intramovement Cooperation." *Journal of Conflict Resolution* 56 (1): 41–66. https://doi.org/10.1177/0022002711429707.

McLauchlin, Theodore, and Margaux Reiss. 2018. "Desertion in Armed Groups under State Collapse: Evidence from Sierra Leone." Université de Montréal.

McPherson, James M. 1997. *For Cause and Comrades: Why Men Fought in the Civil War.* Oxford: Oxford University Press.

McPherson, Miller, Lynn Smith-Lovin, and James M. Cook. 2001. "Birds of a Feather: Homophily in Social Networks." *Annual Review of Sociology* 27 (1): 415–44. https://doi.org/10.1146/annurev.soc.27.1.415.

Mera, Cipriano. 1976. *Guerra, Exilio, y Cárcel de un Anarcosindicalista.* Paris: Ruedo Ibérico.

Mironova, Vera. 2019. *From Freedom Fighters to Jihadists: Human Resources of Non-state Armed Groups.* Oxford: Oxford University Press.

Mironova, Vera, Loubna Mrie, and Sam Whitt. 2014a. "Voices of Syria Project: Summary Statistics for Ex-Fighters in Turkey." April 2014. https://vmironovdotorg.files.wordpress.com/2014/01/exfighters-1-read-only1.pdf.

——. 2014b. "Voices of Syria Project: Summary Statistics for Islamists in Syria." August 2014. https://vmironovdotorg.files.wordpress.com/2014/01/islamists1-read-only.pdf.

——. 2014c. "Why Are Fighters Leaving the Free Syrian Army?" *Washington Post*, May 12, 2014, https://www.washingtonpost.com/news/monkey-cage/wp/2014/05/12/why-are-fighters-leaving-the-free-syrian-army/.

Modesto, Juan. 1969. *Soy del Quinto Regimiento.* Paris: Colección Ebro.

Montalvo, José G., and Marta Reynal-Querol. 2005. "Ethnic Polarization, Potential Conflict, and Civil Wars." *American Economic Review* 95 (3): 796–816. https://doi.org/10.1257/0002828054201468.

Montoliú, Pedro. 1998. *Madrid en la Guerra Civil.* Vol. 1, *La Historia.* Madrid: Sílex.

——. 1999. *Madrid en la Guerra Civil.* Vol. 2, *Los Protagonistas.* Madrid: Sílex.

Morency-Laflamme, Julien, and Theodore McLauchlin. Forthcoming. "The Efficacy of Ethnic Stacking: Military Defection during Uprisings in Africa." *Journal of Global Security Studies.* https://doi.org/10.1093/jogss/ogz015.

Mosinger, Eric S. 2018. "Brothers or Others in Arms? Civilian Constituencies and Rebel Fragmentation in Civil War." *Journal of Peace Research* 55 (1): 62–77. https://doi.org/10.1177/0022343316675907.

Moskos, Charles C. 1970. *The American Enlisted Man: The Rank and File in Today's Military.* New York: Russell Sage Foundation.

Mueller, John. 2000. "The Banality of 'Ethnic War.'" *International Security* 25 (1): 42–70. https://doi.org/10.1162/016228800560381.

Murillo Pérez, María Guadalupe. 1990. "La Auditoría de Guerra de Gijón: Causas Tramitadas por los Tribunales Populares Especiales de Guerra de Avilés, Mieres y Trubia en 1937." In *Justicia en Guerra: Jornadas sobre la Administración de Justicia durante la Guerra Civil Española: Instituciones y Fuentes Documentales*, edited by Archivo Histórico Nacional Sección Guerra Civil, 205–22. Madrid: Ministerio de Cultura.

Nakkash, Aziz. 2013. *The Alawite Dilemma in Homs: Survival, Solidarity and the Making of a Community.* Berlin: Friedrich Ebert Stiftung.

Navajas Zubeldía, Carlos. 2011. *Leales y Rebeldes: La Tragedia de los Militares Republicanos.* Nuestro Ayer. Madrid: Editorial Síntesis.

NBC News. 2014. "Meet the Kurdish Women Fighting ISIS in Syria." September 9, 2014. https://www.nbcnews.com/slideshow/meet-kurdish-women-fighting-isis-syria-56016007.

Neumann, Peter. 2015. *Victims, Perpetrators, Assets: The Narratives of Islamic State Defectors.* London: International Center for the Study of Radicalisation and Political Violence.

Nieto, Antolín. 2007. *Las Guerrillas Antifranquistas, 1936–1965.* Madrid: Ediciones J. C. Clementine.

Núñez Díaz-Balart, Mirta. 2013. "Convivencia y Conflicto de Modelos de Defensa a través de los Periódicos de Guerra Republicanos (1936–1939)." *El Argonauta español*, no. 10 (January). https://doi.org/10.4000/argonauta.1894.

O'Bagy, Elizabeth. 2013. *The Free Syrian Army.* Middle East Security Report 9. Washington, DC: Institute for the Study of War.

Obregón Goyarrola, Fernando. 2007. *República, Guerra Civil y Posguerra en los Valles de Liébana y Peñarrubia (1931–1957).* Santander: published by the author, in collaboration with Parlamento de Cantabria and Braña.

Öğür, Berkan, and Zana Baykal. 2018. "Understanding 'Foreign Policy' of the PYD/YPG as a Non-state Actor in Syria and Beyond." In *Non-state Armed Actors in the Middle East: Geopolitics, Ideology, and Strategy,* edited by Murat Yeşiltaş and Tuncay Kardaş, 43–76. London: Palgrave Macmillan.

Ohl, Dorothy, Holger Albrecht, and Kevin Koehler. 2015. "For Money or Liberty? The Political Economy of Military Desertion and Rebel Recruitment in the Syrian Civil War." Carnegie Middle East Center. November 24, 2015. https://carnegieendowment.org/2015/11/24/for-money-or-liberty-political-economy-of-military-desertion-and-rebel-recruitment-in-syrian-civil-war-pub-61714.

Olson, Mancur. 1971. *The Logic of Collective Action: Public Goods and the Theory of Groups.* Cambridge, MA: Harvard University Press.

Oppenheim, Ben, Abbey Steele, Juan F. Vargas, and Michael Weintraub. 2015. "True Believers, Deserters, and Traitors: Who Leaves Insurgent Groups and Why." *Journal of Conflict Resolution* 59 (5): 794–823. https://doi.org/10.1177/0022002715576750.

Orwell, George. 1989. *Homage to Catalonia.* London: Penguin.

Otunnu, Ogenga. 1999. "An Historical Analysis of the Invasion by the Rwanda Patriotic Army (RPA)." In *The Path of a Genocide: The Rwanda Crisis from Uganda to Zaire,* edited by Howard Adelman and Astri Suhrke, 31–50. New Brunswick, NJ: Transaction Publishers.

Palmer, R. R. 1986. "Frederick the Great, Guibert, Bülow: From Dynastic to National War." In *Makers of Modern Strategy: From Machiavelli to the Nuclear Age,* edited by Peter Paret, 91–120. Princeton, NJ: Princeton University Press.

Paoli, Bruno. 2013. "Et Maintenant, On Va Où? Les Alaouites à la Croisée des Destins." In *Pas de Printemps pour la Syrie: Les Clés pour Comprendre les Acteurs et les Défis de la Crise (2011–2013),* edited by François Burgat and Bruno Paoli, 124–43. Paris: La Découverte.

Parkinson, Sarah Elizabeth. 2013. "Organizing Rebellion: Rethinking High-Risk Mobilization and Social Networks in War." *American Political Science Review* 107 (3): 418–32. https://doi.org/10.1017/S0003055413000208.

———. 2017. "Money Talks: Discourse, Networks and Structure in Militant Organizations." *Perspectives on Politics* 14 (4): 976–94. https://doi.org/10.1017/S1537592716002875.

Parkinson, Sarah Elizabeth, and Sherry Zaks. 2018. "Militant and Rebel Organization(s)." *Comparative Politics* 50 (2): 271–93. https://doi.org/info:doi/10.5129/001041518 822263610.

Payne, Stanley G. 1961. *Falange: A History of Spanish Fascism.* Stanford, CA: Stanford University Press.

———. 1967. *Politics and the Military in Modern Spain.* Stanford, CA: Stanford University Press.

———. 1987. *The Franco Regime, 1936–1975.* Madison: University of Wisconsin Press.

Pearlman, Wendy. 2017. *We Crossed a Bridge and It Trembled: Voices from Syria.* New York: HarperCollins Publishers.

Pearlman, Wendy, and Kathleen Gallagher Cunningham. 2012. "Nonstate Actors, Fragmentation, and Conflict Processes." *Journal of Conflict Resolution* 56 (1): 3–15. https://doi.org/10.1177/0022002711429669.

Peirats, José. 1971. *La CNT en la Revolución Española.* Vol. 1. Paris: Ruedo Ibérico.

Pepper, Suzanne. 1999. *Civil War in China: The Political Struggle 1945–1949.* Lanham, MD: Rowman & Littlefield Publishers.

Pérez Salas, Jesús. 1947. *Guerra en España: 1936 a 1939.* Mexico City: Grafos.

Perry, Tom. 2017. "Exclusive: Syrian Kurdish YPG Aims to Expand Force to over 100,000." *Reuters*, March 20, 2017. https://www.reuters.com/article/us-mideast-crisis-syria -ypg-exclusive/exclusive-syrian-kurdish-ypg-aims-to-expand-force-to-over-100000 -idUSKBN16R1QS.

Peters, Krijn, and Paul Richards. 1998. "'Why We Fight': Voices of Youth Combatants in Sierra Leone." *Africa* 68 (2): 183–210. https://doi.org/10.2307/1161278.

Petersen, Roger D. 2001. *Resistance and Rebellion: Lessons from Eastern Europe.* Cambridge: Cambridge University Press.

Pettersson, Thérése, and Kristine Eck. 2018. "Organized Violence, 1989–2017." *Journal of Peace Research* 55 (4): 535–47. https://doi.org/10.1177/0022343318784101.

Pfeffer, Anshel. 2012. "Syrian Rebel Leader to Haaretz: Assad's Opposition Will Secure Chemical Weapons." *Haaretz* (blog). May 28, 2012. http://www.haaretz.com/blogs /the-axis/syrian-rebel-leader-to-haaretz-assad-s-opposition-will-secure-chemical -weapons-1.433021.

Phillips, Christopher. 2015. "Sectarianism and Conflict in Syria." *Third World Quarterly* 36 (2): 357–76. https://doi.org/10.1080/01436597.2015.1015788.

———. 2016. *The Battle for Syria: International Rivalry in the New Middle East.* New Haven, CT: Yale University Press.

Pons Prades, Eduardo. 1977. *Guerrillas Españolas: 1936–1960.* Barcelona: Planeta.

Posen, Barry R. 1993a. "Nationalism, the Mass Army, and Military Power." *International Security* 18 (2): 80–124. http://dx.doi.org/10.2307/2539098.

———. 1993b. "The Security Dilemma and Ethnic Conflict." *Survival* 35 (1): 27–47. https:// doi.org/10.1080/00396339308442672.

Preston, Paul. 1993. *Franco: A Biography.* London: HarperCollins.

———. 1994a. *The Coming of the Spanish Civil War: Reform, Reaction and Revolution in the Second Republic.* 2nd ed. London: Routledge.

———. 1994b. "General Franco as Military Leader." *Transactions of the Royal Historical Society*, 6th ser., 4: 21–41. https://doi.org/10.2307/3679213.

———. 1998. *Las Tres Españas del 36.* Madrid: Plaza & Janés.

———. 2004. "The Answer Lies in the Sewers: Captain Aguilera and the Mentality of the Francoist Officer Corps." *Science & Society* 68 (3): 277–312. https://doi.org/10.1521 /siso.68.3.277.40298.

———. 2007. *The Spanish Civil War: Reaction, Revolution, and Revenge.* Rev. ed. New York: W. W. Norton.

———. 2012. *The Spanish Holocaust: Inquisition and Extermination in Twentieth-Century Spain*. New York: W. W. Norton.

Prieto Borrego, Lucía. 2013. "Siro Villas Garcia." Generaciones de Plata: Recuperación de Memoria Histórica de Científicos Andaluces Represaliados. November 12, 2013. https://generacionesdeplata.fundaciondescubre.es/2013/11/12/siro-villas-garcia -santibanez-de-ayllon-segovia-1898/

Radosh, Ron, Mary Habeck, and Grigory Sevostianov. 2001. *Spain Betrayed: The Soviet Union in the Spanish Civil War*. New Haven, CT: Yale University Press.

Ragin, Charles C. 1987. *The Comparative Method: Moving beyond Qualitative and Quantitative Strategies*. Berkeley: University of California Press.

Raguer, Hilari. 2007. *Gunpowder and Incense: The Catholic Church and the Spanish Civil War*. Translated by Gerald Howson. London: Routledge.

Richards, Joanne. 2018. "Troop Retention in Civil Wars: Desertion, Denunciation, and Military Organization in the Democratic Republic of Congo." *Journal of Global Security Studies* 3 (1): 38–55. https://doi.org/10.1093/jogss/ogx023.

Richards, Michael. 1998. *A Time of Silence: Civil War and the Culture of Repression in Franco's Spain, 1936–1945*. Cambridge: Cambridge University Press.

Rivero Solozábal, Francisco. 1941. *18 Julio 1936 - 26 Agosto 1937: Así Fue. . . .* Santander, Spain: Imprenta de Alonso.

Rodrigo, Javier. 2008. "'Our Fatherland Was Full of Weeds': Violence during the Spanish Civil War and the Franco Dictatorship." In *"If You Tolerate This . . .": The Spanish Civil War in the Age of Total War*, edited by Martin Baumeister and Stefanie Schüler-Springorum, 135–53. Frankfurt: Campus Verlag.

———. 2012. "Fascism and Violence in Spain: A Comparative Update." *International Journal of Iberian Studies* 25 (3): 183–99. https://doi.org/0.1386/ijis.25.3.183_1.

Roessler, Philip G. 2011. "The Enemy Within: Personal Rule, Coups, and Civil Wars in Africa." *World Politics* 63 (2): 300–346. https://doi.org/10.1017/S0043887111000049.

Rousseau, Denise M., Sim B. Sitkin, Ronald S. Burt, and Colin Camerer. 1998. "Not So Different After All: A Cross-Discipline View of Trust." *Academy of Management Review* 23 (3): 393–404. https://doi.org/10.5465/AMR.1998.926617.

Rudloff, Peter, and Michael G. Findley. 2016. "The Downstream Effects of Combatant Fragmentation on Civil War Recurrence." *Journal of Peace Research* 53 (1): 19–32. https://doi.org/10.1177/0022343315617067.

Ruiz, Julius. 2014. *The "Red Terror" and the Spanish Civil War: Revolutionary Violence in Madrid*. Cambridge: Cambridge University Press. https://doi.org/10.1017/CBO9 781107294349.

———. 2017. *"Paracuellos": The Elimination of the "Fifth Column" in Republican Madrid during the Spanish Civil War*. Brighton: Sussex Academic Press.

Russell, D. E. H. 1974. *Rebellion, Revolution, and Armed Force: A Comparative Study of Fifteen Countries with Special Emphasis on Cuba and South Africa*. New York: Academic Press.

Saideman, Stephen M., and Marie-Joëlle Zahar. 2008. "Causing Security, Reducing Fear: Deterring Intra-State Violence and Assuring Government Restraint." In *Intra-State Conflict, Governments and Security: Dilemmas of Deterrence and Assurance*, edited by Stephen M. Saideman and Marie-Joëlle Zahar, 1–19. New York: Routledge.

Saíz Viadero, J. 1979. *Crónicas sobre la Guerra Civil en Santander*. Santander, Spain: Institución Cultural de Cantabria.

Salas Larrazábal, Ramón. 2006. *Historia del Ejército Popular de la República*. 2nd ed. 4 vols. Madrid: La Esfera de los Libros.

Samaan, Maher, and Anne Barnard. 2015. "Assad, in Rare Admission, Says Syria's Army Lacks Manpower." *New York Times*, July 26, 2015. https://www.nytimes.com/2015

/07/27/world/middleeast/assad-in-rare-admission-says-syrias-army-lacks -manpower.html.

Samaha, Nour. 2017. "How These Syrians Went from Opposition Fighters to Pro-regime Militiamen." *Al-Monitor* (blog). April 3, 2017. http://www.al-monitor.com/pulse /originals/2017/04/syria-south-opposition-defection-army-israel.html.

Sambanis, Nicholas. 2004. "What Is Civil War? Conceptual and Empirical Complexities of an Operational Definition." *Journal of Conflict Resolution* 48 (6): 814–58. https:// doi.org/10.1177/0022002704269355.

Sanborn, Joshua A. 2003. *Drafting the Russian Nation: Military Conscription, Total War, and Mass Politics, 1905–1925.* DeKalb: Northern Illinois University Press.

Sánchez, José M. 1987. *The Spanish Civil War as a Religious Tragedy.* Notre Dame, IN: University of Notre Dame Press.

Savelsberg, Eva, and Jordi Tejel. 2013. "The Syrian Kurds in 'Transition to Somewhere.'" In *The Kurdish Spring: Geopolitical Changes and the Kurds*, 189–217. Costa Mesa, CA: Mazda Publishers.

Schelling, Thomas C. 1966. *Arms and Influence.* New Haven, CT: Yale University Press.

———. 1973. "Hockey Helmets, Concealed Weapons, and Daylight Saving: A Study of Binary Choices with Externalities." *Journal of Conflict Resolution* 17 (3): 381–428. https://doi.org/10.1177/002200277301700302.

Schmidt, Rachel. 2018. "Pariahs to All Sides? Examining Women's Disengagement from Political Violence." Presented at the Annual Meeting of the International Studies Association, San Francisco, April 5, 2018.

Scott, James C. 2009. *The Art of Not Being Governed: An Anarchist History of Upland Southeast Asia.* New Haven, CT: Yale University Press.

Seidman, Michael. 1990. *Workers against Work: Labor in Paris and Barcelona during the Popular Fronts.* Berkeley: University of California Press.

———. 2002. *Republic of Egos: A Social History of the Spanish Civil War.* Madison: University of Wisconsin Press.

———. 2011. *The Victorious Counterrevolution: The Nationalist Effort in the Spanish Civil War.* Madison: University of Wisconsin Press.

Semenov, Kirill. 2017. "The Syrian Armed Forces Seven Years into the Conflict: From a Regular Army to Volunteer Corps." *Russian International Affairs Council* (blog). May 17, 2017. http://russiancouncil.ru/en/analytics-and-comments/analytics/the -syrian-armed-forces-seven-years-into-the-conflict-from-a-regular-army-to -volunteer-corps-/.

Seymour, Lee J. M. 2014. "Why Factions Switch Sides in Civil Wars: Rivalry, Patronage, and Realignment in Sudan." *International Security* 39 (2): 92–131. https://doi.org /10.1162/ISEC_a_00179.

Seymour, Lee J. M., Kristin M. Bakke, and Kathleen Gallagher Cunningham. 2016. "E Pluribus Unum, Ex Uno Plures: Competition, Violence, and Fragmentation in Ethnopolitical Movements." *Journal of Peace Research* 53 (1): 3–18. https://doi.org/10.1177 /0022343315605571.

Shesterinina, Anastasia. 2016. "Collective Threat Framing and Mobilization in Civil War." *American Political Science Review* 110 (3): 411–27. https://doi.org/10.1017/S000 3055416000277.

———. 2019. "In and out of the Unit: Social Ties and Insurgent Cohesion in Civil War." HiCN Working Paper 311. Households in Conflict Network, Brighton, UK.

Shils, Edward A., and Morris Janowitz. 1948. "Cohesion and Disintegration in the Wehrmacht in World War II." *Public Opinion Quarterly* 12 (2): 280–315. https://doi.org /10.1086/265951.

Siebold, Guy L. 2007. "The Essence of Military Group Cohesion." *Armed Forces & Society* 33 (2): 286–95. https://doi.org/10.1177/0095327X06294173.

Six, Georges. 1947. *Les Généraux de la Révolution et de l'Empire*. Paris: Bordas.

Skocpol, Theda. 1979. *States and Social Revolutions: A Comparative Analysis of France, Russia, and China*. Cambridge: Cambridge University Press.

Smyth, Denis. 1996. "'We Are with You': Solidarity and Self-Interest in Soviet Policy towards Republican Spain, 1936–1939." In *The Republic Besieged: Civil War in Spain 1936–1939*, edited by Paul Preston and Ann L. Mackenzie, 87–105. Edinburgh: Edinburgh University Press.

Snyder, Glenn H. 1997. *Alliance Politics*. Ithaca, NY: Cornell University Press.

Solar, David. 1996. "La Guerra Civil en Santander." In *La Campaña del Norte (Abril-Octubre 1937)*, 74–87. La Guerra Civil Española. Barcelona: Folio.

Solé i Sabaté, Josep Maria, and Joan Villaroya Font. 1990. *La Repressió a la Rereguarda de Catalunya: 1936–1939*. 2 vols. Barcelona: Abadia de Montserrat.

Solla Gutiérrez, Miguel. 2005. *La Sublevación Frustrada: Los Inicios de la Guerra Civil en Cantabria*. Santander, Spain: Universidad de Cantabria.

———. 2006. *La Guerra Civil en Cantabria (Julio 1936–Agosto 1937): Política y Administración*. Santander, Spain: Universidad de Cantabria.

Sorenson, David S. 2016. *Syria in Ruins: The Dynamics of the Syrian Civil War*. Praeger Security International. Santa Barbara, CA: Praeger.

Speckhard, Anne, and Ahmet S. Yayla. 2015. "Eyewitness Accounts from Recent Defectors from Islamic State: Why They Joined, What They Saw, Why They Quit." *Perspectives on Terrorism* 9 (6): 95–118. http://www.terrorismanalysts.com/pt/index.php/pot/article/view/475/html.

Spence, Michael. 1974. *Market Signaling: Informational Transfer in Hiring and Related Screening Processes*. Cambridge, MA: Harvard University Press.

Staniland, Paul. 2012. "Between a Rock and a Hard Place: Insurgent Fratricide, Ethnic Defection, and the Rise of Pro-State Paramilitaries." *Journal of Conflict Resolution* 56 (1): 16–40. https://doi.org/10.1177/0022002711429681.

———. 2014. *Networks of Rebellion: Explaining Insurgent Cohesion and Collapse*. Cornell Studies in Security Affairs. Ithaca, NY: Cornell University Press.

Stephens, Michael. 2014. "Analysis: YPG - the Islamic State's Worst Enemy." *IHS Jane's Defence Weekly*, September 12, 2014.

Stouffer, Samuel A., Arthur A. Lumsdaine, Marion Harper Lumsdaine, Robin M. Williams, M. Brewster Smith, Irving L. Janis, Shirley A. Star, and Leonard S. Cottrell. 1949. *The American Soldier*. Princeton, NJ: Princeton University Press.

Strachan, Hew. 1997. "The Soldier's Experience in Two World Wars: Some Historiographical Comparisons." In *Time to Kill: The Soldier's Experience of War in the West 1939–1945*, edited by Paul Addison and Angus Calder, 369–78. London: Pimlico.

———. 2006. "Training, Morale and Modern War." *Journal of Contemporary History* 41 (2): 211–27. https://doi.org/10.1177/0022009406062054.

Sudduth, Jun Koga. 2017. "Strategic Logic of Elite Purges in Dictatorships." *Comparative Political Studies* 50 (13): 1768–1801. https://doi.org/10.1177/0010414016688004.

Szekely, Ora. 2016. *The Politics of Militant Group Survival in the Middle East: Resources, Relationships, and Resistance*. New York: Springer.

Talmadge, Caitlin. 2015. *The Dictator's Army: Battlefield Effectiveness in Authoritarian Regimes*. Ithaca, NY: Cornell University Press.

Taylor, Michael. 1987. *The Possibility of Cooperation*. Cambridge: Cambridge University Press.

———. 1988. "Rationality and Revolutionary Collective Action." In *Rationality and Revolution*, edited by Michael Taylor, 63–97. Cambridge: Cambridge University Press.

Thomas, Hugh. 1994. *The Spanish Civil War*. 4th ed. New York: Touchstone.

Tilly, Charles. 2001. "Mechanisms in Political Processes." *Annual Review of Political Science* 4: 21–41. https://doi.org/10.1146/annurev.polisci.4.1.21.

Toft, Monica Duffy, and Yuri M. Zhukov. 2015. "Islamists and Nationalists: Rebel Motivation and Counterinsurgency in Russia's North Caucasus." *American Political Science Review* 109 (2): 222–38. https://doi.org/10.1017/S000305541500012X.

Tullock, Gordon. 1971. "The Paradox of Revolution." *Public Choice* 11 (1): 89–99. https://doi.org/10.1007/BF01726214.

Ugarriza, Juan E., and Matthew J. Craig. 2013. "The Relevance of Ideology to Contemporary Armed Conflicts: A Quantitative Analysis of Former Combatants in Colombia." *Journal of Conflict Resolution* 57 (3): 445–77. https://doi.org/10.1177/0022002712446131.

UNHCR. 2017. "UNHCR Syria Regional Refugee Response." December 5, 2017. http://data.unhcr.org/syrianrefugees/regional.php.

Valentino, Benjamin, Paul Huth, and Dylan Balch-Lindsay. 2004. "'Draining the Sea': Mass Killing and Guerrilla Warfare." *International Organization* 58 (2): 375–407. https://doi.org/10.1017/S0020818304582061.

Van Dam, Nikolaos. 2011. *The Struggle for Power in Syria: Politics and Society under Asad and the Ba'th Party*. 4th ed. London: I. B. Tauris.

Vidali, Vittorio. 1975. *El Quinto Regimiento: Cómo se Forjó el Ejército Popular Español*. Barcelona: Editorial Grijalbo.

Walter, Barbara F. 2017a. "The Extremist's Advantage in Civil Wars." *International Security* 42 (2): 7–39. https://doi.org/10.1162/ISEC_a_00292.

———. 2017b. "The New New Civil Wars." *Annual Review of Political Science* 20 (1): 469–86. https://doi.org/10.1146/annurev-polisci-060415-093921.

Wedeen, Lisa. 1999. *Ambiguities of Domination: Politics, Rhetoric, and Symbols in Contemporary Syria*. Chicago: University of Chicago Press.

Weinstein, Jeremy M. 2005. "Resources and the Information Problem in Rebel Recruitment." *Journal of Conflict Resolution* 49 (4): 598–624. https://doi.org/10.1177/0022002705277802.

———. 2007. *Inside Rebellion: The Politics of Insurgent Violence*. Cambridge: Cambridge University Press.

Weiss, Michael. 2016. "'I Was an ISIS Jihadist—Until They Arrested and Tortured Me.'" *Daily Beast*, July 22, 2016. https://www.thedailybeast.com/articles/2016/07/22/i-was-an-isis-jihadist-until-they-arrested-and-tortured-me.

Weiss, Michael, and Hassan Hassan. 2015. *Isis: Inside the Army of Terror*. New York: Regan Arts.

Weitz, Mark A. 2005. *More Damning Than Slaughter: Desertion in the Confederate Army*. Lincoln: University of Nebraska Press.

Wesbrook, Stephen D. 1980. "The Potential for Military Disintegration." In *Combat Effectiveness: Cohesion, Stress, and the Volunteer Military*, edited by Sam C. Sarkesian, 244–78. Beverly Hills, CA: Sage Publications.

Whitaker, John T. 1942. "Prelude to World War: A Witness from Spain." *Foreign Affairs* 21 (1): 103–19. https://doi.org/10.2307/20029208.

Wilgenburg, Wladimir van. 2014. "Syrian Kurds Introduce Controversial Conscription Law." Middle East Eye. July 22, 2014. http://www.middleeasteye.net/news/syrian-kurds-introduce-controversial-conscription-law-815152310.

Wood, Elisabeth Jean. 2003. *Insurgent Collective Action and Civil War in El Salvador*. Cambridge: Cambridge University Press.

———. 2008. "The Social Processes of Civil War: The Wartime Transformation of Social Networks." *Annual Review of Political Science* 11 (1): 539–61. https://doi.org/10.1146/annurev.polisci.8.082103.104832.

Wood, Paul. 2016. "The Truth about Islamic State: It's in Crisis." The Spectator. January 9, 2016. https://www.spectator.co.uk/2016/01/the-truth-about-islamic-state-its-in -crisis/.

Worsnop, Alec. 2017. "Who Can Keep the Peace? Insurgent Organizational Control of Collective Violence." *Security Studies* 26 (3): 482–516. https://doi.org/10.1080/0963 6412.2017.1306397.

Wright, Robin, J. M. Berger, William Braniff, Cole Bunzel, Daniel Byman, Jennifer Ca- farella, Harleen Gambhir, Daveed Gartenstein-Ross, Hassan Hassan, Charles Lister, William McCants, Garrett Nada, Jacob Olidort, Alexander Thurston, Clinton Watts, Frederic Wehrey, Craig Whiteside, Graeme Wood, Aaron Y. Zelin, and Katherine Zimmerman. 2016. *The Jihadi Threat: ISIS, Al Qaeda and Beyond*. Washington, DC: United States Institute of Peace. https://www.usip.org/publications/2016/12/jihadi -threat-isis-al-qaeda-and-beyond.

Zaman, Amberin. 2017. "Syria's Arab, Kurdish Women Join Forces to Fight for Future." *Al-Monitor* (blog). November 6, 2017. http://www.al-monitor.com/pulse/originals /2017/11/syria-raqqa-fight-kurds-women-sdf-islamic-state.html.

Zaman al-Wasl. 2017. "Kurdish Security Kill YPG Deserter in Raid on Arab Villages in Hassakeh." *Syrian Observer* (blog). May 11, 2017. http://syrianobserver.com/EN /News/32733.

Zugazagoitia, Julián. 1977. *Guerra y Vicisitudes de los Españoles*. 3rd ed. Barcelona: Edito- rial Crítica.

Index

Tables are indicated by t; figures are indicated by f.